"It's rare for someone to be able to write about life with a special needs child and make it an enjoyable read, but Liane's prose is so good—so smart and funny and lucid and elegant—that even when she's exploring the fears and anxieties a parent faces, she makes it all somehow entertaining. There's real information in these pages for parents going through similar journeys, but it's accompanied by so much empathy and warmth that even those whose lives are untouched by this kind of thing will enjoy reading this. I would recommend it to every parent I know."

—*Claire LaZebnik, author of* Overcoming Autism

"Liane Kupferberg Carter's book is a touching, compelling, and ultimately uplifting account of parenting an autistic son. It is breathtakingly honest about the emotional upheaval and about the many practical and legal difficulties, but also warm and funny. The observations are constantly astute and the book importantly demolishes some of the myths surrounding autism."

—*Adam Feinstein, Editor of* Looking Up (The International Autism Magazine) *and author of* A History of Autism: Conversations with the Pioneers

"Liane does a masterful job leading us up the twisted stairway from denial to acceptance; chaos to freedom. Raising a child with autism can at times feel like we've been thrown in at the deep end. But as we learn in *Ketchup is My Favorite Vegetable*, the waters eventually recede and we can stand on dry land again."

—*Arthur Fleischmann, parent of an adult daughter living with severe autism and author of the bestselling* Carly's Voice—Breaking Through Autism

"In *Ketchup is My Favorite Vegetable*, Liane Kupferberg Carter gracefully articulates the hopes, the disappointments, the frustrations, and the triumphs that are inherent to raising a child on the spectrum and negotiating with the powers that be. The reality of life in a household dominated by autism is artfully conveyed. By the end of the book you are rooting for Mickey and his family, and hoping to read a sequel. Highly recommended!"

—*Chantal Sicile-Kira, author of* A Full Life with Autism

"Liane Kupferberg Carter's *Ketchup is My Favorite Vegetable* is both moving and instructive. It will serve as a helpful and inspirational guide for all parents of special needs children as they transition to the adult world."

—*Priscilla Gilman, author of* The Anti-Romantic
Child: A Memoir of Unexpected Joy

"I will always remember the day that Liane Carter first emailed me an essay for the *New York Times* blog, Motherlode. I knew from the first few paragraphs that I was in the company of a special writer. Her words shine a bright but embracing light on life with a grown son with autism. Never treacly, often funny, always direct and honest, she speaks to parents who have and will walk her specific road. That companionship is a gift to families who are navigating autism. But she's also a gift to parents of all children in every variety. This parenting stuff is joyous and hard, whatever the particulars. Liane captures the whole of that, and gives us all permission to struggle and celebrate at the same time."

—*Lisa Belkin, Senior National Correspondent at Yahoo,*
former reporter and columnist at the New York Times

KETCHUP IS MY FAVORITE VEGETABLE

of related interest

What Color is Monday?
How Autism Changed One Family for the Better
Carrie Cariello
ISBN 978 1 84905 727 1
eISBN 978 1 78450 094 8

When the School Says No...How to Get the Yes!
Securing Special Education Services for Your Child
Vaughn K. Lauer
ISBN 978 1 84905 917 6
eISBN 978 0 85700 664 6

Made for Good Purpose
What Every Parent Needs to Know to Help Their
Adolescent with Asperger's, High Functioning Autism or
a Learning Difference Become an Independent Adult
Michael P. McManmon
Foreword by Stephen Shore
ISBN 978 1 84905 863 6
eISBN 978 0 85700 435 2

Infantile Autism
The Syndrome and Its Implications for a Neural
Theory of Behavior by Bernard Rimland, Ph.D.
Edited by Stephen M. Edelson
Forewords by Temple Grandin, Margaret L. Bauman and Leo Kanner
ISBN 978 1 84905 789 9
eISBN 978 1 78450 057 3

The Complete Guide to Creating a Special Needs Life Plan
A Comprehensive Approach Integrating Life,
Resource, Financial, and Legal Planning to Ensure a
Brighter Future for a Person with a Disability
Hal Wright
Foreword by James Faber
ISBN 978 1 84905 914 5
eISBN 978 0 85700 684 4

KETCHUP *is my* FAVORITE VEGETABLE

A FAMILY GROWS UP WITH AUTISM

LIANE KUPFERBERG CARTER

FOREWORD BY SUSAN SENATOR

Jessica Kingsley *Publishers*
London and Philadelphia

Portions of the book were previously published in slightly
different form in the *New York Times*, 2010–2011.
Some names and identifiable details have been changed to protect people's privacy.

First published in 2016
by Jessica Kingsley Publishers
73 Collier Street
London N1 9BE, UK
and
400 Market Street, Suite 400
Philadelphia, PA 19106, USA

www.jkp.com

Library of Congress Cataloging in Publication Data
Carter, Liane Kupferberg.
  Ketchup is my favorite vegetable : a family grows up with autism
/ Liane Kupferberg Carter ; foreword by Susan Senator.
      pages cm
  ISBN 978-1-84905-715-8 (alk. paper)
  1. Carter, Liane Kupferberg--Family. 2. Autism in children. 3. Autistic
children--Family relationships. 4. Parents of autistic children--
Biography. 5. Autistic children--Biography. I. Title.
  RJ506.A9C388 2016
  618.92'858820092--dc23
  [B]
                            2015026133

British Library Cataloguing in Publication Data
A CIP catalogue record for this book is available from the British Library

ISBN 978 1 84905 715 8
eISBN 978 1 78450 209 6

Printed and bound in the United States

For my beamish boys

"The wound is the place where the Light enters you."

RUMI

CONTENTS

FOREWORD

Let's face it. There are many autism memoirs out there, but so many of the stories are about families who were lost in the autism maelstrom, but who stumble upon That One Thing, and then— their kid is basically saved.

The non-recovery autism book is the one I hungered for. What I'd been through with my son—fairly severe autism with cognitive delays and sensory issues—had been painful, mystifying, challenging. And it remains that way. At 25 Nat is still deeply autistic. New problems keep popping up—with health, caregivers, housing. But still, he has a worthwhile life, sharing an apartment with a terrific caregiver his own age, and he works part-time at a supermarket.

Along came Liane, with her book *Ketchup is My Favorite Vegetable*. I know Liane, I know her work. In reading her story, I found myself nodding my head in recognition, rather than thinking *Been there, done that*. Like me, Liane has been through the wars, the days of Prehistoric Autism, with little known, little information out there, few books, and a fledgling internet.

Ketchup is My Favorite Vegetable is the best kind of autism memoir because it is a family story. Even the pets are included. After all, autism is a family experience, and so I believe that the most helpful kind of story is one that chronicles the entire family's experience. Every member in our families counts, and their stories should be an integral part of the autism book. In Liane's book, you come to know all of them. The Carter family will show you how lives with autism are lived with honesty, hard work, gusto and style.

I had a feeling Liane's book would be different from what's out there because she is the real thing: open, kind, maternal and wise. She is a real autism friend. She will be your autism friend.

Enjoy!

Susan Senator, author of *Making Peace with Autism*,
The Autism Mom's Survival Guide, and *Autism Adulthood:*
Strategies and Insights for a Fulfilling Life, and mother
of three boys, one of whom has severe autism

PROLOGUE

What if a stranger had the power to decide if you were a good enough parent to your child?

Our 17-year-old autistic son Mickey was about to become a legal adult. We were petitioning the surrogate court for guardianship, and had asked our special needs attorney to begin proceedings. My husband Marc and I took Mickey to the lawyer's office so that the paralegal could officially serve him with papers notifying him that we were petitioning the court on his behalf. He must have felt our tension, because he refused to stand. He refused to shake her hand or make eye contact. Standard behavior for him in a new situation when he is scared. Standard anxiety for us.

"As part of the procedure, the court has appointed Mental Hygiene Legal Services for Mickey," the paralegal said. "Basically, their role is to complete some interviews with both of you as proposed guardians for him and with anyone else they feel would be a useful source of information. The court will rely on their report to determine if this guardianship is a safe and appropriate one for Michael."

Appropriate? I was dumbfounded. *We were his parents.* Until that moment, I hadn't known that raising him and loving him unconditionally didn't ensure we'd be able to retain legal influence over his adult life.

Two days later, I got a phone call from a woman who introduced herself as Aretha Franklin.

Could that really be her name? I thought.

She was calling, she said, because the Surrogate's Court had just appointed her agency as guardian *ad litem*. Mickey's temporary guardian.

I understood intellectually that having the state appoint a temporary legal guardian while they processed our appeal was *pro forma*. They did it for every case. It was meant to protect my child's best interests. It was meant to protect all the children in the system. Yet I felt as if someone had called Child Protective Services on us and now a social worker was coming to make a home visit and poke into our personal business. To scrutinize how we had raised our child. What if we didn't pass the test? Did that mean the state got to decide what school he attended? Which medications best treated his seizures? Where, how and with whom he lived?

How do you prove that you are good enough parents?

For 17 years, we'd had therapists, teachers and administrators in our home—in our lives, evaluating him and, by extension, us. Most of them had been lovely. But we had lived with a lack of privacy that most families never have to endure. With ten hours a week of ongoing after-school therapy in our home, we hadn't been able to sit down and eat a normal family dinner in years. Though difficult, we'd learned to expect people would stare at us in public. But no one wants to be observed during intimate family moments. I was tired of well-meaning questions that often felt like veiled criticisms: "Why do you let him wear sweat pants? Why don't you make him use toothpaste? Why can't you get him to eat vegetables?" The underlying message was: "You need to discipline him better. You're not setting the right limits." Marc and I were weary of being watched, feeling we had to defend every parenting choice we'd made.

When Aretha Franklin called to make the appointment, I was my most friendly and chipper. Then I stewed in an icy hot bath of nerves all weekend. Should I bake brownies with Mickey before she arrived, so that she would see what a great mother I was? Or was that what you did when you were showing your house to prospective buyers? Bake something with cinnamon and vanilla, scenting the air subliminally to make the house seem warm and inviting and cozy? Would that look too obvious?

Would she ask him if he liked living with us? If we were kind to him? What if Mickey said the wrong thing? I remembered the time he'd first met his tutor Nikki, gotten that mischievous glint in his eye, and told her, "I like to play with matches." Sometimes he still liked to say provocative things just to get a reaction.

Okay, I decided, bakery-bought cookies would do. She probably wouldn't eat anything anyway. We vacuumed up cat hair, washed a bowl of grapes, brewed a pot of coffee.

"Make sure we hide the bong and the beer bottles," Marc said wryly.

Aretha Franklin was lovely—professional and pretty. And young. So young. She arrived ten minutes early with a large Coach tote bag and drew out a thick manila file folder. "Tell me about Michael," she said.

Do you have a few hours? I thought. *Remember to smile.* "What would you like to know?"

"Where is he in school?" *Wasn't that already in all the documentation we provided?*

"He's in a wonderful life skills program at the local high school," I said. *A program we had to force our school district to create.*

"What activities do you do with him?"

What haven't we tried? His repertory is rigid and limited.

"He loves the beach," I said.

"Museums," Marc said. *Uh, oh, did that make us sound like we were trying too hard to impress? Well, he did like to see what he called the "broken statues" at the Met. He thought they were hysterical.*

"Sports! He loves sports, he's in a recreation program here in town," Marc added.

I thought for a nanosecond of adding, *it's a sports program we started for special needs kids, because there weren't any that would take kids like him.* I stopped myself; it sounded self-serving.

"Visiting his cousins, that's his favorite thing. Books. TV. Video games. But we try to limit them," I hastened to add. *What if she thought we parked him in front of the television?*

"Would you like to meet him?" Marc said.

"Of course." She smiled. We coaxed him into the room, set out a large black-and-white cookie—his favorite—and a glass of skim milk.

Mickey acted silly. He wouldn't answer her questions. "Chicken!" he said. That's what he called people when he was anxious. "I don't want to talk," he said. He gobbled his cookie and left.

"I know this may sound strange, but why do you want to be his guardians?" she asked.

We were his parents. Wasn't it obvious?

Marc said, "Who else? No one loves him as much as we do."

"We signed on for life," I added. "He's our child."

She asked for names and numbers. Mickey's teacher. Mickey's two standby guardians—my brother Marty and our older son Jonathan.

Smiles and handshakes all around. She was so young; how could she have any idea of what being parents to our son truly involved?

As soon as she left, I emailed my brother at work, to tell him to expect a call from Aretha Franklin.

He emailed back: "I will be sure to give her R-E-S-P-E-C-T."

It broke the tension. Marc and I laughed.

"What's Mommy's job?" I used to ask Mickey when he was little.

"To keep me safe," he'd say.

Mickey's answer haunted me. I was angry we had to go through this process. But I was afraid too. Could the court possibly rule against us?

No matter how much I knew logically all we had done for our son, it never felt like enough. The loop that played endlessly in my head: *could've, should've.* After he was first diagnosed, I'd continually felt as if there was one more therapy, one more intervention, one more special diet out there to try. That it would be the critical one, the magical, miraculous one that had eluded us. And that if we didn't try, we weren't good parents.

And the recriminations: what did I do wrong during my pregnancy? Did I not play with him enough as an infant? Not go to enough conferences, seminars and workshops? Or go to too many that took me away from him? Should we have taken him to see other experts? I should have done *more.*

But I don't know what more we could have done. Sometimes, even now in dark moments, I still think, *I have not been a good enough mother.*

Because if I had, Mickey wouldn't be disabled anymore.

[17]

1992: DIAGNOSIS

Because I fell on an icy patch when I was pregnant.

Because I took an Advil before I knew I was pregnant.

Because I bled mysteriously for four weeks during the first trimester.

Because I took the antibiotic the doctor insisted I take for a second-trimester infection.

Because I caught a virus and ran a fever.

Because the amnio was so difficult the doctor had to puncture me three times before she could express even a few drops of amniotic fluid, then told me to go home and drink a little wine to stop the contractions the amnio caused.

Because ten days after Mickey's birth I bound my bruised and bleeding breasts, bundled my baby into a Snugli and snuck him into the hospital to meet my mother, who was dying from end-stage emphysema.

Because I was so emotionally overwrought about her imminent death that I neglected him in some way.

All of these reasons made me the culprit.

My first pregnancy with Jonathan when I was 32 had been uneventful. I spent six days in the hospital, recovering from a long labor and C-section. Jonathan roomed in; my husband Marc spent the last night in the hospital with us. I remember how all that night he kept jumping up from the cot each time the baby snuffled or sighed. He'd held our infant son and crooned to him so gently that I'd felt weepy with love. Marc had lost his own dad when he was only 13 years old; he *needed* to be a father. Having a child of his own helped fill a void in his heart. I'd had no idea how passionately we would both fall in love with our child. Jonathan grew to be an affectionate, mischievous little boy who thought deeply, and asked precocious, startling questions: "What's gravity?" "Is there TV in heaven?" "Are you tired of being a mother?"

I'd been 37 when I'd conceived Mickey. My pregnancy was complicated. Lying on the den sofa after that arduous amnio, I still remember willing the unwelcome contractions to stop. Marc sat beside me, worried. I remember squeezing his hand. "It'll be okay," I told him. "This baby is a fighter."

To this day, I remember how much I thought about autism—or the little I knew about it—during my second pregnancy. I was haunted by a specific character on the television show *St. Elsewhere*, a beautiful, blond, silent and rocking boy named Tommy. I thought about Tommy often. Why? I still don't know. Of all the frightening things mothers-to-be imagine, why had I chosen that one image?

In the weeks after Mickey's birth, I found myself asking anyone who held him, "Is he making eye contact?" Then, at three weeks, he gave all three of us his first beatific smile. I breathed relief.

Soon our baby became a plumpster. A cherub with *pulkes*—fat dimply thighs; sausage-roll wrists; Popeye arms. But at eight months old, he still lay on a blanket on the floor, struggling to reach his Wiggle Worm. *Why didn't he just roll over to get it?* "Oh, don't be so lazy!" I remember my Aunt Adele saying to him.

Lazy? A baby? Her innocent remark touched off a wave of maternal misgivings.

Because there was something about his eyes...something I couldn't name that left me uneasy. A fleetingly disconnected look. As if there were too much white showing beneath his blue irises. *It's nothing*, I told myself.

Then a month later, a tiny bump beside Mickey's eye grew larger. I felt a hard little mass under the skin. Fearful, Marc and I flew to the pediatrician. "That's a dermoid cyst," he said, and sent us to the eye surgeon.

"Once he's beginning to walk, we'll need to operate," the surgeon told us. Our hearts sank.

"How can we do this to him? He won't understand what's happening, he'll be terrified. *I'm* terrified," I told Marc.

"He'll be fine," Marc said reassuringly again and again. But I knew he was trying to assuage his own anxiety too.

Mickey was ten months old, not yet walking but beginning to pull himself into a standing position in his crib when we took him to White Plains Hospital. We changed him into hospital jammies washed soft from much use. Marc and I waited nervously in a cubicle with curtains on rods that screeched each time someone opened them. The anesthesiologist came to take him. "No," I said, "I'm going in there too." The anesthesiologist argued. "He's just a baby. He won't know if you're there or not."

Marc tried to calm me, but I was adamant. "*He'll know*." I donned scrubs, and carried my cherub into a stainless-steel room. The anesthesiologist held the tiny mask to Mickey's face. He struggled, then his blue eyes swam against the liquid whites. "He's gone," the doctor said. "Time to go. I'll find you in the waiting room." Reluctantly, I left.

Forty-five minutes. An hour. My mother-in-law Beverly joined us in the waiting room. The surgeon finally strode in and Marc and I jumped up.

"How is my perfectly beautiful grandson?" Beverly asked.

"He has a perfectly beautiful scar," the surgeon said briskly.

I winced.

Far away, we heard hoarse, harsh crying. It was not until they came to call our name that I realized those sounds were coming from Mickey. He was inconsolable. Half his face was bandaged; blond wisps of hair stuck to the adhesive. I choked back my tears in front of the doctors and nurses.

But days later, he was again joyful and animated. Mickey was back. He smiled and cuddled and watched us attentively. Yet over and over when we tried to play Peek-a-Boo, or How Big is the Baby, Mickey still didn't play back. "Look how intently he's watching our mouths when we speak," I told Marc.

"It must mean he's going to talk early," Marc suggested. Always an optimist.

Again and again I'd say to Mickey, "Wave bye bye." Each time he watched me silently. At every monthly visit with the pediatrician I sought reassurance. "Do you think something's wrong?" I'd ask him.

mothers always know

by natural instincts

"He's fine," the pediatrician said every time. "He's just hitting developmental milestones at the late end of normal. Don't compare your children. Boys often talk later."

Of course, I thought. *Why am I always such a worrier? My fears are foolish.* "The doctor says he's okay," I told Marc. But I wasn't convinced. Something still felt off.

We celebrated Mickey's first birthday with family and friends in our backyard; Mickey, in his stroller, slept through it all. Then, at 14 months, he finally began walking. We were thrilled. Once a week I took him to a "Mommy and Me" class, where we would sing songs, roll little toy cars down ramps, and read story books.

Marc and I listened for Mickey's words. One time he said, *nan-nan-nah*. Banana. Another time he said, *cack*. Cracker. Excited, I called Marc at work. "He said a new word!" We waited eagerly for more words. They did not come.

That Thanksgiving we visited Marc's sister and family; their golden retriever barked.

"Dog!" Mickey said happily.

Thank God. Another word. But just like *nan-nan-nah* and *cack*, we never heard it again.

Weeks later, I took Jonathan to the pediatrician for an ear infection. While we were there, I announced, "I'm still worried about Mickey."

"How old is he now?"

"He's exactly 18 months today."

"And what is he saying?"

"He isn't. The only words he uses are *Ma-ma, Da-da* and *No.*"

"Now it's time for an evaluation," the pediatrician said.

The fear I'd been feeling for months flared. There *was* something amiss. That night I relayed to Marc what the pediatrician had said. Marc was calm. "We'll do whatever we need to do," he said firmly. "We're a team. We'll take him to that appointment together."

The speech evaluation at Blythdale Children's Hospital the following week indicated a "mild" delay; I set up a schedule for therapy. A week later, the "Mommy and Me" class teacher called me at home, asking me to come in. My heart thudded. "What's this about?"

"We're not allowed to discuss this on the phone," she said evasively. Marc was out of town; I remember I didn't sleep that night. The next morning I sat by myself on a little wooden chair in the empty classroom, the teacher across the Formica table from me.

"Mickey's been walking for four months but he's still falling over people and things too often," she said, sounding gentler than she had on the phone. "I think it's great that you already got a speech evaluation, but I think there is something more going on. I used to work with Down syndrome kids, and obviously it's not that. This is new to me. I don't know exactly what I'm looking at here with Mickey."

My heart hammered. Neither did I. Or Marc. Even Jonathan, who was only six, had absorbed our anxiety. That night when I put him to bed, his voice quivered. "Mom?" he said. "Maybe someone dropped him on his head."

∿◉

During that first year of Mickey's life, I had sought out a family therapist, initially to consult with her about handling my mother's imminent death. I had been taking Mickey with me as well, because Barbara also specialized in play therapy for children. In the past few months she'd begun playing with him while we spoke about my fear of abandonment, and how to help Jonathan through the loss of his beloved grandmother. I called Barbara immediately after the school conference.

"You need to get an integrated assessment, not a piecemeal evaluation. Let me get you a referral," she said to me, and asked a colleague to suggest a top-notch evaluation site.

Which is how that cold March morning in 1994 Marc, Mickey and I found ourselves sitting in a series of cubicles at a major teaching hospital in Manhattan, helplessly watching a team of experts spend hours poking, prodding and measuring our 20-month-old son.

I remember the psychologist handing Mickey thick colored pegs. "Put these in the wooden board," she commanded. She sat across the table from him, balancing a stop watch in her lap. *Why was she timing him?* I wondered. He put the first peg in and looked up at her expectantly. No reaction. "Keep going," she said coolly.

Marc and I looked at each other quizzically. *Why this aloofness?* Both of us began to reel quietly at her disengaged manner.

"Come on, honey," I whispered anxiously, "Put the pegs in."

He put in another peg. Again he looked up and waited. When she didn't respond, Mickey clapped his hands, as if to prompt her. *He's looking for praise,* I wanted to say. *Why isn't she responding to him?*

"That's good, Mickey, but you have to go faster," she admonished.

"Come on, Mick, you can do it!" Marc said too heartily.

Again we shot each other anxious looks. *Why was she timing him? Didn't she see he expected her to respond to him? That he wanted her approval? Clearly he was trying to interact with her; wasn't that more important than how fast he could line up a bunch of pegs?*

Midway through the speech therapist's evaluation, Mickey grew irritable. He refused to look at her. While I answered her questions, he fell asleep in Marc's arms.

Finally, the three of us were shunted into the office of the head of developmental pediatrics. "Mother, could you undress him please?" the doctor barked. I pulled off Mickey's hand-knit sweater, his tiny red turtleneck and matching blue overalls. He looked so sweet. Well cared for. So loved.

Again Marc and I watched quietly as the doctor repeatedly put Mickey through his paces, just as the other examiners had done all morning. She weighed and measured him, listened to his heart, examined his skin and manipulated his arms and legs. "He looks well nourished," she observed. She took a yellow tape out to measure his head circumference. Then she shone a pen light in his eyes. Mickey squirmed.

She pulled out a pocket recorder and began dictating: "Full range of motions in extremities. Bilateral retraction of tympanic membranes, with fluid present behind drums." I knew Mickey had the remnants of yet another ear infection; he was still taking antibiotics. *Is that what she saw?* "Cranial nerves intact. Tone within normal limits." She tapped his knees with a small rubber hammer, then briskly ran the tool along the bottoms of his bare feet. "Positive Babinski on the left; right side is equivocal." *Equivocal? What did that mean?*

Finally, she shut off the overhead light.

"You can dress him," she stated, as if he were an inanimate object.

Pale winter light leaked through a sooty sliver of window as Marc and I pulled clothes on our son. The silence felt heavy. Seeking to lighten it, I next said something so ignorant and cringe-inducing to me now that I am ashamed to remember it. "Well, as long as he's not going to vocational school."

Silence.

I hadn't yet been humbled.

"Have a seat," the doctor said neutrally, indicating a chair beside her desk. I sat. Marc leaned on the edge of the exam table, holding Mickey in his arms. I perched forward to catch her words carefully.

"Don't expect higher education for your son."

I felt myself go white; a metallic taste filled my mouth.

"What do you mean?" I asked, barely audible.

"I am saying that he will never be at the top of his class," she said. *What was she talking about? How could she even think this way? He was 20 months old!*

"He is delayed in communication, daily living skills and socialization. Throughout this evaluation he has shown distress and distractibility." Her voice was cool.

"But he has an ear infection," I pleaded.

"Yes. But he hasn't produced any meaningful words. His language is noticeably delayed. There is also a milder delay in his perceptual-motor tasks, and overall motor clumsiness. He is highly distractible."

"So what are our next steps?" Marc asked, his voice tight with fear.

"You should have him tested for Fragile X."

The hiss of my indrawn breath was audible. I knew something about Fragile X; it was genetic. I'd seen a show about it on *Oprah*.

"Fragile X children have language and motor delays, as well as hyperactivity and autistic behaviors. But he doesn't have the distinctive physical signs."

"Which are what?" Marc asked, now hoarse.

"Enlarged testicles. Prominent ears. However, those traits are not always present in younger children. Fragile X is the most common form of inherited mental retardation [that term was still in use] in the United States."

Retardation?

I bit my lower lip; willed myself not to cry. Not now. Not in front of this cold officious woman. "How do we help him?'"

"You're in a good position," she said. "Your son appears attached to you both. You're well-educated parents with an understanding of childhood development. You will be good advocates for your son." Then she reeled off a list of what Mickey would need: early intervention services. A comprehensive program. Speech and language therapy. Educational and behavioral interventions. Physical therapy.

Quickly she stood up. "Good luck to you," she stated as she strode out of the room, leaving us stunned in her wake. We were bodies strewn on a battlefield.

"That's it?" I said incredulously to Marc. "Isn't anyone else going to talk to us?" *Where had everybody gone? What should we do? Where was that social worker?*

"Let's leave. Now!" Marc answered fiercely, jamming sweaters and snacks into the diaper bag.

Wasn't anyone going to say a word to us? Offer some comfort? Escort us to the elevator?

The doctor's words had upended our four lives, with not an ounce of compassion.

As the elevator doors slid open, I noticed the social worker standing near the reception desk. "Goodbye," she called cheerily. "Call me if you need anything."

I was speechless with shock and grief. "Thank you," Marc said curtly, out of a lifelong habit of politeness. Like thanking the executioner who's just offered you a blindfold before he buries the blade in your neck.

Outside, we braced against the rush of icy air, as I clutched Mickey tight, pulling my coat around us both. I began to run to the garage. As we descended the parking ramp, Marc turned to me.

"Are you okay?"

Was I okay?

I glared at him. "What do you think?"

"Talk to me," he pleaded, needing to make sense of what we both were feeling.

"That woman just told us our child has no future. No, I am NOT 'okay.'"

I'd held it together throughout the ordeal; now I was taking it out on Marc, who didn't deserve my rage. Then he startled me.

"I don't want you talking about it to all your friends. Don't tell anyone." He was adamant. Sad. "I don't want anyone to look at him differently."

But I felt angry. It felt as if he was tying a tourniquet around my heart. How could I not talk to anyone? Acting the stoic might work for him. Not for me. Keep this to myself? This pain? Rage? Fear? I couldn't do that. I knew he was shocked and heartbroken. Was he also ashamed? But then, was I?

We drove home in a silence punctuated by my sobs. Who was this child? How could this beautiful boy with his bright blue eyes, soft duck-like blond hair and huge smile be brain damaged? What had I done? I'd taken prenatal vitamins. Eaten carefully. Didn't drink or smoke. Had an amnio and several ultrasounds. His birth had been a planned C-section; the Apgars, normal. I stared at Mickey. Our own son had become a stranger. *What's wrong with you?* I thought, looking at him. *Why is this happening? God make this go away.*

∿❅

Several days later, Mickey and I went to see Barbara. Hugging my knees to my chest, I sat on the carpeted floor of her office, watching Mickey build block towers, then gleefully knock them down. My voice quivered as I told her what had happened at the evaluation.

"I'm so sorry," she kept saying.

"And then," I said, my voice rising, "She said…she said…" A sob caught in my throat; I swallowed hard. "She said he might be…" my voice dropped to a whisper. "'Retarded.'"

"Oh, Liane," Barbara said, so soft and kind. I began sobbing.

And that's when it happened.

Mickey looked up. He put down the block in his hand and stood. Toddled toward me. Was he terrified at the sight of his mother sobbing? He bent down to peer anxiously into my face. Then he spread his arms wide and wrapped himself around me, offering me his solace, his love, his wordless need for reassurance.

I looked at Barbara. Her eyes were streaming too. "Oh my God," I whispered. *"He's* trying to comfort *me."*

∿❅

Empathy. The very characteristic that so many experts told us not to expect. Why does this myth that autistic people lack empathy persist?

EMPATHY +
AUTISM

The reasons are complicated—a convergence of media, popular culture and ignorance. But if you want to lay blame, you might start with the British cognitive psychologists Simon Baron-Cohen and Uta Frith, who in the 1980s coined the term loathed by many, "mind-blindness," for what they considered the core deficit in autism: the autistic person's inability to employ a "theory of mind." Meaning, essentially, that autistic people are incapable of imagining anyone else's thoughts and feelings.

But empathy is a complicated construct. There is cognitive empathy, the ability to read other people's feelings, but there is also affective empathy, the ability to share other people's feelings. Just because you don't have the social/cognitive skill to read someone else's feelings doesn't mean you can't feel someone else's pain. While it's true that autistic people often have a harder time reading social cues, it is quite a leap—and a dangerous one—to assume that a person's inability to interpret non-verbal cues means he doesn't care and has no empathy.

Empathy is the trait that makes us human. In my opinion, to say that autistics lack empathy is to suggest that they are less than human. And once you dehumanize others it becomes "permissible" to do things to them. To taunt and bully and abuse. Consider places like the Judge Rotenberg Center in Massachusetts, a so-called treatment center for people with autism that uses painful electrical shocks to the skin to punish self-injurious behavior. That's not treatment. That's torture.

And if you still don't think this kind of thinking is dangerous, consider this.

In the wake of the Sandy Hook school massacre, as some people speculated that the shooter Adam Lanza might have been on the autism spectrum, hate groups began showing up on Facebook. One group calling itself "Asperger's Prevention Campaign" posted this: "When we reach 50 likes, we will find an autistic kid and set it on fire." (Facebook removed the group.)

Everyone in the autism community knows the saying, "If you've met one person with autism, you've met one person with autism." Some people on the spectrum may struggle with empathy; others can feel overwhelmed by other people's feelings. Then there is everyone in between. You know what? That's why we call it a spectrum. As journalist Steve Silberman, author of *NeuroTribes: The Legacy of Autism and the Future of Neurodiversity*, says, "Calling autistics mind-blind may turn out to be as apt as calling those who don't speak English deaf."

Mickey was exactly the same child we'd had before the diagnosis. Playful. Affectionate. Despite the complications and challenges we would encounter in the next 20 years after that cold March day at the hospital in Manhattan, Mickey's ability to read and respond to others' emotions, whether they are loving or cold, has been a gift. Though it has never been recorded in a medical chart, or documented in any of the countless standardized tests he has taken through the years, it is a key part of who Mickey is. His warmth, his humor, his vibrancy, his sheer resilience pushed us forward.

CHILD'S PLAY

"I called that doctor you saw," Barbara told me at our next visit. "I feel terrible that I sent you there. I wanted to give her a piece of my mind about the unprofessional way they treated you."

I was touched Barbara had done that for me. "What did she say?"

Barbara hesitated. "Essentially, she said the same things she said to you. I told her I won't be sending her any more referrals."

I sighed. "So now what?" I asked, determined to move ahead.

"I'd like to refer you to my mentor, Stanley Greenspan. I think he'll give you a much more hopeful evaluation."

Normally there was a six-month wait to get an appointment, but Barbara made a call. "They're moving you up because Mickey is so young," she told me.

Two weeks later, we told Jonathan he would be spending a fun weekend with Grandma Bev while his dad and I took Mickey to see a special doctor in Maryland who was going to help his brother. "Is he ever going to talk?" Jonathan asked anxiously again and again. Even though we were trying to keep Jonathan's life and routines as normal as possible, it was difficult to conceal the alarm that had taken over our lives.

"We're going to get Mickey whatever help he needs," we tried to reassure him.

The word "autism," which has been in use for about 100 years, comes from the Greek word "autos," meaning "self." Before the 1940s, children who would now be called autistic were labeled emotionally disturbed, schizophrenic or psychotic. In a 1943 paper entitled "Autistic Disturbances of Affective Contact," Leo Kanner, a psychiatrist from Johns Hopkins University, identified autism as a distinct neurological condition. He called it Early Infantile Autism, because it usually appeared sometime during the first three years of life. He described 11 children who shared high intelligence, a profound preference for being alone and an "obsessive insistence on the preservation of sameness."

At the same time, Hans Asperger, an Austrian psychiatrist, identified a similar condition that is now called Asperger syndrome. The symptoms Asperger identified in 1944 were closely related, but not identical, to Kanner's Early Infantile Autism. People with Asperger syndrome experienced the same difficulty with social interactions as the children Kanner studied, but had greater facility with language. Asperger's work went virtually unrecognized until the 1970s. It wasn't until 1994 that Asperger syndrome was recognized as a diagnosis in the *Diagnostic and Statistical Manual of Mental Disorders (DSM)*, the handbook used by health care professionals in the United States and much of the world as the authoritative guide to the diagnosis of mental disorders. People argue about the relationship between Asperger syndrome and autism. Asperger himself believed that the two were distinct disorders, but many today emphasize the similarity between Asperger syndrome and high-functioning autism and consider both to be autism spectrum disorders. In 2013, the revised *DSM-5* folded Asperger syndrome into the umbrella diagnosis of autism spectrum disorder (ASD), which was defined by two categories: impaired social communication and/or interaction and restricted and/or repetitive behaviors.

Though Kanner thought the children's inability to relate to others was probably innate, he also stressed what he observed to be the cold, intellectual nature of their parents, especially their mothers, saying of the parents whose children he studied that they kept their children "neatly in a refrigerator that did not defrost."

Enter Bruno Bettelheim, the renowned University of Chicago professor and child development specialist. From the late 1940s to the early 1970s Bettelheim served as director of the Sonia Shankman Orthogenic School at the University. Building on Kanner's earlier work, Bettelheim declared that autism was an emotional disorder that developed in some children because of psychological harm caused by their mothers. He likened the lives of autistic children to the experience of prisoners in Nazi concentration camps, where he himself had spent ten months during World War II: "The only real difference between the SS guard and the mother of the autistic child is that the mother gets to the child much earlier in life." In his book *The Empty Fortress: Infantile Autism and the Birth of the Self*, which is based on only three case studies, he wrote, "The precipitating factor in infantile autism is the parent's wish that his child should not exist."

The reviled theory of the "refrigerator mother" was unleashed, and mainstream media ran with it. Bettelheim was likable and charismatic, a good self-promoter who easily popularized his theories on national prime-time television shows and in magazines. His book found a wide and willing audience.

Bernard Rimland, parent of an autistic child and a research psychologist, was the first person to challenge this psychiatric orthodoxy. Through his own research Rimland came to believe that the "refrigerator mother" theory was founded on circumstantial and anecdotal evidence. In 1964, he suggested a biological cause of autism in his book *Infantile Autism: The Syndrome and Its Implications for a Neural Theory of Behavior.*

Rimland didn't have Bettelheim's celebrity. His theories went largely unnoticed. But a growing number of parents of autistic children began to hear about Rimland's work, and in 1969, they founded what eventually became the Autism Society of America

(ASA), a public voice for parents of autistic children who rejected the "refrigerator mother" myth. Today autism is considered a neurodevelopmental disorder.

It wasn't until months after Marc and I had taken Mickey to see Barbara's mentor Stanley Greenspan that we learned he was considered the foremost authority in the world on mental health and disorders in infants and young children. What we did notice immediately when we met him, however, was that he was lanky, kind and a bit eccentric. He saw us at his home office, a wood-paneled playroom reminiscent of a camp bunk that was filled with toys, many of them broken or missing pieces. Dolls without heads. Cars without wheels. He greeted us at the door in his bedroom slippers, munching on an apple. "Come in, come in!" he said, smiling gently. "Call me Stanley. What can I do for you?"

I handed him the reports we'd brought. "I'll look at these later," he said. "I'd rather hear from you about what's going on." He listened to us for nearly an hour, as Mickey flitted around the room, picking up and quickly discarding toys.

"What is your biggest fear?" he finally asked.

"There was a boy in our neighborhood named Phillip," I said in a low voice. Phillip had been a developmentally disabled teenage boy with lifeless eyes who sat on the front steps of his home, rocking and sucking his thumb. If you ventured too close, he would swipe at you and make frightening guttural noises. "People used to whisper that Phillip would never grow past the level of a six-month-old," I told him. I couldn't bring myself to look at Marc as I said this.

"That's not going to happen," Stanley said reassuringly. He took out a video camera. "Now it's time to play," he said, directing us to sit on the floor with Mickey. "Okay, Mother, you're first."

"What are you going to do with the tape?" I asked nervously.

"Use it for training purposes," Stanley said briskly. "With your permission, of course."

"I hope it's not a cautionary tale on what *not* to do," I joked. I picked up a tiny toy truck and gently showed it to Mickey, who backed away. No interest.

Stanley jumped right in. "He's being avoidant; don't let him turn away from you. Try being playfully obstructive. Make that truck drive up his leg. Hide it in his shirt. Say, 'Oh, Mickey, where did it go?' Amp it up, you're too soft! You're losing him." I followed Stanley's rapid-fire coaching, feeling self-conscious and embarrassed. It was 20 excruciating minutes before he finally let me off the hook.

"Dad's turn!" he said. Watching Marc play with more animation than I had, I felt as if I'd just flunked Play 101.

We were into the fourth hour of the evaluation before Stanley was ready to give an opinion. He pulled out a pocket recorder. "I'll send you a written copy of everything I'm about to say," he told us. Marc had tensed up; I perched on the edge of the couch cushion, clenching my cold hands.

"Early testing such as the kind your son had at the hospital has no long-term predictive value," he said firmly. "Your son is not 'retarded.'"

Marc and I exhaled audibly.

"Nor is he classically autistic," Stanley went on. "He's got a gleam in his eye: he's got energy and a knowing look. He's happy, he's warm and engaged, and there is nice intimacy. He shows a flirtatious grin. He not only relates to you, he was able to be warm with me after a period of appropriate cautiousness. We can't know how high he'll go until he reaches his ceiling."

"Really?"

"*Really*," he said. "It's no different with your other son; you don't know yet how far Jonathan will go either."

Marc reached for my hand and squeezed hard.

"That said," Stanley continued, "let me tell you what he *does* have. He falls somewhere between two diagnoses: Multi-system Developmental Disorder and Regulatory Disorder. MDD describes children under three who show signs of impaired communication, but have strong emotional attachments. Neither term carries a negative prognosis. They basically describe what is visible at the moment. For insurance purposes, we will call this static encephalopathy, with speech and language, motor, sensory, cognitive and affective dysfunction."

That still sounded negative to me. "How can we help him?" I asked.

"He needs to be energized and pulled into interaction; it's easier for him to withdraw into his own world," Stanley said. "He's having a difficult time regulating all the sensory input around him. He's not quite as responsive to verbal interactions as I would like to see him at this point. He's a little on the under-reactive side, which is why he is so calm and laid back. But he also has some over-reactivity to certain sensations as well."

"Is that why he's so bothered by walking on the grass, and hates touching sand?" Marc asked.

"I've seen him cringe at certain sounds that don't seem to bother other people," I added. "Every time we're in an elevator he covers his ears and hums."

"It's a little like trying to drive a car where the information coming in is distorted," Stanley explained. "There's too much light and an inability to hear what's going on with other cars, and when Mickey presses the gas pedal, the car goes in reverse. Or doesn't move at all. But with lots of practice, Mickey *will* be able to learn to drive his 'car' and overcome the difficult mechanics."

"This schedule I am going to give you is very ambitious," he said. "Our goal is to keep his relatedness cooking." He was speaking quickly, and I struggled to get his words down on paper. *Speech therapy, five times a week. Occupational therapy, three to five times. Play therapy, three to five. Physical therapy consultation. Nursery school. Therapy for parents. Weekly date night…*

Stanley paused. "No need to take notes," he said. "It will all be in my report." Then he looked from Marc to me. "Here is the cornerstone of the program I'm giving you. You are going to play with him."

"We already do," Marc said.

"Yes, but now you are going to be doing the kind of pretend play I've just demonstrated. You'll do it four to five times a day, for at least 20 minutes a session, with two more sessions in the evening when Dad gets home from work." Then he smiled reassuringly. "You know, I've been following many children like yours for many years. All of them are speaking. One young man is even writing poetry."

My voice was tremulous. "Right now, I'd be thrilled to hear, 'Hi Mommy.'"

"I know," he said kindly. "I'll see you back here in six months. Please feel free to call me anytime you have any questions."

In the 1980s, Stanley Greenspan MD developed his Developmental Individual-difference Relationship-based model (DIR), a functional-developmental approach to helping children with a variety of developmental delays and issues. He called it "Floortime." It was based on his work in the 1970s and 1980s as director of the National Institute of Mental Health's Clinical Infant Development Program and Mental Health Study Center in Bethesda, MD. Dr. Greenspan found that babies who fail to connect with their parents for whatever reason—a developmental disorder, for example, or individual sensitivities such as an aversion to being touched—lacked the emotional tools essential to learn and grow. Studying the interactions of mothers with their infants and toddlers, which he video taped and archived, he came to believe that the building blocks of emotional and behavioral development were laid down much earlier than experts had thought.

The premise of Floortime was this: adults can help children expand their circles of communication by meeting them at their developmental level and building on their strengths. Therapists and parents engage children through the activities each child enjoys by getting down on the floor. They enter the child's games, and follow the child's lead, using gestures and words to build warm relationships and expand the child's world of ideas with increasingly complex interactions.

Floortime didn't target speech, motor or cognitive skills specifically. Instead, it addressed them all by focusing on a child's emotional development. Greenspan identified six developmental milestones that are critical for emotional and intellectual growth:

- self-regulation and interest in the world

- intimacy, or engagement in human relations

- two-way communication

- complex communication

- emotional ideas

- emotional thinking.

He called this innovative, sensitive process "opening and closing circles of communication." Today it is used in classrooms and clinics worldwide.

The three of us returned to our car. Marc turned to me as he buckled Mickey into his car seat. "This is going to be hard," he said. He slid into the driver's seat and put the key in the ignition. Then he turned to look at me and took my hand. "Unfortunately the burden is going to fall mainly on you. Are you okay with this?"

"As if you even have to ask?" I said softly.

"I love you, you know."

"I know," I said, welling up. "Me too."

"And we're in this together."

"Yes," I said huskily. "We are." We held hands a moment longer; then he turned on the engine.

I was overwhelmed at everything that lay ahead. We both were. But for the first time in months, I thought maybe—just maybe—we would get through this. Stanley had recognized the same strengths we saw in Mickey. He had given us back our hope.

Play became my vocation. Play as work. Mind-numbing, tedious play, but moments of connection and joy too. Mickey chortled with glee every time we made up games and stories with his favorite plastic Fisher Price Little People toys. Still, it was an emotionally volatile time. Often my moods were only as good as the last therapy session. Advice poured in from relatives and friends, even strangers at the playground. Misguided, insensitive, well-meaning advice. A Greek chorus of advice, rushing to dismiss my fears: "Have you tried speaking more slowly?" "Is English the primary language in your home?" "Boys talk late." "Were you exposed to something during your pregnancy?" "He looks fine; maybe you just aren't disciplining him properly." "He's too little for so much therapy; he'll talk when he's ready." "Every child does things at different times. He'll snap out of it." "Have you had his hearing tested?" "You know, Einstein didn't talk till he was four."

Bed-time reading was a ritual with both our boys. "One more chapter, Mom," Jonathan would plead nightly. I would breathe in the apricot scent of his freshly washed hair and, loath to leave, manage most nights to rasp out another ten pages. He would burrow into my side, sighing, giggling, hiding his face at the suspenseful parts, stopping me to ask the meaning of a new word. Impossible to resist.

Every night I read to Mickey too, the same books again and again. His favorite began, "Once there was a little gorilla, and everybody loved him. His mother loved him. His father loved him…"

I remember the day the sale clerk at Eeyore Books had pressed *Little Gorilla* into my hand and I flipped through the pages. It hadn't immediately grabbed me. "Kids go crazy for this one," she assured me. "Take the paperback version. You'll see."

She was right. *Little Gorilla* became Mickey's favorite book. The text was repetitive and soothing, the words simple and rhythmic. "Everyone loved him… Then one day something happened… Little Gorilla began to grow and Grow and Grow and GROW and one day, Little Gorilla was BIG!" Little Gorilla looked woeful. He was huge. Like a teenager in a new unwieldy body. I couldn't imagine that ever happening to either of my boys, and yet I knew someday it would.

"Everyone in the great green forest still loved Little Gorilla," I told Mickey. "Just like you." Mickey was two. *What a wonderful message for him,* I thought. Even when you grow and change, the people who love you still love you. It was a story about the security and the constancy of love. Even Jonathan, who was nearly eight, liked the book too. I continued to bury myself in both my boys. Reading, playing, feeding, comforting. Again and again, Mickey would put *Little Gorilla* in my hands. "Muh," he would say. More.

Marc travelled often for work. He hated it; I did too. Jonathan, seeing my exhaustion or low spirits, asked over and over, "Are you okay, Mom? Can I help you?" I pretended I was, but I wasn't. I was exhausted. "I wish Daddy wouldn't see clients," he confided. "I want him to stay home with me all day."

Mickey was two and a half and wasn't sleeping. He would keep himself awake some nights till midnight, doze a while, then awaken crying. He'd cling to me, and couldn't be soothed back to sleep. "He is having intense separation concerns," Barbara told me. By then she'd been working with him for six months. Whenever she even said the word "sleep," and began a sleep sequence of play, Mickey would jump into my arms and grip tight. To help him, she devised separation games. She put a stuffed cat on one pillow and a photo of Marc and me on the other pillow. "I don't want to sleep on this pillow!" she had the cat say, and made the cat jump onto the pillow that had the photo of us. Then she would return the cat to his own pillow. Mickey watched her with rapt attention. "Muh!" he said each time.

Mickey also loved to play with a shape sorter box. Once you fitted the shapes into the slots, you could spin the box, and make the shapes tumble out. Repeatedly, purposely, he'd hand this toy to Barbara. "This is useful for separation/reunion play too," she pointed out. Mickey listened intently as she spoke. Then he put the shapes in the box, grinned and clapped his hands. "Do-muh!" he'd say.

Barbara was pleased by Mickey's progress, yet puzzled about him too, as Marc and I were. "He has a wonderful personality," she said. "So enthusiastic. He gets angry sometimes when you set limits, but basically he's happy and even-tempered." Yet there were often times when she couldn't get him to interact. Mickey would play intently by himself, turning the pages of a book. Refusing to engage. He didn't understand "where" questions, or "show me" or "point to the..." Sometimes, Marc, Barbara and I noted with concern, he'd seem to turn inward for a few seconds, not moving or answering when we called his name. None of us understood why he did this, or what caused his behavior. Barbara called him "a puzzle child."

Increasingly Mickey carried spoons, small balls or little plastic people around. He also showed interest in a set of magnetic letters we kept on the refrigerator, recognizing them even if they were sideways or upside down. He'd say "b" for blue, and "gr" for green; he seemed to know colors. Once—thrillingly—he picked up a plastic number and announced, "seben!" He'd begun to jabber, emitting rhythmic streams of sound that sounded conversational.

But at not quite three, he was still banging his head. It scared me. He'd do it when he was angry, or aggrieved. If Marc took Jonathan to the bathroom in a restaurant and I told Mickey, "They'll be back soon," he'd bend forward and clonk his forehead on the table. Or he'd do it to get my attention if I was on the phone. *If only he had more language, he wouldn't need to do that,* I'd think.

Sometimes he'd pull Jonathan's hair when Jonathan wouldn't give him a toy, but he enjoyed playing side by side with his brother. Jonathan would take out a toy garage, and together he and Mickey would take turns rolling little cars and trucks up and down the ramps. They loved to play Caterpillar, a game Jonathan invented. I wasn't sure what the point of it was, but it involved cocooning in a blanket and inching around the floor together. Jonathan was terrific with him. Mickey always lit up and held out his arms for Jonathan. Watching them, I would smile so much my face ached. The game never failed to make Mickey laugh. "Muh!" he'd say.

Mickey loved to hug Jonathan and us. He also showed concern whenever anyone was hurt or upset. Sometimes he would take my father's face and hold it in his hands. "Gaga!" he'd say. Grandpa. He clearly loved him, and showed his affection.

But it wasn't only the sleep deprivation that was making me drag through the days; it was the pervasive sense of guilt that I could not adequately meet the needs of Mickey, Jonathan, Marc and my parents, who were ailing. My father had been diagnosed with prostate cancer; my mother was dying of emphysema. The doctors had sent her home with hospice care. A hospital bed sat in the middle of my parents' living room; an oxygen tank loomed large alongside it, the giant metal canister susurrating ceaselessly. There, tethered, my mother waited, frail and wasted, a translucent umbilical cord sustaining her life. Weekend after weekend, I brought the boys to visit.

The phone never rang late at night without me feeling a sense of dread. I'd imagine Marc's voice going low and even, asking a few questions, then hanging up the phone and turning to face me gently, before he delivered the news. I didn't know how to live day to day. At one point I called her doctor. Anguished, I'd asked him, "What should we expect?"

"It could be tomorrow, or it could be a month," the doctor said. "But I can promise you it won't be five years."

"How come Grandma Joan is so sick all the time?" Jonathan asked. I explained as simply as I could.

"What can we do to help her?" He thought a moment. "We could pray."

"That's a lovely idea."

He looked worried. "I don't know how to pray. I don't know Hebrew."

"You can pray in English."

"Does God know English?"

"Absolutely," I said.

I confided everything to Barbara. "No wonder you're exhausted," she said. "You're putting out a great deal but not much is being given to you. You need nurturing too."

I didn't know how to do this, except to find solace in reading. To myself, and to both my boys. With Jonathan, I read different books he liked, magical stories like *The Borrowers*. But with Mickey, over and over, *Little Gorilla*. Again and again, I snuggled him close, turning the well-worn pages until I intoned the last line: "And everybody still loved him."

Mickey was, in fact, pretty happy much of the time. He had a sunny disposition. He carried his collection of Puzzle Place dolls everywhere, hugging and kissing them, feeding them pretend food. He would line them up against the pillows on my bed, and whisper, "Ssh. Nap." Clearly, he knew how to nurture.

Yet despite those strong moments of connection and empathy, running errands with him was difficult. Particularly shopping. He needed to touch everything. Many kids misbehave, pitching a tantrum in the grocery store aisle; Mickey did more. If I didn't keep a firm grip on him, he'd dart off and disappear in a blink. If I tried to contain him by seating him in the shopping cart, he'd still sweep cartons of cookies in alongside him. One day we went to the local fruit and vegetable market. The aisle was small and narrow. Mickey ran to the green cardboard boxes overflowing with plump strawberries and reached for them. "We can't eat those till we buy them," I said, gently trying to move his hand, and thinking, *does he understand any of my words?* He reached for a pint of blueberries; I stopped him.

Thwarted, he twisted away from me, grabbing fistfuls of green grapes. Again I restrained him, my anxiety growing. He had no impulse control. He needed to touch it all, jam his chipmunk cheeks with food. Frustrated at my pulling his hand away yet again from the tempting fruit, he jerked out of my grasp, kicking the leg of an elderly woman who stood at the counter. I grabbed him, and blurted, "I am SO sorry." She didn't even look at me.

"Young man," she yelled, raising her cane menacingly, "Do you see this big stick? If you come near me again I'll hit you with it."

My cheeks flushed with heat. I scooped down, swept Mickey into my arms, held him tight. I was flooded with horror and shame. I felt her hatred. I knew she was thinking I was a dreadful mother with a nasty child. That it was my fault he acted like this.

I was too humiliated to speak. Shaking and sweating, I struggled to balance Mickey on my hip. Back and forth I went quickly, placing boxes of berries and bags of grapes on the counter. When several strawberries spilled onto the counter, I quickly scooped them up before they rolled over the edge.

"Anything else, ma'am?" the man behind the counter asked.

My eyes blurred with tears. Mutely I shook my head, barely holding myself together. He rang up my purchase and handed me my change. "Let me help you with your bags," he said kindly.

Silently he walked beside me to my car, waiting as I popped open the trunk.

"That woman was horrible to you," he said.

And that's when it all broke loose.

"My son has...something's wrong...he...has special needs. He's disabled." I felt as if I were being strangled, unable to find words that could convey Mickey's inexplicable behaviors. To tell this kind stranger how fears and therapies had taken over our lives. How Mickey would put his hand down his throat till he gagged. Bang his head on the table when he was frustrated. Fling a full plate of spaghetti against the wall. Why would this man even care? Tears coursed down my cheeks. I couldn't look at him. I buckled Mickey into his car seat.

"So what if he has special needs?" the man said hotly. "No one should speak to any child that way. She's a miserable old woman, and if she comes back in I'll tell her exactly what I think. I don't need customers like her."

"Thank you," I choked out.

He nodded. "You take care." I waited till he'd walked back to the store. Trembling so much, I couldn't get my key into the ignition. Instead, I collapsed against the steering wheel. All those fears and feelings that had festered in me for so long finally gushed out. I wailed.

Days later, Marc told me he stopped in to the fruit store for another pint of Mickey's beloved strawberries. "I talked to that man who helped you," he said.

"Really? Why? Did you tell him your wife sometimes acts like a lunatic?"

"You're not a lunatic," Marc said.

"So what did you say?"

"I said, 'I heard what happened when my wife and son came in here, and I really appreciate how kind you were to her.'"

That's why I married you, I thought. *Because you do things like that.* "What did he say?"

"He said, 'Yeah, she seemed pretty upset. That old lady was horrible to her.'"

I felt humiliation running through me again. Was it about Mickey's behavior? About my inability to handle him more effectively? About losing my composure so publicly? I felt shame. Then rage. Rage at people for judging so quickly. Rage at myself, for caring so much what strangers thought. Rage that in fact I couldn't control my own son. That day in the fruit store was the first time I ever saw The Look. Maybe it had been there all along, but now I noticed it. Acutely. At restaurants. Birthday parties. The playground. The barber shop. Oh, the barber shop. Where Mickey would shriek and flail as if the barber were performing surgery on him without anesthesia. One time an old man waiting his turn glared at our reflection in the mirror. "Rotten spoiled brat," he muttered.

Every parent knows The Look. It's the disapproving way people watch your child's behavior. But autism parents know The Look exponentially more.

You see The Look when your child pulls down boxes of Cheerios in the grocery aisle. When he refuses to sit in your lap during circle time at "Mommy and Me" class and instead runs non-stop rings around the group. When he dumps buckets filled with toys just so he can sit on them. When he lines up all the Legos® in rows, and has tantrums if anyone moves them.

The Look bellows, "What is wrong with your child?"

And, "What is wrong with you, that you have a child like that?"

DESPERATION

It was summer but Mickey was still sick. At two, he was still getting chronic ear infections that refused to heal, that muffled his hearing and made him miserable and tuned out. He had only a handful of reliable words. Our pediatrician instructed us to give him a small, prophylactic dose of antibiotics every day, but the infections kept coming. "But he will talk, won't he?" I asked him. There was a silence, a pause that seemed an eternity, before the doctor said, "Probably." Then he sent us to a pediatric ear, nose and throat specialist, who removed Mickey's adenoids and placed tiny tubes in his ear drums to allow the fluid to drain.

He'll finally wake up hearing clearly, I kept thinking. *Then he'll be able to speak.*

But his words didn't, in fact, come any faster. His face still looked gray. Weeks later, at our second visit to Stanley in Bethesda, I voiced my concerns.

"We're doing all the therapies you told us to do," I said. "But Mickey is getting sick all the time. He doesn't sleep well. He bangs his head when he's frustrated. Sometimes he just looks blank and doesn't respond to us at all."

"It's hard to be available for learning when you're feeling sick and in pain," Stanley said, and referred us to Kelly, a developmental nutritionist in Maryland.

"There's a new diet that may help," Kelly told me on the phone days later. "I'll send you the article. It's called 'An Experimental Intervention for Autism—Understanding and Implementing a Gluten and Casein-Free Diet.'"

My stomach lurched. "Stanley said Mickey doesn't have autism," I said quickly. "He said it was either a regulatory or multi-system developmental disorder."

"I still think the diet may be helpful," she said, her voice kind. "It sounds like there are two problems going on. Low immunity, and developmental delays. All his energy is going into getting better, at the expense of his cognitive growth. Children like this often have an immune-system dysfunction that affects the body's ability to break down certain proteins, or combat yeast or bacteria."

We were desperate for help. In 1994, the internet was in its infancy. There was no way at the time to vet any of this information. But Stanley was the foremost authority on children with developmental problems, and he'd recommended her. "Tell me how to do this diet," I said.

Kelly asked us what foods he was craving: bagels? Macaroni and cheese? She explained that the peptides in gluten and dairy weren't breaking down properly, that they had an opiate effect. "That could be why he seems spacey to you. He's addicted to those foods."

It seemed to make sense.

"From now on, no wheat," she said. "No rye, barley, oats or spelt. No dairy of any kind. Use Rice Dream, it's a dairy-free milk fortified with calcium."

Frantically I wrote down her suggestions.

"Supplements," she said. "Use Poly-Vi-Sol multivitamins. Magnesium. B6. Glutathione. Choline, for anxiety. Flaxseed oil. Bifidus. Pycnogenol. You can mix everything into his rice milk."

"Are there any other foods we should avoid?"

"Yes. Ketchup, mayonnaise, vinegar, modified food starch, yeast and chocolate."

What was left to eat? How was I going to feed this child? I became increasingly scared.

In those days, there were no gluten/casein-free products on grocery store shelves. I emptied our pantry, squirreling away contraband pretzels and cookies for Jonathan. Where could we shop? I paced the narrow aisles at Mrs. Green's Natural Foods, reading labels obsessively. I bought organic produce, wheat-free ketchup, frozen rice bread with the consistency of cotton, and a brand of gluten-free, casein-free mixes called Pamela's, which made mealy muffins, bagels and brownies. I kept a separate knife for all these items, terrified of contaminating Mickey's food with a stray crumb of wheat. Saddest of all, it was nearly impossible to eat out as a family. But we didn't want to deprive Jonathan; when Marc was home on weekends, he made sure to take him out for pizza or to the local deli.

∽૭

"What this family needs is a vacation," I announced.

Barbara told me about another family she worked with who'd recently rented a condo on Cape Cod for a week. I asked her to get me the realtor's number. That August we rented a two-bedroom gray shingled cottage covered in salt spray roses that overlooked Nantucket Sound. The car tires crunched pleasingly as we drove along the crushed-shell driveway; blue hydrangeas bobbed over the white picket fence. Inside, the white-washed house was full of light and ocean breezes. Marc and I stood on the second-floor balcony, and looked out at the water. "Look! You can see Martha's Vineyard," he said. It was balm for the soul. I'd been holding my breath so long; I felt as if I could breathe again.

"Are we relaxed yet?" Marc asked.

"We're working on it."

Every morning we walked down to the shore, and I snuggled under the beach umbrella with Jonathan, reading aloud from *The Indian in the Cupboard* while Marc coaxed Mickey into the pool.

We rode the ferry to the Vineyard. Climbed the steep sand dunes at Truro. Ate lobster rolls and Cape Cod potato chips (gluten free). Saw antique cars at the Heritage Museum. Went digging in tidal pools on the bay. Strolled down Commercial Street in Provincetown. "I have a soft spot for this town," I told Jonathan. "We used to vacation here when I was Mickey's age. In fact, this is where my parents first met."

It was not, of course, a postcard-perfect week.

I forgot to pack a bathing suit and ended up having to buy one in a resort boutique where no suit was larger than a size 2 and the dressing room was lit like an airport runway. I spent 45 minutes sweating in line in a quaint, un-air-conditioned candy store so that I could mail chocolate fudge to all the folks back home. Marc endured 37 rounds of mini-golf with Jonathan. "I hate mini-golf. And he cheats!" he complained to me.

"What do you expect? He's only eight."

One morning while Marc ran down the lane to get us muffins and a newspaper, I asked Jonathan to watch his brother for two minutes while I used the bathroom. I returned to find Jonathan's nose pressed to the TV, the front door open, and Mickey playing in the road. When I scolded him, he said, "Well, I only did it once. But if something happens to him, then can we get a dog?"

For seven days I did laundry, cooked, cleaned, swept sand, bathed the boys, spread suntan lotion, packed and unpacked beach toys, and made endless snacks. "But it's a vacation, right?" I said to Marc. "I know it is because we have an ocean view."

"Are we relaxed yet?" Marc said.

"I wish you'd stop asking me that."

It wasn't exactly the pre-parenthood trip we'd taken to Barbados. "Family vacation" might be the ultimate oxymoron. But it was a much-needed break for all four of us from the therapy merry-go-round.

Six months later, Mickey was, indeed, healthier. I was relieved to see his face had pinked again. Marc still had to travel frequently for work, so daily I drove Mickey to the round of therapies that drained us both. Even though therapy was play-based and meant to be fun, it was serious work. We blew bubbles, put Colorforms on the mirror, sorted plastic shapes, built block towers, bounced on therapy balls, fed pretend food to Sesame Street dolls. At times Mickey was joyfully engaged; but his attention was fleeting. Often he was anxious, climbing into my lap, and I would have to coax him to cooperate. Thanks to federally mandated early intervention services, our county health department was paying for two sessions of speech therapy a week, but Mickey's progress was worryingly slow. I was still terrified he might never speak, so we added two more sessions with a private speech and language therapist, in addition to play therapy three times a week with Barbara; extra play therapy with Cindy, a gifted graduate student from Sarah Lawrence College who Barbara had helped us find; and occupational therapy four times a week, with Karen, a practitioner who was also studying therapeutic healing. Karen started him on the Wilbarger Brushing Protocol. She taught us to use a special, soft, plastic surgical brush on his arms, legs and back every two hours, combined with gentle joint compressions, to help reduce his sensory defensiveness. Every two hours was impossible, but we did it as frequently as we could. It helped. Karen also dabbled in cranial sacral work, and did something she referred to as "energy work." I didn't know what it was, but it entailed holding her hands over parts of his body without actually touching him. It sounded like hooey to me, but it was benign, so Marc and I decided to try that too.

The cornerstone of our therapies continued to be Stanley's Floortime, his increasingly well-known play technique that follows a child's natural emotional interests while challenging him to engage more. We were doing Floortime for hours every single day. We still managed to attend a "Mommy and Me" class two mornings a week, because I hoped he might learn to play with other children who were developing more typically. Even with this grueling schedule, Mickey rarely slept through the night, and Marc and I dragged around in a haze of anxious exhaustion.

We worried that Mickey's needs were sucking the air out of the family, that Jonathan was not getting enough of us. We couldn't do things that ordinary families did—eat out, or go to movies. Marc spent Saturdays attending all the soccer practices and basketball games with Jonathan. "Let's go, my bunny rabbit," Marc said to him.

"I'm not your bunny rabbit. Mickey is your bunny rabbit. I'm a man."

"Okay, sir. Let's go bowling."

Jonathan came home that afternoon and told me, "Bowling is very hard, but I almost got a stroke." On the way home they'd stopped to buy Jonathan new sneakers with lights in the heels that flashed whenever Jonathan moved. He loved them so much he insisted on wearing them to bed that night.

Sometimes we took the boys to the Metropolitan Museum. Mickey liked to run through the halls, while Jonathan and I visited the paintings he liked. Jonathan stopped and stared a long time at a Lucian Freud painting, then said, "He's a good artist. How does he stay in the lines so well?"

One afternoon I took Jonathan to Blockbuster Video, and he asked to rent *Mr. Holland's Opus*, a movie about a music teacher. That evening, we sat down with him to watch, until Mr. Holland and his wife began worrying something was amiss with their son. I saw Jonathan freeze. When the doctor delivered the shocking news to the parents that their child was deaf, Jonathan burst into tears. "Turn it off! Turn it off!" he cried, and ran out of the room. Marc and I looked at each other, devastated. We'd been so caught up in our own fears that we hadn't realized how much Jonathan had been affected too. With a sickening thud, I realized why they called it "Pervasive Developmental Disorder, Not Otherwise Specified."

It hadn't only impacted every facet of Mickey's development; it had set up pervasive, permanent residence in each of us too.

Weeks later, running errands in town, I was pushing Mickey in Jonathan's old red and grey striped stroller across a suburban street when Jonathan suddenly said, "Mom? Why did you have to have Mickey?"

I took a deep breath. This wasn't ordinary sibling rivalry, I knew. "I thought it was important for you to have a brother," I answered.

"Why can't he talk?"

"Everyone talks at a different time," I said. "He'll talk soon. That's why we take him for speech therapy. Sometimes kids just need a little extra help."

"Why do you always have to sound like Mister Rogers?" he demanded angrily.

Jonathan was right. I was trying to mask my fears about Mickey to shield him from my anxiety. I wanted to protect Jonathan. I didn't know how.

One night I discovered a large stash of coins in Jonathan's room, and asked, "Where did all this money come from?"

Jonathan hid his head under the pillow. "I can't tell you, I'm too scared."

I sat beside him, stroking his back. "There's nothing so terrible you could do that would ever make me not love you," I said gently. "Don't you know that?"

Finally he whispered, "I took it."

Took it? Did he mean stolen? "From where?"

"Dad's change jar."

"Why?"

He was sobbing. "I'm saving money for you," he said. "So I can give it to you when you're poor and old so you won't die."

My stomach contracted. I remembered how, as a child, my greatest dread was that I would lose my mother, just as she had lost her own mother far too young. Just as Marc had lost his dad.

Naively, I'd thought it was possible to protect Jonathan from that terror. I'd been vigilant about the books we read, and the movies he'd watched. I'd even fast-forwarded through *Bambi* so he wouldn't see the scene when Bambi's mother was killed by a hunter.

"Come here," I said, holding him against me. "I felt like that too when I was a kid. Listen to me: I am strong and healthy. I'm going to be here for as long as you need me, until someday you're married and you have kids of your own."

"But what if you're poor?"

"Then I'll come live with you," I said, smiling. "But only if I can have my own room with a TV and a telephone and Nintendo."

He giggled. "Nintendo? But that's so much money!"

"That's okay," I said. "Look at all the money you've saved up. But you know what we need right now?"

"Butterfly kisses?"

"Yup."

He leaned his hot, tear-streaked face against mine, and fluttered his lashes against my cheek while we snuggled tight.

Sundays were given over to the needs of my increasingly frail parents. My mother, bound to the oxygen tank in the family room, was too ill to travel, so we brought the boys to her. Jonathan liked to curl up alongside her, to watch *Jeopardy* or *Wheel of Fortune*, while Mickey and Marc did puzzles on the floor. I couldn't confide my fears about Mickey to her, though I longed to; I was afraid to upset her. Did she know how hard it was to take care of Mickey, when I so longed for some mothering myself? Neither of us let on.

Occasionally we'd hire a Saturday night babysitter. After dinner in a restaurant, we'd wind up at a book store. Marc would cocoon himself in the history section; I'd start in fiction, but inevitably sneak over to the parenting aisle to look up what I thought of as "the A word." Autism. I was seeking reassurance that Mickey's mysterious behaviors didn't fit the definition. Marc couldn't bear to read those books. "Stop dwelling on it," he'd say. "You're just making yourself crazy." So I read about it secretly. Just as in the weeks after the initial diagnosis, Marc could hardly bear to talk about it, I couldn't bear to talk about anything else.

"Talking doesn't change anything. We know what we need to do, so let's just get on with it," he said.

I felt desperate. There had to be more we could do. I read up on music therapy. Auditory Integration Training. Earobics. Interactive Metronome. Brain Gym. Homeopathy. I filled notebooks with lists: words Mickey was learning to say, skills he was acquiring, more books I needed to read.

As Mickey turned three that summer, words slowly began to appear. His speech therapist referred us to a psychologist for an evaluation, who concluded in her report that Mickey was a child with "at least average intellectual ability who is demonstrating a severe communication delay/disorder with some atypical features." Like Stanley Greenspan, she didn't say "autism."

Barbara and the speech therapist both wondered if Mickey was showing signs of hyperlexia, a language disorder characterized by a precocious ability to read words without understanding them. They each told us not to encourage Mickey's fascination with letters and numbers because it wasn't good to let him develop a splinter skill. I'd never heard the term and looked it up. "Splinter skill: An isolated ability that often does not generalize across learning environments." But Mickey loved playing with the magnet letters on our refrigerator; he delighted in reading off the numbers and letters on license plates. I didn't understand why this was wrong, when it clearly gave him such pleasure. One night Marc was giving Mickey a bath, when suddenly Mickey touched each letter on Marc's t-shirt. "C. A. R. L. E. T. O. N. C. O. L. L. E. G. E. I did it!" Mickey said gleefully.

Marc wiped tears from his eyes. "You think it doesn't get to me too?" he said.

That fall Mickey entered a nursery school program for toddlers with disabilities. I became friendly with another mom there, who went to a conference called "Defeat Autism Now!" When she returned, she was as fervent as if she'd been to Lourdes.

"You *have* to do this," she said. "There's a national network of these DAN! doctors. Their biomedical approach is amazing. You should have heard all the stories about the kids they're curing."

"But those are anecdotes," I said. "And we're still not even sure Mickey has autism."

"How are you going to feel years from now if you don't try their approach and it turns out that this was the answer? Suit yourself, but I'm taking *my* son."

Then Mickey got another ear infection, despite the ear tubes. I felt deep-down desperate. What if there *was* something we were overlooking and this treatment actually was the magic bullet? At three and a half, Mickey spoke perhaps 100 words, if you counted the letters of the alphabet and numbers. The therapies were helping. I was less sure about the diet. But there was no way to tease apart which interventions were working.

"What have we got to lose?" Marc asked. We would try anything. Love is like that. Desperation is like that too.

I called the nearest DAN! doctor, Stephen Lawless, who was only 45 minutes away, the same doctor the mom I had met was seeing for her son. I knew nothing about this doctor except that she liked him. There was no easy way to find information about him. I had recently gotten email, but the internet was still new in 1996; search engines were spotty and primitive, and content was limited. I had joined an online community called Our Kids, and posted questions, but most parents there were dealing with cerebral palsy or genetic syndromes, not our particular puzzling cluster of problems.

Marc and I were upbeat as we pulled into Dr. Lawless' parking lot. "No doctor," Mickey pleaded. The waiting room was crowded with adults; Mickey was the only toddler there. There were no toys. Mickey flitted aimlessly from one side of the room to the other, as he often did. The receptionist handed me a small bag of alphabet blocks. Marc sat on the floor with Mickey, who piled the blocks high, only to knock them down again and again. I filled out 20 pages of questions about his medical and developmental history, distracted by the cascade of tumbling blocks and the glares of other people in the waiting room.

It was more than an hour before we met the man himself. He was tall, trim, with light-brown hair, and looked a vigorous 45. He listened attentively, nodding as I described the special diet we were following for Mickey. "Eliminating gluten and casein is important, but there's so much more you should be doing," he said. *Was that a rebuke? Hadn't we already done so much?*

"We're going to need to run a lot of tests, and I'll tell you up front that your insurance may not cover them. I'll give you kits for urine and stool samples. You'll need to send them to the lab yourself, but my receptionist will give you the paperwork. Once we get results, we'll know how to help your son." He patted my arm reassuringly. "You need to hold him so I can draw some blood."

Mickey didn't understand, but when Marc cradled Mickey against his chest, he cried out, "NO!" I winced, watching him sob and squirm as his blood flowed through a butterfly-shaped loop of tubing. "Go home!" he said. Dr. Lawless took the tubes of blood and disappeared down the hall.

"What do you think?" I asked Marc.

"He sounds so sure," Marc said. "I want to believe him, but..."

"I know, me too," I said. "I think we need our own ground rules. Whatever he wants us to do has to be safe, pain-free and non-invasive."

"Absolutely," Marc agreed.

Dr. Lawless returned. "I've left all your supplements at the front desk," he said.

"What kind of supplements?" Marc asked.

"Similar to what you've been doing," he said. "Vitamins, minerals, antioxidants. I take them myself. I probably swallow 100 pills every morning."

How convenient, he stocks everything we need, I remember thinking.

The visit and supplements cost nearly $1000. It didn't include the lab work.

Getting a urine sample from a child not yet toilet trained was difficult and messy. The kit contained a special plastic baggy with adhesive to be worn inside a diaper. Once we had the sample, we were instructed to send it to another doctor, who, we were told, stockpiled samples until he had enough to send to a doctor in Norway, who would study the peptides and determine if Mickey had a condition called "Leaky Gut," a chronic inflammatory response. It would take nine long months to get results. *He expects us to wait nearly a year?* I was aghast. We sent the stool samples to a special lab in Kansas, where they checked for yeast overgrowth. The blood went to three different labs, for immune assays and costly IgG Elisa testing for food sensitivities. Insurance covered none of it. "It's not as if we're spending money on a trip to Tahiti. It's for Mickey," Marc said. We were desperate parents, willing to try anything.

At our next visit, Dr. Lawless went over the lab work with us. "Just as I suspected, his immune system is compromised. He would benefit from a course of IVIG therapy."

"What does that entail?" Marc asked.

"It's a two-week, daily course of intravenous gamma globulin."

"So you're saying you want to hook up an active toddler to an IV infusion every single day for two whole weeks?" Marc asked skeptically.

How would that even be possible?

"That seems extreme," I stated, looking at Marc, who nodded. *Safe. Pain-free. Non-invasive.*

"Besides, isn't gamma globulin a blood product?" I asked nervously. "What if we find out ten years from now that some deadly prion disease like Mad Cow was in the current blood supply? Isn't that what happened with kids who got the first form of human growth hormone? I saw it on *Oprah*. They all got Creutzfeldt-Jakob Disease and died."

"We're not doing it," Marc said flatly, to my relief.

"Take some time and think about it," Dr. Lawless said smoothly. "Of course it's your decision. But we haven't seen any problems with this protocol." He made a note, pulled out another set of papers and studied them. "The stool sample you mailed to Kansas reveals significant yeast overgrowth. I'm going to give you a scrip for Nystatin. It's an anti-fungal. There's no down side to it, it's quite safe." I took the prescription form, wondering if I should run this by our pediatrician first.

"Are there any side effects?" Marc asked.

"You may see some behaviors from him while the yeast is dying off and toxins are released."

"Like what?" I asked anxiously.

"Spaciness," the doctor said. "Head banging. Sound sensitivity."

"But we already see all of those," I said. "So how will we even know if the Nystatin is helping?"

"Obviously we'll retest him." He sounded annoyed. *Were we questioning him too much? What if he decided we were too difficult and refused to help us?*

Dr. Lawless took a detailed family history. When he heard that Jonathan had been diagnosed with a severe allergy to peanuts when he was four, and that he was still frequently sick with ear infections and strep, he urged us to run some blood tests on him too. Over the course of that year with Dr. Lawless, we shelled out more than $5000 for doctor visits, supplements, pharmacy compounds and scores of lab tests, none of which insurance covered. At our visit that spring, he told us, "There's a scientist out west who is doing promising work on stealth viruses. I think it's advisable to test Mickey. Jonathan too, as a control."

"Why is it called stealth?" Marc asked.

"Because it flies under the immune system's radar. It mutates and infects host cells without causing any inflammatory response."

"Then how do you know it's there?" I asked.

"The scientist's lab has found a way to detect it."

"What does this stealth virus do?" Marc asked.

"Stealth viruses have been linked to everything from chronic fatigue to Lyme Disease, Gulf War Syndrome, fibromyalgia, autism and attention deficit disorder. This may have something to do with your son's developmental problems."

"I read a scary article in *New York Magazine* about early polio vaccines that contained a dormant monkey virus called SV40. Is this the same sort of thing?"

"Yes. Exactly." He sounded pleased. "You've been doing your homework."

Terrified, I agreed to specialized stealth virus cultures for both boys, and wrote a check for $1000.

Dr. Lawless called me the following week. "Mickey tests markedly positive for stealth virus," he said, his manner curt. "Jonathan shows lesser signs of it too."

I was scared. But also confused. *Jonathan wasn't developmentally delayed; quite the opposite. Why would he have it?* I asked Dr. Lawless how he proposed to treat it; he gave me the name of a drug. Ganciclovir.

"Can I call you back?" I asked. Then I called my friend Lauren, the parent of an autistic two-year-old, and a fellow traveler on the biomedical road.

"Dr. Lawless told us Jake has it too," Lauren said. "But it doesn't make sense that Jonathan would too."

Suspicious, I booted up the computer and launched an AltaVista search on the scientist and "stealth viruses." I read, "Live viral vaccines as well as the nation's supplies of blood products, including gamma globulin preparations, should be considered as possible sources of stealth viruses."

I was totally confused. *Gamma globulin? The same intravenous treatment that Dr. Lawless had been pushing us to do could actually cause* this problem? *Thank God we'd refused to do it.*

I also looked up Ganciclovir, the drug Dr. Lawless had mentioned. I learned it was an anti-viral. Potentially carcinogenic; cytotoxic. Used to treat severely immuno-compromised patients. People with AIDS.

He wanted to give this dangerous drug to a four-year-old?

With mounting rage, I read: "The ultimate question to be addressed is whether stealth viral infected patients will improve with anti-viral therapy."

There was no evidence it worked.

Finally, I read, "such patients can provide useful insights."

It was all about doing research.

I called Marc at work. "Listen to this!" I read what I'd found; he was equally horrified.

Livid, I called Dr. Lawless back.

"How many children have you treated with this?" I demanded.

"I'm treating one little boy right now."

"My son isn't a lab rat!" I said. "We're done."

But in the weeks after we fled the DAN! doctor, Marc and I agonized. Should we stop the restrictive diet? What if it was doing something, anything, at all? We'd followed it diligently for more than two and a half years. Mickey seemed more robust, but the diet didn't seem to have made any difference in his developmental problems.

And then one afternoon the nursery school teacher stopped me at the classroom door. She told me that during snack time, Mickey watched the other children eating the pretzels he was forbidden to touch. He handed her back the gluten-free snack I'd prepared, climbed under the classroom table, and scavenged for pretzel crumbs littering the floor. My heart ached. Mickey was nearly five years old; for two and a half years we'd pushed and prodded and withheld foods he loved. We'd probably deprived him for nothing.

Thinking about this story all these years later, I looked up Dr. Lawless on Google to see what had become of him. The New York State Department of Health website recorded that in 1997 (two months after I last spoke to him), the State Board for Professional Medical Conduct suspended his medical license for two years, with monitoring conditions. A Hearing Committee sustained it, because he had been disciplined in Missouri for false statements on his license application, for having a problem with controlled substances, and for making false statements in his New Jersey application. Eight years later, he was again censured and put on probation. Dr. Lawless had written prescriptions for opiates and benzodiazepines to a fake patient, then filled them and used the drugs himself.

I was enraged all over again, realizing how Marc and I had entrusted this charlatan with our vulnerable children.

And what of the other doctor, the "scientist out west"? I wasn't surprised to learn that the State of California Health and Human Services Agency had suspended his license "to conduct clinical studies, and cease all laboratory testing immediately."

And if you Google that lab in Kansas? It comes up on a "Quackwatch" list.

I shared this information with Marc.

"We let ourselves get suckered in," he said ruefully.

"We were so desperate," I said. "It clouded our clarity. We let him sell us snake oil."

I'm sure there are well-intentioned DAN! doctors out there who have the best intentions in helping autistic children. The one we saw didn't. I will never forgive his opportunistic disregard for Mickey's safety. We had come to him in despair, and he took advantage of our anguish.

The summer before kindergarten, Mickey turned five and lost his first tooth. We hadn't even known it was loose, because he still lacked the words to tell us. It was a bittersweet milestone.

I remembered vividly the thrill of excitement when Jonathan lost his first tooth. I had bought some books I knew he wanted. That night while he slept, we wrapped the books in shiny cellophane with yards of glittery ribbons and doodads, sprinkled a trail of sparkly Mylar confetti "fairy dust" outside his door, and wrote him a letter from the tooth fairy. Marc concealed the books and letter under his pillow as he slept. We were awakened the next morning by footsteps stampeding down the hallway. Jonathan burst into our bedroom shouting, "Mom! Dad! It's true! There really IS a tooth fairy!"

Mickey seemed pleased to show off the gap in his teeth. We all cheered for him, but there was no such elaborate pretense this time. The tooth fairy was too abstract for him.

The age of five was also the magic cut-off point I'd always imagined when all would be well. I had hoped that Mickey would be ready for the highly regarded kindergarten in our district, but at the screening he would not cooperate with the evaluators. He refused to look at their flash cards. Eventually he grew playful and began to flirt, and the director of special education noted with delight, "Someone here has a nice sense of humor." Even so, they deemed his current needs "too high management," and said that they didn't have an appropriate class for children like him. Instead, they were opting to send him to an out-of-district class program in a neighboring town. I was crushed. "It's a short-term placement," the director assured me. Mickey would end up spending two years there, until our district realized it was more economical to create its own program.

The first day of kindergarten, I stood in a huddle with the other mothers and watched through the classroom window as Mickey lay on the floor and said repeatedly, "I go home." I was mortified, but the class psychologist wasn't fazed. "He's communicating," she said.

One night at dinner, he suddenly started to sing, something we'd never heard him do. It wasn't on key, but it was definitely singing. He swayed his body to the music. He sang every stanza of a song called "On Top of Spaghetti," to the tune of "On Top of Old Smoky," and he giggled so hard he could barely squeeze out the words, "And then my poor meatball was nothing but mush."

"I taught him that," Jonathan said proudly. "High five, Mickey!" He lifted Mickey's hand and showed him how to do it.

"Jonathan is the best therapy for Mickey of all," I whispered to Marc. My eyes filled; I turned away so the boys wouldn't notice.

"You saved his life," Marc whispered to me.

"No. We all have," I said.

That winter, while stacking blocks with Barbara, Mickey had a seizure.

It wasn't the first time we'd suspected the possibility of seizures. We had noticed two or three times that sometimes he would seemingly turn inward, stare blankly into space for a few seconds, not respond to his name. But these episodes were fleeting. Until that afternoon at Barbara's.

They'd been playing when he suddenly collapsed. His eyes rolled back; he seemed to stop breathing and turned gray. Barbara called 911, as I cradled him, terrified. By the time the ambulance arrived Mickey had begun breathing again. I held him tight during the short ride to the emergency room.

We saw a seasoned neurologist at Columbia Presbyterian, who admitted him to the hospital for a two-day stay. When they glued the electrodes to Mickey's head, it literally took five of us to hold him down. "Mommy, what's wrong? What's wrong?" he cried over and over. Afterwards, he vomited. After two days and nights of EEG monitoring, the neurologist said he could not make a diagnosis of epilepsy, but that Mickey had had two brief "seizure bursts" on the EEG, with no "clinical correlation." It meant that the person looking at the EEG tracing couldn't tell us if it represented a problem or not—but that Mickey was at greater risk of developing a seizure disorder than the general population.

It happened once more. Mickey was sitting at the kitchen table with Jonathan and suddenly disconnected. His eyes turned glassy and vacant. "Bring him in," the pediatrician on call told me. Marc got the car. When Jonathan and I helped Mickey out of the chair, he shook us off, then walked into the wall. By the time we reached the doctor, it was over. "Syncope," the doctor insisted. The medical term for fainting. We were sure it wasn't. We knew what we'd seen.

The neurologist officially diagnosed Mickey with what we had known in our hearts all along. Pervasive Developmental Disorder, Not Otherwise Specified. Autism. But when we received the paperwork, a clerk had assigned the incorrect code to the insurance form. Instead of "PDD-NOS," it said, "Psychosis." Marc flipped out and called the office. "How do you get 'psychosis' when he was there for seizures?" The neurologist called back to apologize. Then he added, "We thought it would be a less stigmatizing diagnosis than PDD-NOS."

∽☉

While Mickey had been hospitalized, I'd asked the neurologist about Secretin, a pancreatic enzyme that was being hailed by many parents and therapists as a new breakthrough treatment.

He shook his head. "Applied Behavioral Analysis—ABA—is the only evidence-based treatment for autism," he said kindly. "If any of those other ones were so effective, don't you think all of us would be doing them?"

I'd read Catherine Maurice's groundbreaking book on ABA, *Let Me Hear Your Voice: A Family's Triumph over Autism* initially because Barbara had pressed it on me. "You should know about other treatments beside mine," she'd urged. ABA was just beginning to be introduced into our community, and wasn't widely available. A standardized teaching intervention, it was based on behavioral principles and originally developed by the neuropsychologist O. Ivar Lovaas at UCLA in the 1970s. Its aim was to foster such basic skills as looking, listening and imitating, as well as complex skills such as reading, conversing and understanding another person's perspective. It could be used from toddlerhood to adulthood. An educational, not a medical strategy, Lovaas's intervention was the first to use the science of behavior analysis in teaching individuals with autism. Lovaas's intervention originally included the use of aversives such as electroshock therapy, but today, most ABA programs only use incentives and positive rewards for desirable behavior. For undesirable behavior, the child is interrupted and steered into more desired behaviors. For each positive act, the child gets a reinforcer, such as a piece of candy, or a sticker on a token board. It is based on the principle that when a behavior is followed by some sort of reward, the behavior is more likely to be repeated.

The Lovaas Institute recommended 40 hours of one-to-one treatment a week. It was endorsed by a number of state and federal agencies, including the US Surgeon General and the New

York State Department of Health. It was intensive and expensive. School districts didn't want to pay for it. It benefitted about half of the children who received it. The methodology reminded me uncomfortably of a trainer tossing fish to a seal. I didn't know it at the time, but ABA is controversial and polarizing in the autism community. Many autistic adults speak out against it, arguing that ABA is cruel and restricts their coping mechanisms.

But Mickey's speech therapist was urging us to try ABA to suppress his "stims"—the odd-looking, ritualistic behaviors he used to soothe himself: humming when he ate; scripting (reciting lines from his favorite TV shows and plays); carrying a bag of Sesame Street finger puppets with him everywhere; talking aloud to himself. "You don't want him to look and act too different," she warned, "or he won't fit in." She called the children she worked with "stimmy." I hated that word. Those so-called self-stimulatory behaviors had a function; they weren't arbitrary. He wasn't "stimulating" himself. He did them for a reason. He was trying to soothe the bodily unease he felt: clothing texture that felt like sandpaper on sunburnt skin; sudden sounds that set his teeth on edge.

Instead of suppressing behaviors, I thought we should be asking, "What purpose does this behavior serve?" If you took away one behavior, wouldn't he just replace it with another? Wasn't he trying to make himself more comfortable in his own skin? His rituals made him happy. He needed them. Don't we all? Only when they are our own rituals, we call them something more benign. We refer to our own hair twirling, nail biting, finger drumming or throat clearing merely as "habits."

Behaviorists talk about the need to "extinguish" behaviors.

Extinguish.

It's a loaded word. Behaviorists use it to mean "to end." To make the undesirable behavior fade away. But I couldn't help reflecting on its more sinister meaning: "to annihilate." Still, I worried that if I dismissed ABA, we might miss out on a methodology that many people, not just the neurologist at Columbia Presbyterian, were calling the gold standard in treating autism. One weekend I drove down to Bethesda with my friend Lauren to attend a joint presentation by Stanley Greenspan and O. Ivar Lovaas—or as I thought of it, Clash of the Titans. Who was right? I thought Lovaas was a swaggering showman, expansive and egotistical; Greenspan was charming, self-deprecating, and to me, far more persuasive. Ultimately, the two men found common ground. "In the end, it doesn't matter what methodology you choose," Stanley said. "Choose something, and do it intensively."

I approached Miss Woods, the new teacher in charge of Mickey's special education kindergarten class, who had firsthand experience teaching in an ABA-based school. "What's your take?"

"Mixed," she said. "A few of the children in Mickey's class have had extensive ABA. Can they attend to table-top tasks? Yes. But once I move them away from that table, they're not generalizing those skills."

I called Barbara.

"I have another client who's hired a woman from New Jersey to run an ABA program for her child," she said. "Her approach is entirely different from the child-directed therapy I do. Frankly, I was a little put off by her at first, but the parent who hired her loves her. You might want to give her a call."

We met to discuss setting up a home program for Mickey. Joyce Wilkes' voice was soft and girlish, her clothes frilly, though she was built like a hand grenade. "He's going to do very well," she assured us.

Mickey was six years old and speaking in five-word sentences when Joyce arrived for their first session. She brought a young colleague named Yvonne with her. They shooed me from Mickey's bedroom and closed the door. Excited but anxious, I sat on the stairs nearby. "Mommy," he called. "Want Mommy." The doorknob twisted frantically. Then, sobbing. "Why are you crying?" I heard Yvonne say sternly. Did her voice have to be so sharp? "Go get a tissue. Go. Get. A. Tissue. Now blow your nose." My hand was pressed so hard against my teeth that later I found red crescents across my knuckles. I knew from the Catherine Maurice book that this was how it went the first time. *These people know what they're doing*, I told myself. *Maybe he needs this. How else will he learn basic academic skills if he can't sit still more than a few moments? This therapy is the gold standard, the neurologist Dr. Silver said so.*

Four times a week after school, for two-hour sessions, Joyce sat in one of the little chairs at the table in Mickey's bedroom. He soon learned to tolerate the intrusive work she demanded of him, working for longer periods of time. Mickey was learning how to learn. She instructed us to buy a file cabinet for Mickey's room, and she filled it with binders, work sheets and flash cards. Over the next two years, we ordered hundreds of dollars of educational materials and supplies she requested.

I plied Joyce with questions about school, curriculum, even how to introduce a kitten into our home. She always had answers. Opinions too. About the books we read him. The foods we fed him. Bed-time routines. Family outings. "He's reading too many baby books," she scolded. "He's too old for *Goodnight Moon*." I thought there was still a place in his life for picture books, but told her I'd put it away; subversively, I stashed it in my office so that it was still available if Mickey asked for it. Joyce was always deliberate and self-assured.

As Joyce became increasingly busy, she delegated more of the day-to-day work to Yvonne, her young partner. Yvonne, in turn, introduced us to her friend Kate, a fellow teacher. Kate was warm and animated, and Mickey adored her pleasingly husky voice. It was Kate who tackled Mickey's dread of haircuts. The first time, they simply practiced strolling by a barber shop. He came home giggling. "Sunglasses on a dog!" he told us over and over.

"What's that about?" I asked Kate.

She grinned. "We saw a dog hanging his head out a car window to catch the breeze and he was wearing goggles. Mick thought it was a riot."

The next week he was eager to go with her again. This time they peered into the window to watch the barbers. They worked up to standing in the doorway. Entering the shop. Watching other people get haircuts. Sitting in the barber chair. Eventually they introduced the cape. The clipper. The scissors. Finally, Mickey allowed the barber to snip his hair. It took months, but by the time Kate was done, Mickey was able to tolerate a haircut.

"You are a miracle worker," I told Kate gratefully.

She was modest. "I'm not. It's just systematic desensitization."

"ABA did that? Well, I'm just floored," Marc said. "Wow. Can we tackle visiting the dentist next?"

Marc and I were excited. Mickey was making progress; he was following directions, working more independently, and mastering arithmetic. He was working on phonics, handwriting, cutting and coloring, but continued to struggle with reading. "Reading really isn't my area of expertise," Joyce said. I appreciated her honesty. By then she and her team had been working with Mickey for two years.

Joyce hired Katrina and Nikki, a mother/daughter pair. Teachers, not behaviorists, they were both expert in the Wilson Reading System, a structured, multi-sensory language program. At her first visit, Nikki sat across the work table from him. Mickey stared her down, testing her. Then he said something he'd never said, and certainly never done: "I like to play with matches."

"No, you don't," Nikki said cheerfully.

Mickey warmed to her immediately.

Over the course of the next year and with more staff at her disposal, Joyce started showing up late. Or she'd call five minutes before she was expected, saying she was cancelling. "Sorry, I won't be there, something's come up," she'd say airily. I was annoyed, but felt uncomfortable speaking up. After all, Mickey had made so much progress in three years; I didn't want her to think I wasn't appreciative for all she had done. I was. But sometimes she'd simply not show at all. She'd take home the data notebook that charted Mickey's progress, and not return it for weeks. Had she lost interest in our case? She still came to our meetings at Mickey's school, but behaved condescendingly to his teachers, then privately excoriated them to me: "None of them has a clue about working with children on the spectrum." She sounded so dismissive. Arrogant. The special education teachers and staff at Mickey's public school were firm, but always kind to him. What did Joyce expect them—or us—to do?

I was afraid to voice my concerns to her. Her staff had helped our son through haircut and dental phobias; his reading was definitely improving, due to the patient tutoring of Katrina and Nikki. I believed we needed her, so I kept quiet.

One afternoon Mickey was sitting beside Nikki on the piano bench when Joyce unexpectedly barged into the playroom.

"Who told you to work on *that?*" she demanded, then turned abruptly to me. "Was this your idea?"

I felt confused. Embarrassed for Nikki. Then, furious. I *liked* Nikki's impromptu lessons. She'd taught Mickey to read simple sheet music. Why was Joyce so enraged? Was she afraid she'd lost control of Mickey's program? That we preferred Nikki to her?

"It's time you made some parenting choices," she said to me coldly after Nikki left. "You're not doing him any favors. He's always running to you for hugs when things get too hard. You're letting Mickey get away with murder."

I recoiled. What was she talking about? She thought I was too lenient? I knew Mickey's needs; he'd been living beneath my skin for almost ten years. Moreover, did she have *any* idea how hard it was on him to have a train of therapists traipsing through the house every afternoon and evening? Or that Mickey's therapy schedule had turned our home upside down? Marc, Jonathan, Mickey and I had been unable to sit down to eat dinner as a family in years; her scheduling requirements had seen to that.

"You've got some decisions to make, or things will only get worse."

I was momentarily speechless. *Was she threatening me?*

Then, abruptly, she set her cup down and stood. "I assume Mickey has homework we need to do," she said coldly.

Completely puzzled by Joyce's outbursts, I sat on the stairs and eavesdropped. "Look at the page!" I heard her scold, voice rising in exasperation, barraging him with questions. "Who's asking the question? Point to the word. So who's speaking? Point to the word that asks the question. What does that mean? No! Not that word."

My fists clenched. Finally, I admitted it to myself: I hated her. I despised the way this woman was treating Mickey. We were *done*.

Striding down our cobblestone path an hour later, she turned and called over her shoulder in a saccharine voice, "Say goodbye to me, Mickey."

"Goodbye," he muttered, waiting until she'd reached her car. "And don't hit me again!" he shouted, slamming the front door.

I froze.

"Mickey, did Joyce hit you?" I struggled to keep my voice even.

"Yeah."

"Where?"

"Here."

"Show me."

He smacked his leg. "Like this."

"Go play, honey," I said to him. "Dinner's almost ready." As soon as he left the room I called Marc at work.

"She did *what*?"

"Mickey says she hit him."

"You're sure he's not making it up? Could it be something he saw on television?"

"Has he ever made anything like this up?"

"Never," Marc said stonily.

"Mickey has no guile," I pointed out. "It wouldn't even occur to him to make up a story like that."

"You're right. I want her *out*. Don't you do it, you're too nice. She's history."

Marc called her that evening, but got her voicemail. He left a curt message. "We're finished with you," he said. "Don't come back, and don't ask us for a reference."

The next day, I called Katrina and Nikki and told them what had happened. I asked them to continue working with Mickey. Nikki finally confided what she'd been afraid to tell me for months. When Joyce had hired her, she'd told her, "Mrs. Carter is nice but clueless. There's a lot of money to be made here. Work for me, and by next summer you'll be buying yourself a vacation house."

I was livid with her, and myself for being too trusting. We hadn't known what a good ABA program looked like when we hired Joyce. I *was* clueless. So frantic to find someone—anyone—to help Mickey, I'd once again gone looking for a miracle cure, sweeping aside any hesitation I'd felt and letting my desperation undermine my own judgment.

Later I learned that two other children told their mothers that Joyce had pinched and scratched them. We discussed calling the authorities. But how could we prove it? It would be her word against that of a suggestible, developmentally disabled child.

Weeks later, Mickey wrote a story in school. The teacher sent it home with a note: "Don't know if this is true or not, but it's good writing! I like the complete sentences, sequencing and punctuation."

Joyce and Jake
By Mickey Carter

Yesterday, Joyce went to Jake's house. Joyce got mad at Jake. Then Joyce hit Jake and sayed [sic] "get to work." Jake poked her. Then Jake got a time out in Joyce's car.

ABA has its place, though it's not for everyone. Just as it is when you choose a doctor or teacher or any other professional, an ABA program's success relies on the skill of the therapist wielding the reinforcers.

When done with kindness, ABA techniques are remarkably effective for Mickey. We hired Shana, a gifted, empathetic young behavior therapist who knew how to motivate and teach our child. She has worked with him and with us for more than ten years.

But even now, Mickey will sometimes ask, "Is Joyce in a big time out? Is she working with other children? Is she in jail?" He is still looking for reassurance.

"Yes," I tell him each time. "Joyce is in a big time out. Forever. She's never coming back here again."

DIZZY WITH LOVE

"I want a dog," Jonathan blurted. He was ten.

"This isn't a good time," I told him.

I felt guilty as I said it. He'd been asking for years. I knew that it was more than a dog he wanted. He hadn't gotten the brother he expected. He was a sensitive, anxious child who needed something that was *his*.

But we were already stretched so thin trying to meet Mickey's many needs. With Marc still travelling frequently for work, and no matter how many promises Jonathan might make to take care of a dog, I knew the burden of tending a pet would fall to me. I wasn't sure I was willing or able to slog through wintry slush every night to walk a hyperactive puppy.

"I need a dog. All my friends have dogs," he pleaded. He didn't let up. He pouted and sulked. Finally, he cried. "Why can't I have a dog, Mom? Why?" he insisted, his big green eyes flooding in tears. I cringed in pain. Then, one night just before his eleventh birthday, he stalked into my office and dropped $50 in wadded-up $1 bills on my desk.

"I'm going to use my own money to buy a dog," he insisted.

I knew I was weakening. "We'll have to talk about it," I said.

He glared. "That means 'No.'"

"No, it means Dad and I will have to talk about it."

Jonathan needed to lavish love on something that would respond to him wholeheartedly, as his little brother could not. But Mickey was terrified of dogs. The sudden, explosive sound of barking made him cover his ears and run. Marc and I agreed a dog wouldn't work for our family. I vetoed hamsters, guinea pigs and ferrets. "Those are just fancy names for rats," I remember saying.

"I wonder if a cat would be too jumpy for Mickey?" Marc mused.

We had a cat once, long before we had children, but Marc and I had been so heartbroken when we had to put her down that we had never gotten another pet. Instead we'd decided it was time to start a family; Jonathan had been born a year later.

There was another pressing problem I had with pets: I am allergic to furry creatures. The wheezing, choking, itchy, streaming eyes kind of allergic. How could I endure weekly allergy shots and take antihistamines every day?

But Jonathan wore me down. I couldn't deny him something he so desperately wanted.

"How would you feel about a cat?" we asked him.

He was radiant. "Yes!" he shouted.

So I downed an antihistamine, asked Milagros, our sitter who has loved and doted on Mickey since he was an infant, to stay with him, and braved the Cat Fanciers regional show. Marc, Jonathan and I strode up and down the aisles, watching fur and tempers fly as we looked for just the right pet.

"Remember, Mom, I don't want one of those snooty Fancy Feast cats," Jonathan told me firmly.

Marc stopped to stare at a woman grooming a spectacular pair of silver-striped Maine Coon cats.

"I thought we said nothing long-haired," I hissed at Marc.

"Just take a look," he urged. "This breed is supposed to be great with children." *How did he know that?* He must have been doing some research.

Which is why five days later we found ourselves driving two hours away to a cattery in rural New Jersey. Jonathan was enthralled. He sat for half an hour on the floor of the cat breeder's bedroom, tickling kittens with a feather duster, before deciding which one would be his. I handed the woman a check, and she handed over our bit of fluff.

"Here's your little lady," I remember her saying.

Jonathan and I sat in the back seat with the kitten in a carrier between us. She mewed pitifully. "I can't believe I have a cat," Jonathan kept saying, with as much reverence as if we'd just been to a religious shrine. At 5am the next morning he woke me. "Mom, she's shaking all over," he said, a panicked first-time parent paging the pediatrician. I placed the kitten in bed between us, and we soothed her until the trembling subsided.

I'd sworn to myself that I wouldn't get so attached this time. But it was already too late. I was a goner. Jonathan called his grandparents to invite them for a viewing that very afternoon.

"Oy. With everything else, what do you need a cat for?" Grandma Bev asked. But she too scooped the kitten into her lap.

We knew how important this pet was to Jonathan. What we hadn't anticipated was how good Dizzy would be for both our boys.

Initially Mickey was skittish. "No cat!" he cried, scaling a kitchen chair to get away from her. He eyed her suspiciously; he startled every time she jumped. He watched her warily, and for several nights insisted on checking under his bed, frightened she might have crawled there without his knowing. But gradually he warmed to her, and began crooning to her as Jonathan did. "Hi, Dizzy girl," he'd whisper. "You're so cute." He started to speak more, and with greater animation, whenever he was near her, a boon we hadn't anticipated. He began to snuggle with her. Eventually he took to resting his head on her as if she were a pillow. "I love you, Dizzy." Dizzy, unusually gentle and forbearing for a cat, stared impassively but never pulled away.

"I could swear she lowers my blood pressure," Marc said. He never failed to light up when he saw her. She always chirruped back. She came as soon as he said her name; she ran when she heard his key in the door. When he took a shower, she would wait patiently outside, then follow him into the bedroom, leap onto the bed, and with a languorous look, roll over on her back. "What a beautiful girl you are. You're in heavy purr tonight, aren't you, sweetheart?" Marc cooed. Dizzy chirped and trilled right back at him. Then she fell over, stared hard into his eyes, and showed him some belly.

"Do you want treats?" Marc said in a lilting, loving voice. "Treat? TREAT?" I raised my eyebrows.

"I'm teaching her to speak," he said sheepishly.

And in fact Marc spoke to her in the same animated tones he'd used with our boys when they were babies. I remembered that first night in the hospital after Jonathan was born, how Marc had insisted on staying, jumping up from the cot every time the baby snuffled or sighed. How gently he'd crooned to him.

"Dizzy's the other woman in your life," I teased Marc. But she was equally a presence in mine. Her fur was so silky; I adored the lion's ruff around her sweet face. "We're all her love slaves," I said.

At six months we took her to the vet to be spayed. Jonathan insisted he had to stay home from school to tend to her. "She needs me, Mom," he begged and I agreed, knowing how much he needed her. He clearly drew strength and solace from caring for her. As soon as we brought her home from the vet, he fussed over Dizzy, making a nest of his old sweatshirts on the floor for her to lie on. He fed her fishy tidbits and carefully brushed her impossibly soft hair.

Dizzy grew quickly, but still behaved like a kitten, to the gleeful delight of Jonathan and Mickey. She loved to dash up and down stairs, leaping over chairs and beds, alighting on window sills and climbing up inside the curtains. Marc and Jonathan bought Dizzy too many toys, which she would play with briefly, then abandon. No matter how many novelties we offered her, she always returned to a tatty brown monkey that she'd carry in her mouth from room to room, meowing plaintively until someone played fetch with her.

That spring we prepared Jonathan to leave for sleep-away camp for the first time. He would be going with his best friend Brett, but I could see he was feeling anxious. Finally he confided his misgivings to me.

"What if Dizzy forgets me?"

I sat on the edge of his bed, and smoothed the hair off his forehead. "She won't," I assured him.

"Can I take a lock of her fur to camp?"

"Of course."

"And you'll send me lots of pictures of her?"

"I pinky swear." We locked little fingers.

"Look at her, Mom!" he said. Dizzy was sitting on his pillow; the pink tip of her tiny tongue protruded. Jonathan gently nudged it back in her mouth. "I don't want her to look like a bimbo," he explained.

Where had he learned that *word?* I wondered.

Dizzy wasn't a bimbo, but she certainly was a coquette. There was something healing about this small, affectionate creature. She'd not only given us consolation; she'd restored a measure of joy and light to our lives. All four of us were bonkers over our dainty, animated, loving fur muff. Dizzy filled a need we hadn't had time to realize we had.

When Jonathan returned from camp at the end of the summer, Grandma Bev came to welcome him home.

After watching him sulk all the way through brunch, my mother-in-law turned to me and said sympathetically, "He must be getting his period."

I knew exactly what she meant.

"Snap out of it," I felt like saying to him. I realized he couldn't. He was suddenly and firmly in the grip of his emerging hormones. I remembered my own mother's statement: "You started crying when you were 11, and didn't stop until you were 16."

"Were you like that?" I asked Marc.

He smiled. "Who remembers?"

Jonathan was in the thick of it. Suddenly he was rolling his eyes in disgust, oozing exasperation, or sighing theatrically at how overburdened he was by our demands—*such* a chore, having to brush his teeth, feed Dizzy, *and* hang up his towel. He was devouring entire loaves of bread with jam and family-size cartons of Cheerios. One morning he stood scowling in front of the refrigerator. "Don't we have milk?" he accused.

"Yes."

"Well, where is it?"

"Gee, I don't know. Maybe you should check the bathtub," I said.

Both boys had just started in new schools—Mickey, in a self-contained second-grade classroom, Jonathan in sixth grade at middle school. Eleven is an odd age. Jonathan had one foot mired in childishness, the other foot dipping in toe first to the bracing waters of adulthood. No longer a child, not yet a teen, he was nestled between the safe harbor of home and the open, uncharted sea ahead. All I could do was hug the shore and watch him drifting away from us, drawn by the tidal pull of teenagehood. Other parents who'd mapped this passage warned me of rough water and hidden currents ahead.

Yet unlike me, uncomfortable talking to my mother about the changes in my body, Jonathan reveled in his. He asked for a stick of deodorant, and in front of us applied it enthusiastically from armpit to waist. He was thrilled to show off the one hair that had sprouted under his arm. He studied himself in the bathroom mirror for extended periods, blasted his boom box and said things like, "No offense Mom, but if you were my age, I wouldn't marry you. You're not my type."

"Oh? What is your type?" I asked.

"Smart," he said. "Blonde. And tall."

A part of me (not the part that was hurt at being told I wasn't smart) was glad he still trusted me enough to say things like that.

One Saturday morning Marc returned from running errands. It was nearly noon and Jonathan still slouched around in t-shirt and boxers. "You think you could manage to get dressed?" Marc asked. Jonathan glared and slunk into the kitchen after me. "Dad's *insulting* me," he said.

Yet Jonathan confided in his father steadily, asking questions about his body he was no longer comfortable asking me. The one question he did ask me was a doozy.

"What is oral sex?"

"What do *you* think it is?" I said, stalling for time.

He looked thoughtful. "I guess it's when you talk about it."

That night when I leaned in his door to say goodnight, I found him in bed wearing a baseball hat, listening to the Mets game, and clutching the worn, white bear I thought he'd put aside months before.

Part of me missed the incandescent child whose face grew radiant at the sight of mine. Where was my boy smelling of milk and mud? Now it was all sweat and rancid sneakers. I listened to the voice that was beginning—ever so slightly—to deepen; looked into gray-green eyes that were suddenly level with my own, and wondered: how can this be the downy blond duckling I gave birth to?

And sometimes, suddenly, I would be pierced with the fear of what Mickey would be like when he reached the middle school years. Autism and adolescence were sure to make a volatile mix.

"You just don't get it," Jonathan said often. Of course I didn't. What parent ever did? Sometimes I was tempted to say, *you didn't invent these feelings, you know. Been there, done that.* But in truth I hadn't been where he was. Obviously I had never been an adolescent boy. But more importantly, I hadn't had a disabled brother whose behavior was increasingly becoming an embarrassment— behaviors like obsessing endlessly over Thomas the Tank Engine trains, or talking loudly to himself in public. This voyage was Jonathan's alone. At 11, he was learning to negotiate between our complicated family life and the world outside, figuring out how to navigate it all. We could only loose the moorings, hoping that the vessel we'd given him was sea-worthy, the compass sound, and then…bit by bit, let him go.

BESIEGED

It wasn't long before Mickey began swimming through the shoals of pre-teen years too.

One night when he was ten, I lay alongside him at bedtime reading a book to him called *Arthur's Teacher's Pet*, when he suddenly blurted, "All of my friends are being mean and playing tricks on me." He started to sob.

Mickey was not a crier.

My heart constricted with pain and fury. I knew children with special needs were often bullied, but until now we'd been lucky. I'd read several studies that said children on the spectrum are at greater risk, and that of all bullying reported, 65 percent of these incidents targeted kids with autism spectrum disorders. I don't know who the perpetrators tend to be, but what I've noticed is that any time Mickey has been singled out, it has always been at the hands of other students in special education. I suspect there's a pecking order, even—or especially—among them.

Mickey's expressive language was still limited, and Marc and I couldn't get too many details out of him. But the emotion was loud and clear. Eventually, we were able to piece together that Tommy and Lucie, both new students who'd recently joined Mickey's self-contained fourth-grade classroom, had been picking on him. "They tell me to go wrong places!" he told us. Tommy and Lucie would say things like, "you're supposed to go to the art room," and when Mickey got there, no one was there. They were repeatedly giving him wrong directions, so that he would wind up places in the school building where he wasn't supposed to be. He told us, "They laugh at me." It made me livid.

"I'm not going to school," Mickey said the next morning. "Everyone doesn't have to." Somehow I coaxed him onto the bus, then immediately called his teacher Samara. She was aghast. "No one does that to my Mickey!" she said. "I'll get to the bottom of it."

That afternoon, she wrote me a note in the chatter book, the marble notebook that went back and forth between home and school. "I can tell he's having some anxiety about school. There's been shouting out and lots of hugging," she wrote. "Today at the end of recess he actually did a somersault in the classroom. When I told him to sit down quietly for a few minutes, he got weepy. He pulled himself back together but then did not want to sit with anyone. I'll call you tonight."

"Tommy and Lucie both came to us from mainstream classes," she told me that evening. "I bet they were probably being teased themselves, so they are targeting Mickey the way they were targeted. Not that the reason matters, because it's still completely unacceptable."

"Mickey keeps asking to read that same Arthur book over and over," I told her. "It's the one about teasing."

"I'm going to talk to the class tomorrow and put everyone on a behavior contract," she promised.

The next afternoon she wrote in the chatter book, "Mickey was very upset again today. He was not teased himself, but saw Victoria being teased. He seems to not distinguish between the teasing directed at him or just in his vicinity."

That didn't surprise me. I wrote a note back. "Mickey is sensitive to other people's moods. You know how people are always saying kids with autism don't have empathy? Totally untrue."

"Things are much better today," she wrote the next day. "He got through all his math independently, and told me, 'I'm so smart!' I need to tell you the other good thing that happened this afternoon but it's too much to write."

We spoke that evening. She told me she had sat the class down in a circle to talk about teasing. Then she asked Mickey to tell his classmates how he felt. "And, boy, did he let them have it!" Samara exclaimed. "He crossed his arms and glared at the other kids. He was fierce! He told them they were being mean, and how angry that made him, and that they'd better stop it immediately. I was amazed. The kids were too. I think sometimes they think that because Mickey's language is limited, he doesn't have the same feelings as everyone else. You should be very proud of your son."

Marc and I were more than proud. We were awed. Mickey had just advocated for himself for the first time. He was clear. And everyone got it.

Late one winter afternoon, his tutor Nikki came into the kitchen looking puzzled. She said, "I think Mickey is playing a game. He's staring and he won't answer me." My stomach lurched as I tore into his room. I found him sitting cross-legged and immobile. His stomach gurgled strangely; his eyes were locked to the side. I took hold of his arms. "Mick? Mick?" I called.

Jonathan, who was watching this, said, "Maybe he's just joking, Mom," and tried to tickle him.

"No, he isn't," I said, struggling to stay calm. "Go next door and get Eileen." Jonathan raced out into the snow without shoes. Our neighbor Eileen was a doctor; she would know what to do. Minutes later, she crouched beside Mickey. "He's still ictal," she said. *Ictal*. It was the first time I heard that word. From the Latin: *ictus*. A blow. A stroke. A seizure. We held him and waited. Finally,

Mickey sighed heavily and slumped forward, as if a puppeteer had suddenly released the strings, and he returned to us. "I'm so tired," he said, and climbed into his bed.

We did not yet know that somewhere between 30 and 40 percent of children with autism eventually develop epilepsy. According to the Epilepsy Foundation, epilepsy and seizures affect 3 million Americans of all ages; 326,000 school children through age 15 have epilepsy. Mickey was entering adolescence. Puberty was about to wreak neurological havoc.

We saw a new neurologist, Dr. Orrin Devinsky, director of the Comprehensive Epilepsy Center at NYU Langone Medical Center, who admitted Mickey to the hospital. My friend Lauren and her son Jake were staying on the same floor. A lucky coincidence; Jake was there for seizure monitoring too, so we arranged for the boys to share a room. Mickey slugged any technician who tried to come near him. He was so belligerent they needed to drug him. But by day's end, both boys wore identical sets of 32 electrodes glued to their scalps. Their heads were covered with gauze stocking caps.

For five days, a standard stay for seizure observation, Lauren and I shared the room too. We collected sheets from the nearby linen closet, made beds out of reclining chairs, and slept in our clothes. We took turns taking showers down the hall in a cold, tight stall with a warm trickle. "You know," I remarked, "the spa services here suck."

On the third day—or was it the fourth?—I made the mistake of glancing at a magazine for a few moments, only to hear Mickey say delightedly, "Ah. I feel *much* better." I looked up to discover that he had yanked off the cap—and all 32 electrodes. They would have to wire him up all over again.

Despite all this, they were still unable to document seizure activity.

The seizures and bullying continued. One morning, his middle school teacher Dori called me from the nurse's office. "Mickey just had a seizure," she said. "He's asking for you."

Mickey was sitting on a couch, leaning his head against Dori. He looked dazed. While Marc sat with him, I took Dori aside and asked what happened.

"I'm not sure what precipitated it," she whispered. She had noticed Mickey seemed agitated in class. He'd burst into tears and told her, "I'm going to have a seizure." Then his eyes had rolled back in his head; his limbs started shaking. When it was over, she and a classroom aide had walked/carried him to the nurse's office.

"How are you feeling now, buddy?" Dori asked him.

He looked angry. "Brandon York is a bully!"

Brandon York was a boy who had briefly been in Mickey's self-contained second-grade classroom before his parents decided to pull him out mid-year and put him back a grade. We hadn't thought of him in years, till Mickey began complaining, "Brandon York is following me." Brandon wasn't in Mickey's class.

"What's going on?" I asked Dori.

She frowned. "I'm not sure," she said. "I didn't actually see anything because the kids went to music with my aide, but I've noticed Brandon lurking by our door a lot lately."

"What happened, honey?" I asked Mickey.

"Brandon York kicked me! He gave me a seizure! He's evil. He needs to go to jail."

Dori looked grim. "I'll take care of it."

She called that afternoon. "I read Brandon York the riot act. I told him if I ever, *ever* catch him lurking outside my classroom again or bothering any of my students, I will march him straight to the principal's office."

Several weeks later Marc and I attended the bar mitzvah of our friend's son who has Asperger's. Her son was in the same small middle school program as Brandon York. All the bar mitzvah boy's classmates were there. I was sitting at a table eating a salad when Marc returned to the table. He was red-faced.

"I just had quite a conversation with Brandon York," he told me grimly.

Marc had been on the buffet line when he noticed Brandon standing next to him. "Hi, Brandon, I know your parents. I'm Mickey Carter's dad."

"Mickey Carter? That kid is an asshole."

"I was so shocked I didn't know what to say," Marc told me. "I told Brandon he was being rude and inappropriate and then I tried to change the topic. I asked if he was still playing baseball. He said, 'No! I stopped coming to sports because Mickey ruins it for me! He's a jerk! He has a lot of issues! He needs to be on medication!'"

"He said that to you?" I was aghast. "Who talks to a parent that way?"

"That kid has some serious problems," Marc said. "And they have *nothing* to do with Mickey."

I worried. How could we best protect our son? The middle school was divided into four houses. Fortunately, Brandon wasn't just in a different program than Mickey's; he was in a different house altogether.

Days later we got a call from Dori. "Your son is amazing."

"Why? What did he do?"

"I just got a call from Mickey's house counselor, who said she'd just had a call from Mrs. Beni, the house counselor for Butler House. Mrs. Beni told her that Mickey came to see her."

"But she's not Mickey's house counselor," I said. "What's going on?"

"Mrs. Beni said that during lunchtime today Mickey marched himself into her office and said, 'Mrs. Beni, Brandon York is bullying me. You have to make him stop.'"

"He did that all on his own?" I asked. "Figured out Brandon was in Butler, and who he should talk to? All by *himself*?" I was giddy.

"Absolutely on his own," Dori said. "I had nothing to do with it. I can't tell you how proud of him we all are."

Mickey was proud of himself too. So much so that it emboldened him to take another step.

Literally.

One afternoon after school, we waited for the school bus to bring him home from the middle school. I was in the kitchen when I heard the sound of the front door opening. I looked up to see Mickey flushed and grinning.

"Oh, I didn't hear the bus," I said.

"I didn't take the bus!" he exclaimed. He was vibrating with more excitement than we'd ever seen. "I walked home all by myself!"

We lived a few short blocks from the school, but to get there you had to cross a busy road. So busy that for years the town had been lobbying the state—unsuccessfully—to install a traffic light. There was a crossing guard during drop-off and dismissal times, but not during the rest of the day.

"What do you mean you walked home?"

"I didn't take the bus! I walked home all by myself from middle school! I did it!" He pumped his fist in the air, nearly manic in his excitement, the words tumbling out faster than we'd ever heard. "Are you proud of me? I did it! I did it! I didn't get hit by a car! I didn't get killed!"

Oh my God.

I looked at Marc. He was equally stunned.

I struggled to keep my voice even. "I'm very glad you didn't get killed, but you can't just walk home without telling anyone at school."

"Mickey, what you did wasn't safe," Marc said.

"But I'm safe! I didn't get killed! I did it!"

"How could this have happened? Don't they have a dismissal protocol? Didn't the bus driver notice someone was missing?" I asked Marc.

Apparently with all the end-of-the-school-day tumult, no one had. "I'll call the house counselor and find out," Marc said.

I suddenly remembered the time Mickey had been in kindergarten and I'd arrived ten minutes early one afternoon to pick him up, only to intercept him as he'd bolted out of the building. Alone. I'd walked him back into his classroom—a class of 11 students, one teacher and *six* classroom aides. No one had noticed him slipping out the door. I was horrified. To her credit, so was the teacher, who the next day installed a track of jingly bells on the classroom door.

Breathe, I thought. Mickey wasn't in elementary school anymore. He was 12. Nearly a teenager. Verbal. Able to advocate for himself. It was achingly clear how much he wanted to be just like all the other kids on our street who walked to and from school each morning and afternoon.

How were we going to make him understand the danger, I wondered, without quashing his burgeoning independence?

For Mickey's thirteenth birthday, Jonathan, Marc and I took him to see *Charlie and the Chocolate Factory*. The theater was crowded; finally we found four seats in the front section, so near the screen that we were engulfed in flashing colors. Mickey seemed to enjoy the film, but after an hour he began to squirm, unable to get comfortable. I grew uneasy. The movie was nearly over when he leaned into me. His body went rigid. I heard the sound of air being forcibly expelled from his lungs, and his head began to jerk rhythmically, as if something were pulling him. Again. Again. Again. Drool frothed from the corner of his mouth. I grabbed Marc, and we both watched in helpless horror. I tried to cradle Mickey's head to keep it from striking the hard seat back. When the spasms subsided, the left side of his face was paralyzed. He was confused, and spoke with difficulty. "I blew up like Violet in the movie," he said.

The movie ended. We held him, waiting for the paralysis to abate, as people swarmed into the central aisle behind our seats. *How was it possible no one had noticed us?* Despair rose in my throat; I felt splayed open. We stood him up. Somehow the three of us got him to the car, home, and into bed. I said to Jonathan, "You must have been so scared."

"You're the one who was scared. I'm fine," he said, trying to sound dismissive. I didn't believe Jonathan; I'd seen his distraught face in the theater. Once again his brother had commandeered all our attention. How could he not resent that? Or be guilt-ridden at feeling that way? Despite the denial, Jonathan's fear was palpable. So was his rage. I didn't know how to assuage either.

"Even though we haven't captured any seizures on an EEG or seen anything unusual on the MRI, we usually diagnose epilepsy after a person has had at least two seizures that are not caused by a known medical condition," Dr. Devinsky told us. We started Mickey on a course of anti-epileptic medication. But months later, it happened again. First, in the back seat of the car; then, while the boys were playing video games with Marc.

"Mom! Come quick!" Jonathan yelled. Marc and I flipped Mickey to his side, cushioning his head. Horror-stricken, we waited helplessly until the convulsions subsided. "I'm sorry, I have to get out of here, I can't watch," Jonathan said, his voice cracking as he fled. My heart broke, for both my boys.

For centuries people believed that someone with seizures was possessed by devils. We know better now, but why does it feel as if treatment is still in the dark ages? In the years since Mickey was diagnosed with epilepsy, we have seen terrible side effects from medications that at best achieve partial control of his seizures. Cognitive slowing. Mood shifts. Agitation. Exhaustion. We worry, every day, every hour, about all the things that can trigger seizures. Summer heat; missed meals; too little sleep; drinking too little water; drinking too much water; flashing lights; 3-D movies; anxiety. Even joyful anticipation: he has had seizures going to a Chanukah party; eating dessert at the Thanksgiving table; watching the Super Bowl with his cousins.

Every time he has a seizure, friends and family ask, "Was it a bad one?" Sometimes I feel like retorting, "I've yet to see a good one." I know they mean well; they are asking: did he fall to the floor? Lose consciousness? Convulse? Not all seizures look that dramatic; each one has a different texture, a different set of symptoms. I am at a loss how to answer. They don't realize that when it is your child, every seizure is bad. He is literally seized: snatched up in an electrical storm that sucks the air out of him before it spits him out, disoriented and spent. What is it like, I wonder, to wake up lying on a couch or floor, your body sore, your head aching, unable to recognize familiar people around you? Unable to form words? Struggling to speak, only to see uncomprehending faces? To have no memory of what has caused you to land there, nothing but the ominous sense that something bad has happened? Doctors have told us, "A seizure is like getting kicked in the head." How many kicks can a child sustain before there is permanent damage?

When my children were infants, I checked them throughout the night to reassure myself they were still breathing. All these years later, I am still checking. The fear has a name: SUDEP. Sudden Unexplained Death in Epilepsy. Each year, 50,000 people die as the result of a seizure. For people with autism, it is the leading cause of death. Every four months, we still must take him for a 30-minute EEG in the neurologist's office. Each time he tries to fight the technician; sometimes we need to call the doctor in. When we do, Mickey's whole affect changes: he likes Dr. Devinsky, and really wants to please him. He tries so hard to comply. But the strobe light, the confinement and the discomfort of electrodes all terrify him. You cannot reason with him. Panic takes him to another place.

Mickey fought technicians; Marc and I were suddenly waging a Kafkaesque fight of our own.

We received a terse letter from our health insurance provider informing us that they would no longer cover Mickey's epilepsy medication unless we switched from the brand-name drug to a generic form. They would re-authorize covering the brand-name medication only if he took the generic drug for a month and had what they called "a documented clinical failure."

In other words, they'd decided that Mickey had to have a seizure to prove that he needed the brand medication the doctor had given him.

Once a drug has gone off patent, this allows multiple generic companies to make the drug, in addition to the brand manufacturer. The problem is that "equivalent" doesn't mean "the same" when it comes to generic drugs.

Generics contain the same type and amount of medical ingredients as the name brand, but have different inactive ingredients—colorants, fillers, binders, disintegrants, lubricants, colors and flavors. Dissolution properties may vary from one generic to the next. There is a potential for allergic reaction. Many epilepsy drugs are absorbed and metabolized in more complex ways than other drugs.

Generic drugs don't have to deliver precisely the same amount of medicine, or do it at precisely the same rate. Even generics for the same drug can differ from each other. The Food and Drug Administration allows a 20 percent variance in bioequivalence for generics—a 90 percent confidence interval, within the acceptance range of 0.80–1.25. Which made me wonder: if 80 percent was good enough, could 120 percent be considered an overdose? If a generic only had to be 80 percent equivalent, was that like asking for change for a dollar but only getting back 80 cents?

Generics to control high blood pressure or elevated cholesterol do the job. But for some patients with seizure disorders, there is little margin for error. It's the difference between epilepsy that is fully controlled, and breakthrough seizures. There was mounting evidence that switching to other versions of anti-epileptic drugs often didn't control seizures as effectively.

Marc called our insurance company and argued. Dr. Devinsky filed an expedited appeal. The insurance company turned us down anyway.

I was livid. Had anyone at the insurance company bothered to look at Mickey's full medical profile? How was it possible that a clerk, relying on the medical guidelines of a panel of experts who had never met, let alone treated, our child, could possibly decide what was best for him? That they could over-ride the clinical judgment of the doctor who was actually treating him?

What about the sheer cruelty of forcing a child to undergo more seizures, just to prove a financial/medical point? Doctors follow the fundamental principle of "first, do no harm." Shouldn't that apply to insurance company medical panels too?

Brand-name drugs are expensive. I wasn't opposed to using generics to cut costs. But not at the expense of efficacy. Not at the expense of my child. How much was actually saved, if cost-cutting measures resulted in breakthrough seizures? Had anyone at the insurance company factored in the financial impact of paying for EMS services and hospitalizations? The time and wages lost when patients and parents miss school or work? The social and emotional repercussions on those patients and their families?

According to the Epilepsy Foundation, a study in the July 2009 issue of the journal *Pharmacotherapy* concluded that patients who had "an epileptic event" requiring acute care were about 80 percent more likely than the control group to have recently had an anti-epileptic drug substitution.

"For the vast majority of patients, there probably isn't a problem with switching to a generic," says Jacqueline French, MD, Co-Director of Epilepsy Research and Epilepsy Clinical Trials at the NYU Comprehensive Epilepsy Center. "But some people are on relatively thin ice when it comes to seizure control. They're sensitive to small changes in blood levels." According to Dr. French, there are no well-performed studies to assess risk from switching between generics, and although switching is probably safe for most people, patients taking multiple AEDs—like Mickey—are at risk for drug interactions.

Both the Epilepsy Foundation and the American Academy of Neurology oppose generic substitution of anti-convulsant drugs for the treatment of epilepsy without the attending physician's approval. The stand-off pits insurance companies, health plans and pharmacies against doctors and people living with epilepsy. Even though relatively few people with epilepsy may be vulnerable, "for some of them, a new seizure can be a threat to their livelihood, or even their life," says Shlomo Shinnar, MD, spokesman for the American Academy of Neurology.

I was angry that short-sighted cost considerations could take precedence over patient welfare.

The insurance company's experiment was a clinical failure. After three weeks of taking the generic form of his medication, Mickey had a seizure. They finally agreed to pay for the brand-name medication they had no business taking away in the first place.

~◎

After a new drug suddenly made Mickey agitated and aggressive, we were forced to admit him to the medical center again. This time Jake and Lauren were not there to buffer us.

Using foul-smelling glue and the ear-splitting air gun, they wired the 32 electrodes to his scalp. They covered his head with a cap that looked like the cut-off top of a pair of pantyhose. He was tethered to the wall behind the bed; he slept on a plastic pillow. The video camera mounted to the ceiling let the staff watch from an EEG monitoring lab down the hall I never saw. They talked to us through a speaker. "He's moved out of view," they would say. Or, "You're blocking him, Mom, please don't sit on the bed." There was no privacy. The florescent light fixture stayed on all night. I could not tell day from night unless I strained to see out a soot-smudged window. I knew there was an outside world; far below in the street you could see movement, notice that it was raining, hear the sound of sirens heading to the unseen emergency room below. Mickey felt miserable. He was angry, ready to hit anyone who tried to touch him. Each time anyone, even the lady who brought the food tray, entered the room, he said beseechingly, "Excuse me, ma'am, can you please take the stickies off my head?"

The nights were long and lonely. Marc was home with Jonathan. I remember trying to sleep on a flimsy fold-out cot with a paper-thin blanket, listening to the muted midnight sounds of the hospital. I waited till morning when someone arrived who could stay with Mickey long enough so I could shower. Dawn was an arbitrary marker. All the days in the hospital seemed to flow into each other, unraveling in a seamless ribbon of time— punctuated only by the visits of doctors; nurses; food trays.

The doctors told us we would need to wean him from one medication before starting a new one; it took 24 hours before he had a seizure. I was watching when he began to stare. He slid sideways, head wedged against the bed rails; his hands clenched.

the endless separation from a parent

Gone. I pressed the video button to mark the tape, as I had been instructed; then I rang for the nurse. "Mickey? Mickey?" she said, then announced for the video camera, "2:43pm. Patient unresponsive." She placed plastic cushions that looked like crib bumpers against the bed rails. We waited it out. It lasted less than a minute before he returned to us. He was stunned in the aftermath, and slept. Finally, after years of trying, we had finally documented a seizure. We had a confirmed diagnosis. Temporal lobe epilepsy. I felt vindicated, thinking of the resident on rounds who earlier that day had suggested that perhaps I was mistaken, that my child merely had migraines. Had he thought we, his parents, were making it up? No migraine looked like that.

The next day, Marc took my place at the hospital so that I could attend Jake's bar mitzvah. The rabbi asked us to join hands for the *Misheberach*, the prayer for healing the sick. I was sitting alone. Still, I sang. I sang with the congregation, "Bless those in need of healing with *refuah sh'leimah*, the renewal of body, the renewal of spirit," and as we sang the final "amen," I pictured my boy in that hospital bed, the endless, unspooling days and nights, the doctors and nurses, technicians and residents all poking at him. I blinked hard to keep the tears from running, and thought, *who will heal our child?*

HEALING OUR WORLD

"Okay, here I go!" Mickey said.

He was standing at the *bimah*, a lectern at the front of the synagogue, beaming a mega-watt smile at the 50 gathered friends and relatives who had come to celebrate his bar mitzvah day with him. He had just finished reciting his *parshah*, in transliterated Hebrew, a passage from the Book of Numbers that contains the Priestly Blessing heard weekly in synagogues around the world. He was about to read his *d'var Torah*, the traditional short speech on the significance of the weekly Torah portion.

"Shabbat Shalom!" he began, reading carefully and clearly from the large index card I had typed for him the night before. "Amen means complete, and I just finished my Torah portion. Amen! The part of the Torah I just read is the Priestly Blessing. It is our oldest and most important blessing, and it wishes for all people to have peace. This is very exciting for me and I am so proud to lead everyone here in prayer and song and to read from the Torah. I want to give special thanks to my teachers Dori, Shana, Stacy from Matan and Rabbi Angela; to my brother Jonnie, and to my parents. I love you."

Our neighbors Nancy and Chuck Clarvit passed one soggy Kleenex back and forth between them, finally sending my eight-year-old niece to the ladies room to bring back more tissues. She returned with a wad of rough brown paper towels which made their way up and down the aisle.

We were completing a journey that had started 12 years earlier, when Mickey's first speech therapist at Blythedale Children's Hospital had gently suggested the possibility that he might never speak at all.

But here we were.

For years, we danced with the idea of a bar mitzvah. Thirteen is a milestone for all Jewish children, and we were determined that our son would take part. I knew he could learn a few simple prayers and songs; he has amazing memory skills, not uncommon for children with autism. But Hebrew was out of the question. Mickey often grappled with speaking and understanding the most rudimentary English, though at times he was startlingly direct and clear. We wanted him to have the experience of preparing for his bar mitzvah, to mark that passage, whatever it would be, just as Jonathan had done, in his own accomplished way.

Initially our temple hadn't known what to do with Mickey. We attempted religious school when he was nine, putting him in a class for much younger children. But even that proved too academically rigorous and language-laden. He lasted three sessions.

"The Torah says you're supposed to teach your children," I said to the director of the religious school. "It doesn't say *some* of your children. Isn't it a sacred obligation to teach *all* our children?" Although we could instruct Mickey about holidays and observances at home, it felt important to us that he have the experience of learning within a community.

With that in mind, Marc and I met with the senior rabbi at our synagogue to express our hopes and frustrations. He steered us to the Center for Jewish Life. Physically separate from the main temple, the CJL is an intimate and airy light-filled meeting house with 12-foot-high ceilings and wonderful acoustics. It offers a more private worship experience, and is usually reserved for small life cycle events—a baby naming, a *bris*, an *oneg Shabbat* (celebration of the Jewish Sabbath)—unlike the large, imposing and formal sanctuary where we had celebrated Jonathan's bar mitzvah four years earlier.

Each Saturday morning we took Mickey to Sharing Shabbat at the CJL, a spirited, family-centered service suffused with song, that was designed for younger children. At first Mickey was reluctant; it was new and unfamiliar, and he insisted on carrying his collection of small plush Nintendo characters, jamming Mario and Luigi in opposite pants pockets, bringing them out whenever it was time to sing. Sharing Shabbat was led by the aptly named Rabbi Angela. She truly had the voice of an angel as she guided the children in song and prayer with her guitar. Mickey loved the small sermons and stories she told. "She's a nada-rator," he would say. "Like Martin Sheen." He meant "narrator," somehow equating Angela's tales to his favorite Eyewitness Animal Video series. Angela was kind and welcoming. I suspected that she, too, had probably grown up having to field insensitive questions; as the daughter of a Korean Buddhist mother and a reform Jewish father, she knew firsthand about feeling marginalized from mainstream Jewish life. Angela was trained as both a cantor and a rabbi, the first Asian-American to graduate from the rabbinical program at the prestigious Hebrew Union College. Marc and I began to talk with her about how we might shape Sharing Shabbat into a bar mitzvah service.

Still, we worried. What if a large crowd unnerved him? What if he panicked in mid-speech, declaring, as he often did, "That's it! I'm out of here," and bolted? We shared these fears with Angela.

"You know, a 13-year-old child doesn't *have* to read from the Torah," Angela said. "It's not mandatory. Turning 13 just means that he has earned the privilege. We can do this however you feel most comfortable."

To help him prepare, Angela sang all the Torah blessings, songs, prayers and *parshah* (Torah portion) into a tape recorder for Mickey. Each night that spring Mickey lay in bed listening. Often I lingered outside his door, loving the crystalline purity of Angela's voice singing him to sleep.

Traditionally, a bar mitzvah child in our congregation undertakes a mitzvah project—a good deed that helps others. It is part of our ethical heritage of *Tikkun Olam*, a Hebrew phrase that means healing or repairing the world. "No gifts," we told everyone. "Please take whatever you would have spent and give it to the National Alliance for Autism Research." Astonishingly, in the weeks before the bar mitzvah more than $40,000 from friends, family and congregants poured in.

Several days before the event, the four of us met with Angela to rehearse in the CJL. We invited our friend Ellen to be the appreciative "audience" so that Mickey could practice in front of others. It was an uncommonly warm day in early June; I fanned myself with a prayer book. Angela flipped on the air conditioning, and turned to Mickey. "What should we sing first?" she asked him, and before she could even take out her guitar, he said, "V'Shamru!" and launched in, confident and unselfconscious. He sang every single verse. In Hebrew. We were stunned.

"Mickey! That was *wonderful*," Angela said.

I was incredulous. "I had no idea he knew that."

We sang several more songs, and then Angela took the Torah from the Ark. The silver spindle ornaments tinkled and jingled as she placed it in Jonathan's arms. She asked him to practice carrying it slowly around the periphery of the room. Mickey trailed him, grinning as he clutched the tail of Jonathan's t-shirt. Ellen grabbed my hand, and I realized that we were both wiping tears.

It was a beautiful, blazing Saturday morning when workmen arrived to set up a tent in our backyard for the barbecue in Mickey's honor we would host the next day. Inside the house, Marc and I dressed Mickey in a blazer, French blue shirt, red foulard tie and gray pants. Just like a typical family, we joined grandparents, aunts, uncles and cousins at the synagogue an hour before the service to pose for family portraits. "Today would have been my dad's eightieth birthday," Marc whispered to me. Tenderly, he draped Mickey in a white and gold *tallis*, a prayer shawl that Mickey's great-grandmother had brought from Israel 50 years earlier. The room was radiant with mid-morning light as it filled with the people we loved most.

After Mickey's speech, amidst the sound of much sniffling and throat clearing, and after Mickey returned to his seat between us, each of us hugging him, Angela began speaking to everyone gathered. She talked about the significance of the Priestly Blessing, the ritual and meaning of this day, the privilege of working with our son. What I remember most, though, is the welter of feelings: the palpable longing that my own mother might have lived long enough to reach this hard-won happiness with us, even as I felt the communal embrace that drew in my husband, our two sons and me, and held us fast.

In her achingly lovely voice, Angela sang *"Lechi Lach"*—literally, "let us go forward," a modern song that is based on God's words to Abraham to seek his destiny:

> *Lechi lach* to a land that I will show you
> *Lech li-cha* to a place you do not know
> *Lechi lach* on your journey I will bless you
> And you shall be a blessing, you shall be a blessing
> You shall be a blessing, *lechi lach*.

"Michael Gabriel Carter," said Angela, looking at him, "You *are* a blessing, to everyone in this room."

"Thanks! You too!" he said, in such a chipper tone that everyone laughed.

"May God bless you and keep you," said Angela. "May God shine upon you, and be gracious to you, may God lift up his countenance upon you, and give you peace," she said, concluding the service. The room erupted in applause.

Mickey raced over to my father. "Grandpa! I did it!" he cried. "Are you proud of me?"

My father hugged him. "You made us all proud today," he said.

We crossed the hall into the airy room beyond, to tables heaped high with buffet platters, and vases bursting with sunflower bouquets. My cousin Mark, who had already had the pleasure of seeing the first of his own three children through a bar mitzvah three years earlier, pulled me aside into a bear hug. "That," he said, "was the best bar mitzvah I have ever seen."

It was a journey of faith and healing for us all. And there was joy. Different from our wedding day; different too from the births of either of our children, both born beneath the glare of a surgeon's spotlight. This joy was unique; it had a texture all its own. For one beautiful, blazing day in June, we were a normal family.

FAMILY LEGACY

My father was indeed a proud grandfather. He doted in his own quiet way. He thought his grandsons were perfect. When Mickey had finally been diagnosed at age five with Pervasive Developmental Disorder and I'd broken the news to my father, I remember Dad's bewilderment clearly. "What's all the fuss about?" he'd asked. "I was a late talker too."

I'd tried to explain. "It's not just a speech delay," I told him. "It's a whole cluster of problems."

Dad just didn't get it. Finally, he patted my arm lovingly. "Maybe he'll snap out of it," he said.

My father could fix anything. A sparking light socket, a misfiring carburetor, an overflowing dishwasher. He could fold paper into an origami cat, untangle a fine gold chain necklace, or disassemble a car engine and put it back together again. But over the years, he came to realize that Mickey was something he couldn't "fix." Even though Dad didn't understand what was wrong with his grandson, he was determined to help us the most practical way he could. He offered to help us pay for private therapy for Mickey.

My father, my uncles and many of my cousins have pursued physics, electronics, medicine, engineering, even herpetology. Mickey comes from a family of scientists. The only science I have ever undertaken has been biological: combining my genes with Marc's to make our two boys. But even though the science gene seems to have (mostly) skipped me, I suspect we are all living with its unexpected legacy.

Research suggests there is a correlation between families with highly analytic skills and autism. Simon Baron-Cohen, Professor of Developmental Psychopathology at the University of Cambridge and director of their autism research center, has a number of highly controversial theories, but there is one that makes sense to me: families filled with scientists, engineers, physicists and mathematicians are more likely to produce children with autism. While this doesn't describe Marc's family, it certainly fits mine. All of my first cousins on my father's side who have had children have at least one child with some form of a learning difference, whether it is an attention deficit disorder, or a non-verbal learning disability. Mickey, with a pervasive developmental disorder, has the fullest expression.

My father was a highly self-educated engineer. I did not take after him. Although I did well enough in science, I took after my mother, who loved literature and art. In her younger days she had been a life-of-the-party kind of girl, a counterpoint to my shy but steady dad. He was neat to a fault, slow and methodical. Everything I was not. Not an emotive man, he rarely said he loved me. But I knew it from the way he was forever taking out his pocket comb to smooth the snarls in my long hair. "People say your dad is a rock," my mother often said. "And you know what? He is." He was certainly the steadiest man she'd ever met, the kind of analytical and resourceful guy you'd want to get shipwrecked with, because he'd figure out how to get you home.

Both Jonathan and Mickey loved doing puzzles with my father, or playing Connect Four, a two-dimensional game like Tic-Tac-Toe, where players take turns dropping colored discs into a vertical grid. The object of the game was to connect four of one's own discs of the same color next to each other vertically, horizontally or diagonally before your opponent did.

"They're both good at this," Dad observed.

"They get that from you," I said. Actually, Jonathan was more like my mother: outgoing, funny, talkative, a voracious reader; Mickey was more like my father, slow to speak, a spatial thinker, adept at finding visual patterns.

Watching Dad play with the boys, I would often think about the time I was 13, and had asked for a stereo. Dad had decided we'd build one together. "These are skills you'll have forever," he'd said, his head bent low to watch as I grasped the soldering iron gingerly. We were assembling a Heathkit stereo, a do-it-yourself kit that supplied everything but the tools. He was determined to refine the wiring and soldering skills he had begun teaching me two years earlier when I devised my fifth-grade science project, an electronic question and answer game board. I'd won third prize in the Queens District Science Fair that year.

Dad was a child of the Great Depression, one of seven children, all born at home. With little or no money, they'd learned to rely on their ingenuity. At 12, Dad and my Uncle Jack had built a working car from the parts of some abandoned vehicles they'd found. My dad taught himself to drive, shifting gears in his parents' driveway. Eventually he and Jack took to the roads, blithely unaware that they might need at least one driver's license between them.

Shy and modest, Dad rarely volunteered information about himself. When I was in seventh grade, my class read an anthology of stories about people who had demonstrated different kinds of courage. One in particular impressed me: a scientist at Los Alamos named Louis Slotin, who, in the midst of a radiation experiment gone wrong, had thrust his hands into the tank to halt a nuclear chain reaction. He shielded the other scientists in the room, taking the brunt of the radiation himself. Slotin died nine days later. When I recounted this story at the dinner table, my usually silent father spoke up.

"Yes," he said. "We were friends. I used to ski with Louie in New Mexico."

I was incredulous. "You *knew* him? You were there? During that experiment?"

"No," he said. "But I was in an accident later on."

"The radiation knocked out all your dad's white blood cells," my mother added. "Everyone was quarantined in a hospital. No one was expected to live."

"How scary," I breathed. Until then I don't remember ever giving any thought to what my father's life might have been like before we were part of it.

Dad got up from the table and returned with a large manila envelope filled with stacks of black-and-white photographs: pictures of himself in army fatigues, head bent in concentration over a table of electrical parts; at the controls of an airplane; by a Quonset hut on a tropical island; waving from the cockpit of a B-29 plane painted with the name "Great Artiste." It was the first time I heard what my father had actually done during World War II. I was awed.

"I was drafted in 1941," he told me. "Eventually I landed up at Fort Knox as a radio instructor. Your uncles Max and Ken both enlisted. We were all out in New Mexico, working on a top-secret project." Both Max and Ken, fraternal twins, had graduate degrees in physics, but the secret project needed the skills of an electrical engineer. My father, a boy from Queens with only a high school education, had precisely the complex skills the project required.

"The government ordered me to travel secretly," he continued. I didn't remember ever seeing my dad so animated. "I had to wear civilian clothes. It was like a movie. My contact person told me to go to a certain bus stop, and make a phone call from there to find out where I was supposed to go next. I wound up at Los Alamos."

"What was the secret project?"

"The Manhattan Project," he said with excitement and pride.

Dad had been recruited for the ultimate science project: developing the first atomic bomb. He handled measuring instrumentation and assembled radioactive materials that no one today would dream of doing by hand. In the summer of 1945, he shipped over to Tinian, a south pacific island in the Marianas that was the final staging ground.

"I was in charge of monitoring instrumentation for 'Fat Man' and 'Little Boy,'" he said. "Those were the code names we had for the bombs we were going to drop on Japan. I ran the equipment. I flew in one of the two escort planes that accompanied the Great Artiste, the airplane that detonated the second atomic bomb over Nagasaki." Then he handed me a photo: the terrible, iconic mushroom cloud over Hiroshima. I saw the photo had been signed by the Enola Gay's pilot Paul Tibbets and the other men who accompanied him that day.

Suddenly I felt my own emotional detonation. "Didn't you feel horrible about killing so many people?" I asked nervously.

He bristled. "You have to understand. We were at war. We were facing a land invasion of Japan that would have meant losing another million American lives. What were we to do? It's so easy now to sit in judgment. You don't know what it felt like then." Still, I've often wondered how my father lived with such ultimately disturbing moral ambiguity.

My father and I had difficult times during my rebellious teens. It was the early 1970s: the war in Vietnam was raging, and my conservative father and I disagreed on everything. My mother was our intermediary, carrying messages back and forth across our own enemy lines. Dad barely spoke unless it was to tell me that I was wearing too much makeup. Eventually we reconciled when I was in my twenties. My mother no longer needed to translate us to each other. Both my parents were thrilled to welcome Marc into the family. "I hope you realize," my mother said lightly, "That if you and Marc have a fight, your dad and I will take *his* side." The man I married isn't what you'd call handy, but he and my dad grew close—even though only one of them was a talker. Marc cemented the relationship by giving my dad Jonathan, his first grandchild.

I remember one afternoon, not long before my mother died, when we arrived for a visit. Mickey was four; Jonathan, nine. Mickey had run ahead into the den to greet Grandma. He tore out, eyes big with fear, and flew into Marc's arms. I stepped inside. My mother was hooked up to a BiPap machine, an apparatus to help get more air into her lungs. I knew immediately why Mickey had recoiled. Mom was wearing a face mask; a hose hung like a giant snout from her grey, wasted face. We had all grown used to seeing her wear the clear nasal cannula that tied her to a tank of oxygen; this new breathing machine made her look monstrous.

Mickey had always loved my reticent father openly and unreservedly. But after my mother's death, we noticed that Mickey was wary around my father; every time Dad sneezed explosively, Mickey would flee.

"I think something about it reminds him of your mom," Marc said.

Mickey wouldn't—couldn't—talk about Grandma. Every time I mentioned her to him, he'd stop me: "No! No talking."

We tried to shield Dad from Mickey's nervousness around him. But every time Dad reached for a handkerchief, Mickey would freeze, his eyes locked on Dad's movements.

"I think the sound of your sneezing frightens him," I said apologetically one evening after Mickey fled the dinner table.

"You think so?" Dad said, surprised. "Am I that loud?"

"No, you're not," I assured him. "He's just sensitive to sound." Gingerly, I added, "I think there's something about it that reminds him of Mom and how hard it was for her to breathe."

"Really?" He was incredulous. "Does he even remember her?"

"Most definitely!" I said. "He was nearly five when she died. You'd be amazed at how much he remembers."

"You need to create some new memories," Mickey's therapist Barbara suggested at our next visit. "Find an activity they can both enjoy doing, and take some pictures. We can write a story about it and make it into a book for him."

The following weekend, we drove Dad, Jonathan and Mickey to an empty nearby field and flew kites. Dad, of course, was expert at it; as he helped the boys untangle and tug their kite strings, I snapped photos of the three of them. Afterward, we warmed up with hot cocoa at the deli, and both boys leaned up lovingly against their grandfather. Mickey's fear had begun to abate.

The landscape of the brain is vast and mysterious, much of it still uncharted. As Mickey developed epilepsy in puberty, I found myself poring yet again—or still—over books and journals, trying to decode the mysteries of our synapses, and wishing I had paid better attention in biology class. This time, though, not only for Mickey's sake, but for my father's as well.

Dad was nearly 90. He still drove to his office every day, where he read the *Wall Street Journal* and monitored his stocks online. But I saw with sorrow the inevitable cognitive changes that time had effected. Worried that I detected a slur in his speech, concerned about his memory lapses, I took him to a geriatric specialist. It was like being with Mickey all over again in the early years, watching as doctors and technicians administered their myriad tests. The MRI confirmed what I suspected: my father had had a series of small strokes. But what was more telling to me, before any expensive tests were even run, were the small pen and paper tasks the doctor set before him. She asked him to draw the face of a clock. The man who once read schematics for pleasure, a spatial thinker who could manipulate three-dimensional models in his mind, this brilliant electrical engineer who had with his own hands assembled not one but two atom bombs, drew a lop-sided oval. He placed the clock numbers at odd intervals, the four and five scrunched together so tightly they pushed the six into the seven. My heart was squeezed somewhere in between. I knew about cognitive loss. Mickey, too, had lost ground. We did not know whether it was the seizures, or the powerful medications he took to control them. In sixth grade he could multiply and divide fractions; now he struggled with the most basic addition and subtraction.

In his final years, my father became more my child than my parent. Like Mickey, he often perseverated on the small, the irritating, the insignificant detail. But like his grandson, he was also loving and sweet-tempered. And I felt grateful that the same skills Dad had instilled in me—patience, perseverance, attention to detail, trying to make all the pieces fit together—still served me well with both of them.

We were supposed to have Sunday brunch with my father the day in July he died. Driving out to Long Island that morning, I telephoned repeatedly to say we were on our way, only to hear the answering machine pick up again and again. By the time we tore into the parking lot I was frantic. "You stay in the car with Mickey," Marc said, racing into the lobby. Minutes later, he reappeared and motioned me out of the car. "He's dead," he told me, wrapping his arms around me as I struggled to stifle my cries. "I called 911." Mickey flew from the car.

"Grandpa is dead?" he asked.

We could hear the rising wail of sirens, saw a stroboscope of flashing red lights as cars and cruisers careened into the courtyard. I drew Mickey tight and covered his ears.

Two days later, I clutched hands with Marc and Jonathan as we buried my father. Briefly, as we waited for the limo to the cemetery, Jonathan broke down. He was so tall now that I had to reach up to hold him tight in my arms. "We will get through this," I told him. "We will be okay." Mickey was home with Milagros. He had already seen too much. I didn't want him to see that coffin being lowered into the ground. Hear the flat and brutal thump of the first shovelful of dirt.

Friends and family followed us home for the ritual lunch. Baskets of bagels, bowls of hard-boiled eggs. Round objects, to symbolize the eternal circle of life. Mickey wandered solemnly from room to room, stopping in front of a group eating at the kitchen table.

"Are you here because you're sad about my grandpa?" he asked them.

Months later, as I stowed away Mickey's summer clothes, I noticed that he had taken all his photos of his grandfather and put them in the closet, facing the back wall. I returned them to his book shelf. A day later, they were back in his closet. I asked him why he had put them there.

"No, no, no. No talking," he said.

I understood. It was all I could do to look at those pictures myself.

"Do people come back from heaven?" Mickey asked repeatedly. Over and over, I told him no.

"Do they come back from shopping?"

I said yes, of course.

"What about James' parents?" he asked.

I knew who he meant. He was talking about the book *James and the Giant Peach*. On the first page, James' parents go shopping in London, where they are eaten by an angry rhino, and James has to go live with his wicked aunts. Was this why Mickey often waited up late at night when Marc and I went to dinner and a movie?

Sometimes he would look up at the sky and ask if Grandpa was up there.

"I don't want him to be dead," he'd say. "Make him come back."

"He can't come back," I said.

"But I want him to!" he cried.

Crying over grandfather's death.

Other times he asked for concrete details: "Who buried him? Is it with sand or dirt?"

Mickey played Nintendo games endlessly, watching characters who "die," only to be reborn in the next game level. A high-tech version of Wile E. Coyote and Road Runner, forever chasing each other through an undulating landscape of cliffs and chasms. Or he pored over my wedding album. "The married pictures," he called them. Pointing out all the relatives who had died, asking me to name them. Inexplicably, he found the name "Bernie" hilarious, repeating it to himself again and again for days. When we drove by a cemetery, he would ask, "Is that a cemetery? Are strangers buried there?" I thought of Elisabeth Kübler-Ross' Five Stages of Grief, which were not unlike the stages I'd gone through when Mickey had been diagnosed years earlier. I had learned then that grieving wasn't linear. I had cycled through each stage repeatedly. Just as Mickey was now doing. How could I explain death to him? I couldn't explain it to myself. Often I woke in the dead of night, awash in a wave of nausea. How would he cope with my death? With Marc's? What would he do without parents to care for him? Who would love him when we were gone?

Mickey wrote stories. He began doing this a few months before his grandfather died, whenever we took my increasingly frail father out to eat at Bruce's Deli. Waiting for food, Mickey busied himself by writing stories about his grandpa on the back of a paper place mat, filling every available bit of white space with inky words. Now he wrote stories whenever we went out to eat. The stories were all the same. They were always about someone who had died. In every story, a zoo animal escaped, invaded that relative's home and made a big mess. The animal broke the computer, the dishwasher and TV. It ate everything in sight. Every story had a title: "Aunt Tessie and the Bison." "Aunt Selma and the Okapi." "Grandma and the Warthog." The stories didn't vary much. The syntax was off. He would only write them on a piece of paper torn from a small spiral notebook in my purse. And yet, these stories were powerful, filled with action and anger. Most of them ended along the lines of, "Aunt Tessie yelled get out you ugly mean bison. But that bison didn't listen. That bison at Aunt Tessie's house forever. The End." Sometimes he resolved them with: "Uncle Jack has to call 911. The police arrest the monkey to put the monkey to jail. The End."

Aunt Harriet and the Panther

One day Aunt Harriet went out for a walk. When Aunt Harriet left a evil panther came in Aunt Harriet's house to make a mess. A evil panther broke the stove, refrigerator, television, windows, computer, tub, shower, cupboards, chairs, table. But when Aunt Harriet came home. She saw the mess the panther made. Aunt Harriet got angry and Aunt Harriet yelled get out of my house you ugly panther. But the evil panther didn't listen. The Evil Panther stayed in her house. That Evil did not leave Aunt Harriet's house.

The End

A year later when we held the unveiling, the Jewish tradition of honoring the deceased with a marker or headstone, we took Mickey with us to the cemetery, thinking that seeing the grave might answer some of his questions. Surprisingly, he walked through the group of gathered relatives, shaking hands, happily greeting people by name, as social as a politician working a crowd. Standing front and center by the grave, he eyed the unfamiliar rabbi. "Hi, I'm Mickey. Who are you? Are you helping us pray?"

Driving home, he asked suddenly, "Who buried Martin Luther King?"

"The people who work in the cemetery," I answered.

"Can God make people alive again?"

I said no.

"But he has to!" Mickey said, now angry.

"People's bodies die. But we still love them, and think about them, and talk about them. Our thoughts and feelings about them will always be in our heads and hearts," I answered, trying to appease his wrath.

"My family is in my heart?" he asked.

"Yes."

He thought a moment. "Are they buried in my stomach?" He needed answers I didn't have.

Mickey stacked all his stories in a cubby hole in his desk. "Sit with me, Mom," he said one afternoon, and I perched on the bed beside him. He wanted to nap, so I covered him with a quilt. "Mom," he said, "You're being like a flight attendant."

I smiled. "I'm right here."

"Do you miss your parents?" Mickey asked.

"Yes," I said. "Every day."

"Me too," he said, and sighed. "Mom? When are my cats going to die?" Dizzy had by then been joined by several more cats.

"Not for a very long time."

Clearly, he was wrestling with angels.

Then one day, at City Limits Diner, he looked up from the story he was writing and asked, "Are people in stories alive?"

"Not exactly," I said. "People who have died stay dead. But it's very good to write about them."

"Will they come back?"

"No," I repeated, trying hard to help him understand.

And then he smiled radiantly. "But they're alive in my stories!"

"Yes," I said. "Absolutely. They are."

He'd surprised me once more. I was pierced with the realization that the legacy he'd inherited wasn't only from my father, but from my mother as well. Like her—like Jonathan, like Marc, like me—Mickey felt acutely the healing power of story.

That love of words runs like a plumb line through our family. The power of the written was sacred in my parents' home, and my mother taught me to worship it.

One Saturday afternoon, soon after Marc and I had become engaged, I sat in the den at my parents' house, reviewing the brochures on silver and china patterns I'd collected. I picked up a pamphlet and read aloud to my mother:

"'Other silver makers will tell you that theirs is the original Queen Anne Williamsburg pattern, but don't be misled.'"

My parents' heads both shot up. "Could we have that again?" my father said.

"'But don't be misled,'" I said.

"Let me see that," my mother said. Then she whooped.

"That's not 'my-zulled,' it's 'miss-led,'" she said, and everyone burst out laughing.

"You mean M-I-S-L-E-D isn't pronounced 'my-zulled'?" I said. "Doesn't it sound like 'reprisal'?"

Everyone laughed harder. "Oh, honey," my mother said finally, "We're not laughing at you."

"Oh yeah? Well, you're not laughing with me, because I'm not laughing." My face was hot with embarrassment. "It *looks* like my-zulled," I said. "My-zull" was part of my reading vocabulary (as opposed to a speaking vocabulary), one of many words I had seen or written but never spoken. My reading vocabulary was extensive: I'd majored in English, and at that time was finishing a Master's in journalism, while working as a copywriter for Simon and Schuster. I believed that whoever said "the pen is mightier than the sword" was the kind of guy who probably got picked last for the team, and as I was an athletically challenged child, I had turned to books early on. Got a question? Get the book. Or even better, books, and make that plenty of them.

So I gave birth to my-zulled. "Don't be my-zulled!" everyone in my family cautioned each other for years. Whenever we wanted to deflate each other, we would trot out that phrase. Over time, family jokes grow as individual and unique as fingerprints, and our family was rife with them. As my Great-Aunt Mae used to say, "If it's not one thing, it's the same damn thing." I was finally vindicated years later when Russell Baker wrote a column on the op ed page of *The New York Times* revealing that for years he too had mispronounced the word "misled," thinking it rhymed with "King Faisaled." "You see? You see?" I scribbled triumphantly across the page, and mailed it to my mother.

I may have been my-zulled, but my mother never was. She was a stickler for grammar, spelling and punctuation. Though she was too poor to go to college, she was quick, well-read, and so precise in her speech that people often mistook her for a school teacher. She gave the dictionary a place of honor in our living room. Perpetually open, it lay atop a mahogany book stand, beside a soapstone statue of Nathan the Wise, who was mounted on an electrified base so that he could shed literal light. As a child I liked to run my hand over the cool drapes of Nathan's pale robes, and would smooth the enunciated and intricately carved fingers. The shelf below this table was always filled with piles of *National Geographic*, *The New Yorker* and my father's electronic supply catalogs.

My mother bought *The World Book* when I was in the third grade, a beige, fake-leather-bound set with yearly updates. I would sit and look up one of my current heroines, such as Madame Curie or Helen Keller, read the entry; then, seduced by words on the opposite page, curl into the barrel chair next to the dictionary stand, and read the rest of the encyclopedia. I'd turn page after page from entries on Kennel Club dog breeds to Kenya, Khartoum, Kinescopes and the Kremlin, the jolly drawings of Kris Kringle giving way to terrifying photos of Kwashiorkor-swollen babies, until I had exhausted "K," and would rise, dazed and stumbling, to put away the volume and vow to tackle "L" another day.

My parents received three newspapers a day, *The New York Times*, the local *Long Island Press* and *The Wall Street Journal*, as well as a wealth of magazines. My mother was such a hungry reader that during the Depression, when my grandmother washed the kitchen floor and laid newspapers down while it dried, my mother would sit and read three-week-old papers as avidly as if they were the latest screen magazines. At ten she read Fitzgerald, Hemingway and Woolf. "I didn't understand any of it," she told me, "I just read whatever I could get my hands on." She developed her own method, reading so fast that, as a high school student, she was sent to Columbia University for testing to see just what her system was. I often wonder if Evelyn Woods, who coined the phrase "speed reading" and developed the system known as Reading Dynamics, was part of the team that studied my mother. Reading, all reading, was a sacrament. Years later, even as other parents clucked and commented, my mother allowed me comic books. "I don't care what she reads, as long as she's reading," she'd say.

Before I learned to read, my mother read aloud to me until she was hoarse; merciless, I'd beg for just one more chapter, and she usually gave in. I loved to nestle against her, to feel the resonance of her voice. She read all of Frank Baum's Oz books to me; *The Secret Garden*, and best of all, *A Little Princess*. I wanted to be Sara Crewe, the bookish heroine who begins life as a beloved daughter and becomes a lonely and abused orphan, but is sustained through much hardship by her inner nobility and powerful imagination. (Eventually, she triumphs; this was children's literature, after all.)

Initially, I struggled with reading; I still remember the humiliation when my second-grade teacher assigned me to the slow group of readers in our classroom. But some time during that winter, I sneaked home our classroom reader because it was filled with intriguing pictures and I wanted to puzzle it out for myself. It was like learning to ride a bicycle; for weeks, I wobbled and fell, and then, suddenly, I was soaring. I tore through all the Nancy Drew mysteries, the Cherry Ames nurse stories, the Vicky Barton stewardess saga, *Little Women*, *A Wrinkle in Time* and *The Diary of Anne Frank*. I was voracious. Reading became my parallel universe: I could flee the frenetic press of family life into an imaginary room of my own. And reading also kept the unnamed, free-floating dread at bay. Immersed in a book, I temporarily stopped thinking the sad and scary thoughts that often kept me awake long into the night.

Reading by flashlight under the covers, I didn't have to think about my Cousin Ruthie's fatal heart defect, her brother Stevie's death from meningitis, or my grandmother Anna, whose leg was amputated before she died on the same dreadful day as her daughter Frances. I didn't have to think about my mother's pervasive sadness for the early loss of her own mother. Reading lessened the loneliness and fear. The world disappeared when I read; I was oblivious even to the sound of my own name being called. I loved it more than any other activity. I still do.

When I was pregnant with Jonathan, I read every volume on pregnancy in the town library, showing great panache as I tossed around terms like "alpha fetal protein," "chorionic villi sampling," or "effleurage" (which, despite its floral-sounding name, was not a feminine hygiene product). While I read *The Miracle of Life*, Marc read *Goodnight Moon* to my belly. In those early, anxious days of new motherhood, I pushed aside all those labor and delivery volumes to make way for the baby care books: Spock, Brazelton, Leach, Greenspan and Turecki. But even that was not enough: it was imperative to subscribe to four different parenting magazines. Never was redundancy so reassuring. When Jonathan was only a few weeks old, Marc began a nightly ritual of cradling him in one arm, and reading out loud, with great expression, from *The Wall Street Journal*.

Not surprisingly, Jonathan's first sentence was "Read the book." Jonathan dictated his first stories to me at the age of three, while sitting in the bathtub, and I happily wrote them down word for word. Reading came easily to him, and by the time he was seven, he read even more hungrily than I had done. His room was heaped with books piled like ziggurats, cantilevered towers tilting so haphazardly on his bedside table that more than once they fell over on him as he slept.

His reading delighted my mother. We each saw our younger selves in him. And I suspected that Jonathan, too, used reading to tamp down fearful thoughts. My mother, after a lifetime of smoking, was slowly smothering from emphysema, and in those last years of her life, Jonathan and I clung to our comforting nightly custom of reading aloud. Leaning up against his headboard, his head pressed into my shoulder, together we escaped into magical realms like *The Indian in the Cupboard* or *Half Magic* that offered respite. Mickey, too, sought us out to snuggle and turn the pages of his beloved picture books: *No, David!, Do You See a Mouse?* or *Little Gorilla*. As my mother became increasingly bedridden, we toted mystery books and video tapes to her bedside. Though she was tethered to an oxygen tank, Jonathan would snuggle against her, and when she was too weak to talk, they would simply watch television together.

"That child is the darling of my heart," she confided.

Jonathan was nine when she died. Again, I turned to books, this time on grief and on how to explain death to children. I longed to lose myself in a book, but found I was unable to concentrate. Instead, I embarked on a frenzy of cleaning. Going through her dresser drawers one day, I discovered a letter she must have been writing to Marc on the eve of our wedding. My mother was known for dashing off witty quatrains, or parodies of show tunes, whenever there was a birthday or anniversary. But this note was earnest and unrhymed. It simply said: "May Liane give you as much joy as she has given us."

My boys have given me the same joy, despite an abiding sadness that I cannot share my love of books with Mickey as I have with Jonathan. I took solace that Mickey managed to take from stories the things he needed. Again and again, he chose books with short, powerful words and evocative imagery. The absurdities of *Cloudy with a Chance of Meatballs* always made him laugh—just as watching Jonathan grow could make *me* laugh. I was happily reminded of my mother's love of words, as I savored Jonathan's precocious malapropisms, confusing "eclectic" for "electric," "cousin" for "cuisine." When he told me about a friend who got braces, he said, "Mom, the poor guy has to wear a recliner all the time!" All I could picture was a kid wedged in a Barcalounger. Once when I told him how handsome he looked, he said, "Good enough to be on the cover of Vague." Halfway through the first act of *The Lion King*, just after the evil uncle murdered his brother the king,

Jonathan, then age ten, nudged me. "Mom," he said. "It's just like Hamlet." And I thought, no one's going to my-zull this kid.

And just as I understood Jonathan's need to read, he knew mine. Not quite two weeks after my father passed away, the final book of the Harry Potter series was released. When the package from Amazon arrived at our doorstep, Jonathan claimed it first. He devoured the 800-page book in a single night. Then he handed it to me the way one passes a jug of water to a marathon runner. I settled into the club chair in our library, cranked open the casement window so I could smell the Casablanca lilies blooming below, and immersed myself in the world of Magic and Muggles.

Jorge Luis Borges wrote that he "always imagined that Paradise will be a kind of library." I do too. And I like to imagine that my mother is there. Three-week-old newspapers line the checkerboard linoleum floor. She sits contented in a comfy chair, a much-thumbed copy of *Webster's Unabridged* beside her. She is healed and healthy, and she is reading.

FELINE FATALE

Daffy was meant to be a companion for our cat Dizzy. She looked identical. The same kohl-rimmed eyes. The same silky, silver fur. The same sweet face. She was Dizzy's Doppelgänger.

But inside?

A heart of darkness.

Dizzy, our Maine Coon cat, was a year old when I began to wonder if she might be lonely. "What do you think she does all day when no one is around?"

"She's a *cat*," Marc said. "She's fine."

"She needs a friend," I insisted. We adored Dizzy. Her charming chirps and trills. Her languorous looks. People always remarked on her beauty. "Let's get another one who looks just like her."

"If you're looking for a lap cat, this one's a honey," said Mrs. Klase, Dizzy's breeder, days later. She placed a tiny tortoiseshell tabby in my arms. "I call her Funny Face." One side of her face was the color of cream; the other, chocolate. A yin-yang cat. She nestled against me and purred loudly.

"She *is* sweet," I agreed. "But do you have any silver ones like Dizzy?"

She did. A seraglio of long-haired kittens, all looking as if they were wearing furry harem pants. Jonathan played with Funny Face while Mrs. Klase fetched a silver brother/sister pair.

"I want *this* one, Mom," Jonathan said, an iron grip on Funny Face.

But I couldn't let go of the idea.

"How would you like to take home two?"

His grin was huge. *"Really?"*

We spent 20 minutes playing with the silver siblings. The boy was friendly and adventuresome. His sister wasn't.

"Take the girl. I don't want a male cat," Marc whispered.

"Why not?"

"I can't stand the thought of having to get him 'fixed.'"

"Are you *serious?*"

Marc crossed his legs.

"What can you tell me about her personality?" I asked. Mrs. Klase shrugged, non-committal.

We drove home with two kittens. Funny Face, whom we immediately renamed Fudge, and the silver girl we decided to call Daffy. "Like Dizzy and Daffy Dean," said my husband, the baseball historian.

But Daffy was not a team player.

Dizzy loathed her immediately. She leapt to the back of the sofa and glared, as if to say, "What's this bimbo doing here?"

Fudge slunk away; Daffy stood her ground, growling. After much hissing and swatting, they reached a clawed truce.

Daffy was testy as a teenager. One moment she'd play the cat coquette, all fun and flirty, inviting you to play. Then she'd rear back, grooming her fur frantically as if to erase any trace of human scent. She got high licking the glue off packing tape; she'd roll around ecstatically on top of a damp peppermint teabag. If you called her name, she'd stare impassively. Gorgeous but vacuous. The Paris Hilton of cats.

"Does she seem a little off to you?" I asked Marc.

A year later, when we visited a cat show, Mrs. Klase was selling two smoky grey kittens. Jonathan reached for the feather tickler.

"Don't fall in love," I warned.

"Too late, Mom," he said.

That's how Moxie came home with us.

Daffy was not amused. She expressed her displeasure by leaving little piles of poop in odd places. Beside the basement door. Beneath the playroom window. Behind the litter box. She was sneaky; we never saw her do it. We bought new litter boxes. Different brands of litter. Nothing helped.

But Daffy had a champion: Shana, Mickey's behavioral therapist.

"I *adore* her!" Shana gushed. "All your cats are beautiful, but this one is Miss America. I'd take her in a heartbeat." She squeezed Daffy, who squawked crossly. "Does that sound shallow?"

"It's a mistake to pick pets for their looks," I said. The rueful voice of experience.

"Please can I have another kitten?" Mickey asked.

In a final, fatal lapse in judgment, we brought home another cat. Mickey named her Ketzel—Yiddish for "kitten." We quarantined her, as the vet suggested, then slowly introduced her to the rest of our feline family.

Daffy was *really* not amused.

We found our fluffy towels mysteriously pulled off the bathroom towel bars, with yellow puddles pooling in them. Then puddles appeared everywhere. Mickey's book shelves. Jonathan's bed. Marc's desk. The living room sofa.

"Maybe it's a kidney problem," I worried. "Let's take her to the vet."

Seven hundred and seventy-five dollars later, the vet said, "Clean as a whistle."

"You have to get rid of her," my mother-in-law Beverly said.

"I can't. She's family."

Instead, I bought a special ultraviolet light like the ones forensic experts use on cop shows to reveal crime stains. It was worse than we thought. The house was a feline latrine. Daffy had marked nearly every piece of upholstered furniture we owned.

The vet gave her tranquillizers. Then Pet Prozac. No change. One night Daffy sat in front of the reading lamp, blocking Marc's light. When he tried gently to move her, she bit him.

"I am so *done* with this cat," Marc said.

I called the vet back. "The only thing left I can suggest is a behavioral therapist for pets," she said.

The irony did not escape us.

I would have done it too. But then my father died suddenly. That meant crowds of visitors...and Daffy's wrath. Desperate, I called Shana.

"Take her," I begged.

I packed her off with a trousseau. A pricey cat carrier. Buckets of food and litter. Bundles of bedding and toys. "Daffy's having a sleep-over with Shana," I told Mickey.

Shana called that evening. "I put her behaviors on extinction. She gets Tuna Treats every time she uses the litter box properly. Then I'll fade the prompts."

"I'd still put a rubber sheet on your bed."

"No worries," she said.

With Daffy's disappearance, the four other cats reappeared, much like the Munchkins creeping out after Dorothy dropped a house on the Wicked Witch.

"Is it my imagination or do they seem...happier?" I said to Marc.

"I know *I* am."

"When do you want me to bring her back?" Shana asked a week later.

"How about never?" we chorused.

Shana still claims Daffy is friendly and well behaved. No sign of Dizzy's Evil Twin. She's pretty pudgy too, from all the treats.

Shana admits she's afraid *not* to give them. She fretted when her fiancé Dave moved in with a Boston terrier named Iggy.

"She swats Iggy if he gets too close, and she eats Iggy's food right out from under him. Otherwise, she's an angel. I told Dave all about her but he doesn't believe me," Shana said, then described how Daffy also liked to put her head in the fish bowl and lap up the fish's food. Amazingly, the fish swam up to watch. "I swear, they even kiss!" she said. She showed me a video on her phone to prove it. One day the fish went belly up. Daffy missed her pet. She was moping and cranky, so Dave bought her another fish. It lasted six hours.

"I think she scared it to death," Shana said.

Kind-hearted Dave bought another fish. Two days later, Shana emailed me.

"Last night we walked into a crime scene. The cat and dog looked innocent enough but laying there on the floor was... Daffy's latest pet. The murderess! I am beside myself. I don't know how she did it. We think she picked him up with her mouth and flung him on the floor and then watched him die."

She added, "We will make her wait a couple of days before her replacement friend is bought."

Clearly Daffy had the upper paw.

"Is Daffy still our cat?" Mickey asked.

"Yes, but she lives with Shana now," I told him. "Would you like to visit her?"

"No, thank you," he said.

That said it all.

THOSE KIDS, THOSE PARENTS

The phone rang late one afternoon as I was chopping salad. Cordless receiver wedged between my shoulder and my ear, I lined up a row of cherry tomatoes on the cutting board.

"Hi, my son Jeremy is a volunteer in your sports program," a woman who identified herself only as "Jeremy's mom" said. "I'm going to need you to write something up for him for the school volunteer awards ceremony next month."

"Hmm-hmm," I said.

"I need an evaluation that describes your program, what my son has contributed, and what kind of growth you've seen in him. And also, what he's learned from working with those kids," she said.

Those kids.

"I'm sorry, what did you say your son's name is?" I said, starting a slow seethe.

"Jeremy."

Who was Jeremy? I honestly didn't remember him. We had so many volunteers, all trying to fulfill their school's community service requirements by volunteering at the Alternative Sports League, the weekend program in our community for children with disabilities that Marc and I had started several years earlier.

But as usual I was polite. "Sure, happy to," I said, savagely chopping the tomatoes, thinking, *if it's your kid's community service, why isn't he calling me himself? Why isn't he writing his own report?*

"Oh, just one more thing. Could you have it for me before Friday? I can pick it up, just leave it in your mailbox. I know it's short notice, but I'm just overwhelmed and I'm taking my daughter up to Canyon Ranch this weekend," Jeremy's mom said, and laughed. Was she trying to draw me in? Sound apologetic?

"You know how it is," she said.

No. Actually, I didn't.

"No problem," I said, and hung up. Mad at myself, I whacked at a pile of carrots, and thought, *so you're stressed having to make your kid rack up his community service hours to pad his college application packet? Let me save you the trouble. I'll just give him a t-shirt that says, "Look how selfless and wonderful I am: I volunteer with autistic children."*

Our sports program got a lot of traction from the middle-schoolers in the neighborhood. It was customary for children going through a bar mitzvah or church confirmation to do a service project—collecting clothing or canned goods for charity. Then some parents cottoned on to the fact that their sports-loving kid could get more mileage out of our program. The problem was that once the confirmation, bar mitzvah or Boy Scout project was over, so was the kid's commitment. Most of them never showed up again. I wondered: what were their parents teaching them?

One Saturday morning, Marc and I sat in the synagogue listening to a boy we knew from our town deliver his bar mitzvah speech. "For my mitzvah project I'm so proud of all the work I did for the Alternative League," he said. "I'm really good at sports, so I was able to share all my skills with those kids."

There it was again. *Those kids.*

"I hope I helped their lives in some way," he added.

Marc leaned in. "Did he come to any of our games?" he whispered.

"I saw him there once. Maybe twice?" I whispered back.

Here's what particularly galled me: this kid, all self-congratulatory smiles, actually lived in our neighborhood. He's close in age to Mickey. But in all those years, this boy had never— not once—rung the doorbell to ask if my son wanted to come out and play. It reminded me of that old "Peanuts" poster, a cartoon of Lucy Van Pelt with a bubble over her head that said, "I love Mankind. It's people I can't stand." I had seen how this boy's sister looked the other way when my son walked by. Like many of the children in town, they simply ignored my child. In six years of elementary school, Mickey had never been invited to one birthday party. In middle school I saw kids in the neighborhood walking to and from school together; not once had any of them ever asked my son to walk with them. Yet Mickey always glowed with delight when he saw them. "Hi, Lindsay! Hi, Shawn! Hi, Kelsey!" he would sing out happily. He gave his heart so freely. It made me wince. He thought the neighborhood kids were his friends. Sometimes they mumbled back, then looked away. I could see he made them uncomfortable.

It hurt. All these kids were accumulating community service brownie points to impress the colleges; my child wasn't going to go to college at all. I was jealous. How could I not be? I didn't mean to begrudge other parents their good fortune. It was just that there was so much that I knew Mickey would never be able to do, things which those other families took entirely for granted. He wasn't going to get a license to drive. He probably wasn't going to go to the prom. When Marc and I wanted to go to a movie, we still had to hire a babysitter, even though our "baby" was a teenager.

"We're studying disability for English class," an eighth-grader told me one morning at our sports program. She was big-eyed and bubbly, and had just shown up at the sports league toting a video camera. "I want to show how caring this community is."

"You'll have to get permission from the parents before you tape anyone," I said.

"How did you feel when your child was diagnosed with autism?" she asked me. "Can I interview you? We're learning about tolerance."

The dictionary defines tolerance as "the act of enduring." Could this really be what the teacher had in mind?

I don't want you to tolerate my child, I thought. *I want you to accept him.*

My friend Susan, also a parent of a child with a disability, told me that some boy on her block who had an assignment for his church's confirmation class asked to "borrow" her son Jacob. They played basketball in the driveway for ten minutes, till the boy's mother came running to document the event with her digital camera. Susan showed less forbearance than I might have.

"I'm sorry," she said, stepping firmly between Jacob and the camera. "I feel very uncomfortable with you photographing him. My son isn't a project. He's a person."

One morning a reporter and a cameraman from *The New York Times* showed up at our middle school. Among other things, they wanted to report on a newly launched club that invited mainstream students to share snacks and board games after school with a class of autistic students. It was a front-page story, and it began: "The privileged teenagers at S— Middle School are learning to be nicer this year, whether they like it or not."

Could one really teach empathy? I wasn't sure. What I was sure of was this: I was tired of other parents who expected me to go all soft-eyed and grateful because their kids spent one hour a week on a soccer field kicking a ball around with my son. My child wasn't someone's mascot. He wasn't a charity case. He wasn't a community project. He was a kind-hearted, teenage boy, and he wanted so much to have friends.

Clearly we needed more social opportunities for him.

Perhaps I was naive, but I had always proceeded with the assumption that all parents with special needs children had inherent bonds. Toward that end, I had co-founded our town's special education PTA when Mickey was still in nursery school; co-written a manual for parents new to special education; created a bowling group for children with special needs. I wanted to smooth the way not just for Mickey, but for any child, any family, struggling as we had, because I assumed we were all in this together.

I was wrong.

Betsy was a mother who had a daughter in Mickey's class. We had created programs together and worked on the annual autism walk. We had even vacationed together with our families. Betsy had recently taken a job as a program coordinator at a local community center, and was eager to set up a new social program for teens with developmental challenges.

"I'd love to pick your brain," Betsy said. "Can you come to a meeting?"

I had seen all too well that when kids with special needs reached adolescence, the social skills gap widened significantly between them and their typically developing peers. Mickey would be 15 soon; this new program could be just what he needed.

Excited, I described the program to Shana, Mickey's behavioral therapist who still worked with him after school. One afternoon Betsy dropped off a flyer just as Shana was arriving; I introduced them, and they talked at length. Betsy called me that night. "Shana is terrific!" she said. "Would you recommend her for one of the teaching positions for our new program?"

"Absolutely. She's a gifted therapist. Not to mention kind-hearted and patient. Kids love her."

So Shana did meet with Betsy and the center's director, Cynthia. Betsy told me Shana had offered several suggestions for activities and ways to structure the classroom. Cynthia was so taken with her that she'd offered Shana the job immediately.

"And I'm so excited about being able to work with Mickey in a group setting!" Shana told me. "This will be so good for him."

Betsy called frequently. "She's starting to sound like a chipmunk on speed," Marc whispered, his hand over the phone's mouthpiece, after Betsy's breathless third phone call that night. "Tell her to pace her excitement."

"Ssh!" I hissed, taking the phone from him. "Betsy?"

"Don't forget to get us your paperwork!" she enthused. "And you're going to need to make an appointment to bring Mickey in for an interview."

"An interview? Aren't we already part of the program?" I asked, taken aback.

"Oh, the head teacher just needs to meet all the applicants," Betsy said.

"You're going to have a great time," I told Mickey the day of our interview. "All your friends from school and sports will be there too." He didn't look convinced; I think he recognized my excessive chatter for what it was: nerves. Mickey didn't necessarily handle meeting new people well. Unfamiliar places and experiences could alarm him, bringing out what we euphemistically referred to as his "off behaviors." Sometimes he'd refuse to answer questions, or say things like "Leave me alone!" or "I'm outta here."

"Remember, best behavior!" I reminded him as we walked into the lobby. "Hi, Betsy!" Mickey said happily, waving. Betsy was talking with a woman in a suit who turned out to be Cynthia. The two of them disappeared into their shared office; Mick and I sat at a small round table in the lobby. There was nothing on the table.

No books. No puzzles. No crayons or craft materials. Nothing to engage his attention. He stirred restlessly as we waited 15 minutes, watching other parents come and go with their children.

Finally the head teacher, an enthusiastic young woman who introduced herself as Melanie, sat down with him at the table. She asked some general, get-acquainted questions. "Where do you go to school?"

"Middle school."

"What do you like to do?"

Mickey looked away. Silence.

"What's he doing for the summer?" she asked me.

"He's going to sleep-away camp for three weeks," I said. "But it's his first time and he's kind of apprehensive, so why don't we talk about something else?"

"Mickey, you're going to *love* camp!" she said. "It's so much fun. You'll get to sleep in a bunk with your friends, and go swimming every day, and go on hikes and nature walks, and do arts and crafts, and sing songs around the campfire, and..."

Mickey glared. "Chicken! I'm not talking to you. I'm out of here." He stood.

"Just a little while longer, honey," I said, anxiously, placing my hand on his arm. He shook me off.

"Would you like to visit my classroom?" Melanie offered.

"No, thank you. I'll. Do. It. My. Self." Not a good sign when he starts to clip words and over-enunciate that way. He looked baleful.

"Why don't you take a little walk by yourself and see what's down that hallway?" I said quickly. As soon as he'd gone, I turned to her. "He's very worked up about camp," I explained. "His anxiety is sky high. That's why he doesn't want to talk." Instead, I let loose a barrage of my own words, to make up for his resistance. I described his struggles with language; talked about his seizures; told her how he was initially resistant to anything unfamiliar, but that once he got comfortable she would see his delicious sense of humor. "He's really a funny kid," I said. I wanted them to understand his challenges, but also to recognize his many strengths. I didn't stop jabbering until Mickey returned.

"Come have a seat, honey," I said, patting the chair.

"No. Thank. You." He flung himself to the floor, leaned against the wall, crossed his arms.

"So, Mickey, are you excited about starting a new camp?" Melanie asked all over again.

Was she obtuse?

"I'm. Not. Talking. To. You."

"Excuse me a minute," Melanie said, and disappeared into Betsy and Cynthia's office. She emerged with Cynthia.

"Thank you so much for coming in today," Cynthia said. "We've enjoyed the opportunity to get to know Mickey."

Get to know? They hadn't spent more than five minutes with him.

"As you know we have a lot of applicants for this program," she continued. "The need for a program like this is very great."

"Yes," I said. "I'm thrilled that you're going to focus on social skills. It's a huge concern for our kids."

"I understand," Cynthia said soothingly. "Many of our families tell us that. Unfortunately there just aren't enough programs to fill the need that's out there, and space is limited. I know you've expressed interest in our program, but I don't think that Mickey would be comfortable here."

What? Wasn't this a done deal? Weren't we already in? I'd been invited to planning sessions. They'd hired our therapist.

"I don't understand."

"I don't think we will be able to meet his needs. He seems unhappy to be here, and he's having trouble getting along."

"He goes to school every day and gets along just fine," I retorted.

Wasn't the point of this program to help bolster social skills for kids who needed it?

"I know it's a disappointment," she said consolingly. "But I'm sure you wouldn't want to put him in a place that's not a good fit for him."

They were rejecting him? Angry tears welled up; I choked them back.

"We're hoping to start a class next year for more challenged children that would be a better fit for Mickey," she said. "I'll let you know." *But this program was designed for teens aged 13 to 15; by next year he'd be too old for their program.*

"Thank you so much for coming in today and giving us the opportunity to meet you both." Cynthia stood. We were done.

I drove home in a fury. Angry at Betsy. Enraged at Cynthia. Even mad at Mickey; why couldn't he just *behave*? I knew he knew how. "Am I going to a new school?" he asked. "No, honey," I said tersely. "You aren't. We'll find better things to do."

Had I been used? Asked to contribute ideas and a therapist, then elbowed out? How could a special needs program reject a child with special needs? Wasn't that the whole point of creating this program—to meet those needs? Livid, I called my friend Lauren. "They rejected Jake too," she said, trying to console me. "Once they said they couldn't take him without an interview I knew they didn't want him."

"Do you think it's just about behavior? Or do you think it's the seizures?" I asked Lauren. "Did the epilepsy scare them off?" Once Mickey had started having seizures, Betsy had been too nervous to have him over for play dates at her house unless I agreed to stay too.

"They just want the easy kids," Lauren said, angry but resigned. "Don't you know that yet? That way the program looks good and they get to feel good about themselves for 'addressing special needs.'"

I stewed. I assumed Cynthia would go directly back into their shared office and tell Betsy that she wasn't going to allow Betsy's friend's child into her precious pilot program. But I was sure Betsy would plead my case. She would fix it. She would talk to Cynthia and to Melanie and persuade them that Mickey just had a hard time meeting new people. She'd say she'd known him since he was seven and that he was really a great kid. She'd be able to straighten this out. I waited to hear from her.

And waited.

It was appalling enough to be thrown out of a program; but Betsy was my friend. Why wasn't she calling me?

"Maybe she's embarrassed," Marc suggested.

By the time five days had passed, I was seething. Not about being tossed; about Betsy not caring enough to call. I was hurt. Crushed. I couldn't believe she wasn't going to call.

I don't do confrontation well. Instead, I poured out my outrage into an email. I told her I was shocked that as my friend she had let nearly a week go by without checking to see how I was feeling. "I've learned that the world at large doesn't treat my son well," I wrote. "I just never expected to be excluded by my own special needs community."

She called several hours later. Initially shaky, her voice turned clipped and cool. She claimed Cynthia had not told her anything about our interview. She claimed my email was the first time she was hearing about Cynthia's decision to reject us. I thought— but did not say—that this seemed unlikely; after all, the two women shared an office, and it had been nearly a week. It was inconceivable to me that Cynthia wouldn't have said anything. Or rather, it was inconceivable that my friend wouldn't have asked. She was defensive. "I'm sure Cynthia had her reasons," she said.

"We're still waiting for grant money. We need to do what's best for the program." We. Not once did I hear the words, "I'm sorry."

I told the story to Shana as neutrally as I could. "If this job is important for you career-wise, you should take it anyway. It's fine. You'll still be working with Mickey other nights." I hoped she wouldn't take the job, but I was scrupulous not to say so. Shana said she'd think about it. She called Cynthia, then called me back.

"The very first thing Cynthia said to me was, 'I heard the Carters were very upset,'" Shana told me. Betsy must have showed her my email. Shana also told me that she asked Cynthia to give Mickey another chance. "I could be there this time," she had told her. "I know he'd do great if I was in the room."

Shana told me that Cynthia had said no. That she'd added, "I've already made my decision. But Shana, there's another child who didn't do too well at the intake. She was so shy she wouldn't lift her head off the table. We're screening her again, and you can be present for that interview."

I sighed. "Honey, you do what is best for you. I would never tell you to turn down work. It's okay."

Shana called me back the next morning, outraged.

"So I called Cynthia and told her I wasn't comfortable taking the job because of the way she treated you," Shana blurted out. "And oh my God, she got so angry at me! She said, 'If I'd known you were so close to the Carters I never would have hired you.'"

"What does *that* mean?" I asked.

"I have no idea! Then she accused me of behaving unprofessionally," Shana said.

"You didn't deserve that."

"*Really*," Shana said. "I'm not even working for her yet and this is how she already treats me? I could never work for someone like that."

Months later when we crossed paths, Betsy and I both looked the other way. I was too angry to speak to her. Several parents mentioned Betsy's "exciting new program" to me. Each one added, "And I was so surprised Mickey's not in it." One mother said, "Mickey would be perfect for that class."

"They didn't want us," I said each time, and changed the subject.

I remembered Mickey's therapist Barbara, who'd often told me, "Try not to take it so personally when someone mistreats you. Usually that person isn't singling you out; she treats everyone else that way too."

"I have a theory," my friend Miriam said. "Just because you have a kid with special needs doesn't magically turn you into a different mother. You're still the parent you would have been anyhow. And some parents just aren't team players."

I thought I'd already learned lessons on betrayal, but this one was worse; it walloped my kid too. I'd wanted to believe that we were one big accepting family. I hadn't seen—or perhaps, hadn't wanted to acknowledge—the hard truth.

Which is this: even special needs parents discriminate. Against each other. Parents jockey for position and placements for their children, and sometimes even throw each other under the bus. They curry favors with gifts to special education program directors; they insinuate themselves into the inner workings of programs and bureaucracies, seemingly to help everyone's kids, but in reality helping just one. Their own.

I realize we are all warrior parents, doing what we do to make the best lives possible for the children we love so fiercely. But sometimes some parents also eye each other's children and make judgments. They weigh and categorize and judge and exclude, just like people everywhere.

"My son is higher functioning than yours."

"Your child brings my child down."

"I hope my child doesn't pick up any of your child's poor behaviors."

"I don't know how you do it. Thank God I don't have to deal with what you're dealing with."

"My child is nothing like yours."

"Your child is too special."

And even this: "Your child is more autistic than mine."

Betsy and I still spun in the same special ed orbit, but we had circled away from each other. Two years after this falling out occurred, we found ourselves sitting next to each other at a conference on— ironically—inclusion. We spoke. She said she had had no idea that Cynthia had said or done any of those things to us or to Shana. Revisionist history? Maybe. I let it slide. "You know," she ventured, "There's a second class open now if you'd like to try again." She sounded warm and sincere.

The bad taste was too strong. I wondered only a moment if I was refusing a program that might have something to offer Mickey. Then I looked her straight in the eye.

"Absolutely not," I said.

But for every Betsy, there has been a Lauren. "You two need to know each other," the speech therapist had said when she'd introduced us years earlier. We'd become close friends; our sons were too. It had been a lonely time when Mickey was first diagnosed. I'd felt as if I were stumbling around in an unlit room of my dark imagination. When I'd finally connected with other special needs parents like Lauren, it was like taking a deep breath after holding it too long. We talked with bottled eagerness, like war veterans sharing their foxhole experiences.

"We're trying a new seizure med for Jake," Lauren told me one afternoon. "It's called Keppra."

"We saw bad side effects on that one," I warned.

"I know. The doctor told me Jake might even have hallucinations. So I said, 'Really? How would we be able to tell?'"

We both cracked up. We convulsed with hysterical laughter.

This is what passes for funny with special needs parents. Gallows humor. Our personal shorthand. It's how we cope.

"There are two kinds of days," Lauren often said. "Bad days, and good days that haven't gone bad yet." And exhausting days, when it felt like too much effort to talk to anyone, because I just didn't want to have to explain living with autism.

"Did you read today's book review in *The New York Times?*" I asked. "Listen to this: 'A Gallop Toward Hope: One Family's Adventure in Fighting Autism. Rupert Isaacson took his autistic son, Rowan, on a trip to Mongolia to ride horses and seek the help of shamans two years ago. His new book, *The Horse Boy*, tells the story of their journey.'"

"Gee. If only we'd known."

"Yeah," I said. "Maybe witch doctors are the way to go. Do you think Blue Cross would cover that?"

Like our family, they'd seen shamans too in the beginning, and pursued crazy treatments. We both knew families who'd depleted life savings on expensive and unproven treatments. Woo-woo stuff. Snake oil. We often talked about how there was a whole cottage industry of people who sell hope.

There's a *New Yorker* cartoon I love: two women are sitting in a bar. One says to the other, "Talk to me. You have wounds. I have salt."

Miriam was another fellow traveler. Her son James was friends with Jake and Mickey. The boys liked to eat dinner out on Friday nights. Mickey called it, "The Gentlemen's Club." They sat at one table; Lauren, Miriam and I sat at our own. Riding home in Miriam's van one evening, we listened to James issue driving directions. "You have arrived at your destination," he said.

"You think he can make a career being the voice of GPS?" Miriam asked.

"When am *I* going to drive?" Jake asked Lauren. She didn't miss a beat.

"When you're 50," she said.

Cracking jokes was our version of whistling past the graveyard, but it also felt rich and restorative. A form of hard-earned bravery. Edgy humor kept us afloat.

Lauren told us she'd seen a story on the AP wire. "Is Facebook addictive?" the article asked. "A British scientist says all that time online could be changing how the brain functions—shortening attention span, even contributing to autism."

"Is that so?" I said. "But last week some researchers in Seattle insisted it was all the television kids watch on rainy days."

"It wasn't *television*," Miriam pointed out. "They blamed autism on the constant *rain*."

"Well, they got it wrong. Obviously, it's *umbrellas* that cause autism."

Ba-dump-bump-ching!

"There's a post going around Facebook saying that mothers who breathe while pregnant are more likely to have a child diagnosed with autism," I said.

"Has the Centers for Disease Control weighed in yet?" Miriam asked.

"In related news," Lauren said, "a new study says autism moms have stress levels similar to combat soldiers."

"Someone actually spent money to study that?" I said. "They could've just asked us."

Miriam laughed. "Ladies, we need Brownie uniforms. With merit badges. Then we could say, whoa, learned that one already. See here? I got this one in Guadacanal."

I was lucky to find my posse. My tribe. Together we strip-mined the sometimes lonely landscape of special needs parenting, sifting for gold nuggets of humor. Jokes insulated us against despair, because sometimes there's nothing better than a bracing bite of sarcasm to bolster your spirits.

But my biggest bolster is Marc. He is my buttress and bedrock, my best friend, lover and companion, the guy who in the aftershock of a 5am earthquake that jolted us awake could still turn to me in bed and ask, "So did the earth move for you too?"

"We're going too fast," I said on our second date, pulling out of a long kiss. "I think we should put the brakes on a little."

"We can put on the physical brakes," he said readily. "But please don't put on the emotional ones." That just about did me in. A man who wasn't afraid to feel, to admit he felt, who welcomed emotional intimacy?

The story of how we met played out like a rom-com movie. I first saw him in the airport in New York. He was cute. Twenty-something, with dark hair and beard, intense blue eyes. But what most caught my eye was that he was carrying *Flannery O'Connor: The Complete Stories.*

What kind of guy carried a book like that on a Club Med vacation?

I always peek to see what people are reading. What everyone seemed to be reading that week in June 1980 was *Class Reunion,* a trashy bestseller by Rona Jaffe. Cute Guy's book choice wasn't exactly chick magnet material. But to a book nerd like me, it was catnip.

I was vacationing with my college friend Bari. I didn't see the Cute Guy again till mid-week. He was with a guy named Rich who had spent days pursuing Bari. Rich introduced the Cute Guy as his roommate. I was miffed when Cute Guy didn't even glance at me. I shrugged. *His loss.* But it rankled.

The last day of our trip, Bari invited me to watch Rich play in a tennis tournament. She introduced me—again—to Cute Guy, who, I knew from Bari's description, had spent the last two days busily chasing Bari too. We chatted between sets. We discovered we both majored in English. He mentioned that *Annie Hall* was his favorite movie. "Me too," I said, thinking, *too bad he likes Bari.*

On the plane back to New York the next day, I pulled out my copy of Henry James' *Washington Square* and started reading.

"I live near Washington Square," someone said. I looked across the aisle. *How did he wind up sitting next to me?*

"Me too," I said. "Tenth Street and University Place."

"Ninth Street and Fifth," he said. "We're neighbors."

We talked about our jobs; when I told him I handled publicity for authors at Simon and Schuster, he asked what was the best book I'd worked on lately. I told him it was a biography by Scott Berg called *Max Perkins: Editor of Genius.*

"Oh, sure, he was Ernest Hemingway's editor. Scott Fitzgerald too," he said. *Wow, how many guys would know that?* Then he asked, "Have you read Fitzgerald's short stories?"

Excited, I nodded. "'Bernice Bobs Her Hair' is my favorite."

He opened the Flannery O'Connor paperback. "If you like short stories, you *have* to read this one."

"You want me to read it right *now?*"

"It won't take long."

So I read. I felt his eyes on me. *Why is he watching me read...are my lips moving? It's a test...he expects me to say something all English major-y and brilliant.*

"I like the way she mixes grotesque characters with violence and colloquial humor. It's part of that Southern Gothic tradition..." *Oh, Jeeze, did I sound pretentious or what?* I leaned forward and handed him the book. He touched my hair gently. "You have a silver streak."

"I know, can you believe it? Going gray at 25. I hate it."

"Oh no, it's very attractive." His voice was low. Intimate.

"It's my Susan Sontag impersonation."

"So now you have to tell me the worst book you've worked on," he said. I described a novel based on a true story about a serial killer in Detroit.

"But in a weird way that has something to do with why I came on this trip," I told him. "Even though the book was awful, I got friendly with a reporter in Detroit. I told her I was thinking of cancelling this trip because I had too much work, and she said, 'If you don't go, ten years from now you won't even remember what you were doing that week. But if you go, you'll remember exactly where you were.'"

"And now you will," he said.

"And now I will."

"I almost didn't come on this trip either," he confided. "I was all set to go camping in Newfoundland till my mother said, 'Are you nuts? Do you really want to spend your vacation in a cold damp tent in the fog?'"

"I think I like your mother," I said.

We smiled. Suddenly he reached his hand across the aisle and linked fingers with me. "You are really a good person," he said, squeezing.

My heart raced. *I could marry a guy like this*, I thought wistfully. *Lucky Bari.*

As we were getting off the plane, Bari turned to me and said, 'Do you like him?'"

"I do," I admitted. "But you met him first. I would never do that to you."

"It's fine!" she said cheerfully. "He's not my type."

He insisted on helping me with my luggage. I saw my parents chatting with a woman I didn't recognize. I pointed. "That's my mother, but I don't know the woman she's with."

"I do," he said. "That's *my* mother."

"We just ran into each other," my mother explained. *Our folks already knew each other? I'd travelled a thousand miles to the Bahamas, to meet the boy next door?*

As soon as I got back to my office I mailed him a copy of the Max Perkins book. Two days later he called; I invited him to my office. He was nonchalant as he browsed my book shelves.

"Take anything you want," I told him.

Which he did. Because two weeks later, he asked me to marry him.

And I did.

"*Two weeks?*" my best friend Pat from college worried. "Are you sure?"

I was.

And still am. We share sensibilities. We steer with the same moral compass. Though we could never have anticipated the demands that parenting a child with special needs would bring, our certainty in each other and as a couple hasn't wavered. Our marriage has been a decades' long conversation that nurtures and sustains us both.

STICKING MY NECK OUT

"Turn on *Oprah*," Lauren said on the phone one afternoon. "They're curing autism again."

I groaned.

Oprah's guest was actress/Playboy Playmate of the Year Jenny McCarthy, promoting her latest book. Apparently she had figured out the cure for autism. Or as she called it, "vaccine injury."

She popped up everywhere. She was interviewed on *Good Morning America* and *Larry King*, telling the world that she had loved her child enough to cure him. That she was "recovering" him. That he was "no longer in the world of autism."

Cured? Recovered?

Those words made me cringe.

How do you "cure" someone's neurological wiring? I've seen many kids who have made good progress in a therapeutic setting, my own son included. But these children still are and always will be autistic. The road to "recovery" she was extolling sounded exactly like the one we'd been down, thanks to Dr. Lawless and our own desperation. A road we'd abandoned. She was misleading parents with unproven, even potentially dangerous biomedical interventions. I was livid. I wrote a vehement essay I titled "Cure du Jour" and emailed it to Lisa Belkin at *The New York Times*. Lisa ran it as a guest blog in "Motherlode":

We've watched so-called miracle cures come and go: Secretin, a pancreatic enzyme; intravenous gamma globulin; the "metabolic enhancer" DMG; hyperbaric chamber therapy; mercury chelation; stem cells from China; the Lupron protocol, a form of chemical castration. All junk science. There's nothing wrong with reasonable hope. Parents need to cling to something…[but] it's distressing and hurtful to hear McCarthy say her son is cured because she "was willing to do what it took." McCarthy, who describes herself as one of a tribe of "warrior moms," seems to imply that if our kids are unrecovered, it's because we didn't do the diet right, weren't willing to let doctors inject our children with unproven drugs or somehow just didn't love our children enough. I've heard McCarthy say on national TV, "Evan is my science." I'm sorry, one little boy is not "science." Warm and fuzzy anecdotes don't do it for me. Give me hard science any day, with its double blind studies and rigorous peer review.

My piece posted at lunchtime. By 3pm, I was fielding phone calls from TV producers and journalists. At day's end, there were hundreds of comments posted about my article. I received more than 100 personal emails and two dozen friend requests on Facebook from people I'd never heard of.

It wasn't only what I'd said—it was when I'd said it. Purely by coincidence, earlier that morning, the respected medical journal *The Lancet* had retracted its publication of Andrew Wakefield's 1998 study in which he had linked vaccines to autism and ignited a firestorm around the world.

"Cat's out of the bag now," Marc said. "Brace yourself."

Our friend Alison Singer, president of the Autism Science Foundation, emailed me. "Have you seen the front page of the *Age of Autism*?" she asked. "They took some nasty shots at you."

Indeed they had. I read comments that I was "bitter," "two-faced," "angry," "defeated," "lazy," "lame," "clueless." I was admonished to "Grow up and quit crying." There was much paranoid speculation, including the suggestion that Lisa Belkin and I had orchestrated "a planned hit job."

"Don't read that stuff," Alison advised.

Alison herself is routinely demonized in the blogosphere. She's been called "a pharma-whore" and a "child-killer." A year earlier, after she said publicly that there was no connection between vaccines and autism and that it was time to move on, the *Age of Autism* blog had Photoshopped her face into a picture of people seated around a Thanksgiving table, brandishing knives as they prepared to carve up a dead baby in the center.

"Don't bother trying to defend yourself, it'll only make it worse," Alison said. "People will say anything on the internet because they can hide behind their anonymity. Just remind yourself that those are people who don't know you. Focus on what your friends and colleagues are saying. Easier said than done, of course."

"I'll post something in your defense!" Jonathan loyally offered.

"I appreciate that, but I don't want to see you get attacked too."

"Tell me again why I am sticking my neck out," I asked Marc.

"Because you want to help parents who are struggling the same way we did ten years ago," Marc said. "Alison's right. Ignore it. Focus on the comments in the *Times*. They're almost all supportive." He was right: the positive comments far outnumbered the critical ones. I was gratified to see such remarks as "Amen," "Someone needed to say it," and "Thank you for being the voice of reason and an advocate of science."

"If you're going to put yourself out there this way, you'll need to grow thicker skin," Marc said.

Did I really want to do this? To be so…public?

I received a heartening email from Paul Offit, MD, author of *Autism's False Prophets: Bad Science, Risky Medicine and the Search for a Cure*:

A brave, clear, forthright opinion. For which, no doubt, you will be hammered by those who hold a different opinion and, instead of engaging in honest debate, make things personal and mean. Hang in there… Sometimes doing the right thing isn't the easy thing.

This was a man who knew a thing or two about "personal and mean." After the publication of his book, he had literally received *death threats*.

I was still smarting from the verbal attacks two months later, when I wrote a piece for the *Huffington Post* blog on the eve of World Autism Awareness Day, called "Autism: Time for Civility." I meant it to be a rebuke to all the fighting in the autism community. I was asking if we could all pull together on the issues we *could* agree on. I talked about how I had experienced the rift in our community firsthand after my "Cure du Jour" piece ran. I concluded it with:

> On the eve of World Autism Awareness Day, I'm pleading for more civility in our community. Open debate that is not personal, petty or mean. There's just too much at stake. How can we expect Congress to listen to us, when we are so divided among ourselves? Our children deserve our respect. Our commitment. Our hope. We aren't the enemies. Autism is.

I know. I KNOW.

I was wrong. Horribly wrong.

I drew a hailstorm of outrage down on myself with that last sentence. I deserved it. The comments were fierce. Furious. Insulting. They said I hated my child. Hated people with autism. Was no better than a Nazi advocating eugenics. Those were the *moderated* comments. I could just imagine the ones the *Huffington Post* wasn't letting through. The more civil ones called me "divisive," suggested that I lacked compassion for my child, and told me that autism wasn't a disorder, but a different way of being.

One polite comment summed it up neatly: "You ended very badly. Many people with autism feel that autism is a part of who they are. When you say that autism is the enemy, you are suggesting that an integral, unchangeable part of a person is an enemy. Ending with this sort of attack is hardly conducive to finding common ground."

She was dead right.

I should *never* have said that autism was the enemy. I've done a lot of soul-searching since I wrote that dreadful sentence. What I'd meant to convey was that all of the issues the autism community faces—lifetime struggles to obtain services, accommodations and treatments; comorbid medical problems like epilepsy; lack of medical insurance coverage; the paucity of affordable, safe housing and employment opportunities; the lack of acceptance— are the commonalities that should unite us. Instead, I'd been glib. I had thoughtlessly, stupidly, opted to close the piece with what I'd then thought made for a punchy ending.

Since then, I've read many blog posts by self-advocates, autistic adults who write eloquently and persuasively that autism isn't a disease, but a different way of being. An identity. A disability, yes. But not a disease. I've come to understand why they feel the search for a "cure" for autism is demeaning and futile. They see their autism as an inextricable part of their being. If you want to get rid of the autism, you want to get rid of *them*. And I agree with them. Wholeheartedly. We need to do a far better job of respecting everyone's diversity. There's an internet meme that says, "Autism is not a processing error. It's a different operating system."

But if I am going to be completely truthful, I have to admit that there are times I feel jealous. Jealous of autistic adults who are often able—and yes, I realize, often at enormous personal effort— to live and survive in an inhospitable world, to attend schools of higher learning, to drive a car, to hold jobs and manage their finances and medical needs, to have families of their own. In no way do I mean to minimize their very real struggles.

I am jealous because their autism isn't our autism. Mickey will never be able to do those things.

Our son is cognitively challenged. His anxiety is crippling; his seizure disorder potentially life threatening. Of course I wish we could "cure" him of those debilitating problems. I want better drugs and therapies to ease Mickey's core challenges. But I'm no longer a "curebie." I don't want to change his very way of being. I love who he is. But I ache to remove the barriers that hold him back from living the fullest, most enjoyable and independent life possible.

"Cure" is something you hear mostly from the parents of newly diagnosed children. They are the families who still believe in miracles. Love is like that, but desperation is like that too.

We've met so many families who struggle far more than we ever have. Families without insurance. Families with no access to quality services. Families whose children hurt themselves, or have intractable seizures. We know how fortunate we are. We have financial security. A comfortable home in a safe community.

Even so, there are many nights I wake panicked, gripped by the suffocating sense of my own mortality, and I agonize: *how will Mickey live without us?* Who will take care of him? Jonathan can't be expected to take on that full burden. In those darkest moments in the middle of the night, I resolve to live forever.

I can't ever die.

MOMENTS OF AGITATION

More honesty.

Maybe my fear of loss has run most of my life.

Okay, maybe there's no *maybe* in that sentence.

Everything I've done has been in the service of creating safe spaces. I'm terrified of not being in control—of myself. I hate taking risks. I have unbounded and probably misplaced faith in organization. If I can just find the perfect system—and by that I don't just mean cooking and freezing a week's worth of meals once a week, or figuring out the best way to organize a closet—I can somehow throw a net of protection over everything and everyone I love. I even make sure to stay awake on an airplane flight, because somehow that helps keep that plane aloft. Of course I know it's magical thinking. It's illusory. I know my vigilance and worry doesn't keep us safe. Yet I keep at it. Hope triumphs over reason.

I realized just how hypervigilant I'd grown one day that fall, when Marc's sister Jill called me and announced, "I'm going to Paris!"

My niece was spending a semester in Europe, and Jill intended to visit her daughter. Jill knew that I love all things French. "Why don't you come with me?"

I sighed. "I wish."

The idea gnawed at me. I felt envy, and a *soupçon* of fear. I mentioned it to Marc, trying the idea out on us both. "It's nice of her to ask, but of course I can't."

"Of course you can!" he said. "Don't you think I can hold down the fort for a week?"

A few days later Jill called and asked again.

"Want to come? We could have such fun," she wheedled.

"Yes," I said, surprising us both.

Yes.

I hadn't been to Paris since the summer I was 16. I hadn't even been out of the country since our honeymoon. I had never left my children before. The thought made me nervous and giddy.

Jill speaks no French. She told me she was depending on me. Ever the dutiful student, I borrowed Jonathan's high school French grammar review book, and grappled with conjugations, irregular verbs and the subjunctive. I listened to French radio stations, understanding perhaps every fifteenth word, and those were only the helper words—*avec, avant, après*—nothing substantive. Frustrated, I wanted to beg the radio announcer, *"Plus lentement, s'il vous plait."* Please. Slow. Down. While I struggled to decode one sentence, the radio voice was already two paragraphs ahead. I felt adrift in the sea of language. Reclaiming my high school French was sheer physical exhaustion as I strained to decipher the foreign sounds. I was still floundering with first-year phrases like *La plume de ma tante est sur la table*, while it sounded as if the speakers on the air were parsing Proust.

Laboring to master the rudiments of French all over again, I couldn't help but wonder: is that what it was like for Mickey every day, struggling to make himself understood in English, a language that felt innately foreign to him? The fatigue, the mental strain, the confusion of idioms? I pictured his mind like the old PBX telephone switchboard I manned one summer in college, his brain a bundle of clustered, colored cords, a cerebral scramble as he strained to locate the right plug. "What did you did today?" he often asked me. No wonder he still napped every afternoon. He must be exhausted.

My friend Ellen, a former student at the Sorbonne, tried to help and spoke French to me. When I tried to answer, it felt like striking two keys at once on an old manual typewriter: the keys jammed in mid-air, metal trapped over metal. The words stuck; my throat throttled. I could think only in the present tense.

Marc offered to buy me the Rosetta Stone Language Learning software program, which I refused. Too expensive. But it occurred to me how aptly it was named. After all, I had spent the last 16 years looking for my own personal Rosetta Stone, the key to decoding the mystery of our younger child.

The French grammar book I studied told me the *passé simple* tense is for actions that have been completed; while the *passé composé*, though in the past, is still connected to the present and may even still be happening. That was a tense I knew too well, from my endless replay of Mickey's first few years of life, when it had felt as if Mickey was an ambassador from another world and it was our job to learn each other's language.

The more I studied my French, the more I found myself remembering Mickey's battles with English. I thought about how at the age of three, he had recognized all the letters of the alphabet, known numbers up to ten, and shown a keen interest in reading signs and license plates. How he had loved to stack alphabet blocks into towers, and knock them over. "More go," he'd said again and again. How the speech therapist had wondered aloud if he might have hyperlexia, a precocious ability to read words without understanding them. How she'd asked me when he was four to make a list of his words. It had numbered close to a hundred and consisted mostly of nouns he struggled to combine into three-word sentences: "I go home." "Want more juice." Verb tenses had been difficult, and pronouns, slippery and situational, had often eluded him. I had waited for a breakthrough, when, miraculously, Mickey would suddenly begin speaking in fluid, full sentences. But just as I would never speak French that way, had it been an unfair expectation of him? Even now, he was still sometimes like a foreigner who spoke laboriously and often ungrammatically as he made his way in a foreign city.

The past few years I'd been dreaming repeatedly that Marc and I were finally traveling to Europe. Sometimes it was the hill towns of Umbria, where my college roommate Pat had a home; sometimes the outskirts of London or Rome. But it was always the same dream. I would realize we had been there a week and that it was time to leave but we hadn't seen or done anything I wanted. I would grow frantic in the dream. I'd embark on a frenzy of sightseeing, only to meet frustration. Mickey would refuse to enter a museum. Gag on new foods. Talk too loudly to himself. Jonathan would be embarrassed and blame me. I'd wake up feeling thwarted. It would hit me: Mickey still couldn't cross a street unassisted. Would we ever be able to travel as a family?

I bought my ticket. Jill and I made hotel arrangements. I realized I was living too much in the conditional tense, imagining dire events: what if my plane crashed; the train derailed; a terrorist detonated a bomb in the Metro? I could die. What if Marc had to raise Mickey and Jonathan alone? How could I chance leaving my children without a mother?

I distracted myself with a flurry of housecleaning, file-purging and bill-paying. I unearthed a pile of old love letters I didn't even remember saving from a college boyfriend and extracted a promise from my friend to toss them out if I should not return from my trip. How dare I take a vacation without my husband? He deserved a respite as much as I did. They say travel broadens; was this still true when it terrified?

The imperfect tense—*l'imparfait*—is an ongoing state of being. It is hard to accept life in the imperfect tense. And yet, somehow, we do. We must. The imperfect, the present and the future co-habit within us.

On some days the tenses loom like landmines: the future, and the conditional. But we live, too, in what my French grammar book calls *le subjonctif*, the tense we use to express wishes, emotions and possibility.

Perhaps Mickey would someday read at sixth-grade level. Perhaps he would grow up to have a job that gave him pleasure; friends; a place in a community that welcomed him. Perhaps someday, our family would travel to France, and I would use my grade-school French.

More likely, it would be Quebec: closer to home, but still French.

For now, I realized, I needed to stay firmly rooted in the present, and focus on the regular verbs:

Mickey *is* speaking. He *is* loving. We *have* hope.

Worrying didn't ultimately change anything, I was realizing. It only throttled you. Maybe it was time to think again about sending Mickey away to summer camp. Marc and I had waffled for years about it. Once we'd even gone so far as to put down a deposit on a highly regarded special needs camp in the Adirondacks I'd worked at the summer after I'd graduated college. But it was a seven-week program, and they offered no mini-sessions. It seemed too long. Mickey had never been away from home. I worried too about Mickey's epilepsy. We were still having a hard time stabilizing him. The camp was a five-hour drive away. What if he had a medical emergency?

What clinched it, though, was that when I expressed concern that Mickey still tended to bolt, the director had hesitated. "Those woods around camp are pretty vast," he said.

And suddenly I was picturing search helicopters with spotlights combing the trees for my kid.

thinking about
sending Mickey
to
Summer
camp

The camp director was very gracious when we asked for our deposit back.

Lauren had been sending Jake to Camp Ramapo, 90 minutes north of our town, a summer program for children and teens with special needs, for years. She sang the camp's praises, even appearing in one of their promotional videos. Yet each summer I'd resisted her urging to take a look at the program. The thought filled me with dread. He wasn't ready. Marc and I weren't ready.

"Jake and Mickey are so different," I'd say to Marc. Where Jake was sensory-seeking, Mickey was sensory-avoidant. At Saturday swimming class, Jake would dart deep in the pool; Mickey had to be coaxed in. Jake loved the zip-line and high ropes; Mickey hated heights. Jake rode horses; Mickey had taken one look at a horse riding past him at the Vermont State Fair, wrenched free of my hand and fled. Jake thrived on rugged outdoor activities; Mickey seemed to think nature was something best viewed in a half-hour Eyewitness video tape.

But at 14, Mickey aged out of the local special needs day camp program, so we made an appointment to visit Jake's camp. A counselor named Frankie gave us the tour. Frankie was about the same age as Jonathan; Mickey warmed to him immediately. We toured the waterfront and hiking trails, and visited the Quiet Cabin, which was filled with books, games and puzzles. "It's the chill-out place for kids on sensory overload," Frankie explained.

"I could use a room like that," Marc said.

"Couldn't we all," Frankie agreed. He showed us the open, airy dining hall, the pool, the playing fields, and a corral. Mickey eyed the horse warily. Next he escorted us into an immaculate, pine-paneled camp bunk. "Remember Jonathan's first camp bunk?" Marc said, and we both rolled our eyes in amusement. Jonathan had attended a venerable, beloved camp in the Berkshires. The cabin had been primitive, the cots separated by particle board dividers. There were bats. And the bathroom had been…unspeakable.

It had been years since Mickey wandered, but we were relieved to learn that the ratio of counselors to campers was virtually one to one.

"I'm impressed," Marc announced.

"Me too. I like that it feels just like a typical camp."

At the end of our tour, we returned to the camp director's office. "What's your name?" Mickey asked.

"I'm Mike." They shook hands.

"Hey, that's my name! I'm Michael."

"What activities do you like to do, Mickey?" Mike asked.

"I don't know!" Mickey said.

"Sure you do," I said. "What are some of your favorite things?"

"Computer and Nintendo."

Mike smiled. "Well, we don't have video games here, but I think there are lots of things you'll enjoy. We have soccer, and volleyball, and woodworking, and fishing. We even have high ropes. Do you think you'd like that?"

"Maybe."

"And we have boating. Have you ever gone canoeing?"

"Mom's hat fell in the river!"

"He's talking about the time we went canoeing in Vermont," I explained.

"We have a beautiful waterfront here," Mike told him. "Do you like swimming?"

"Sure!"

"Thanks for coming to see us today, Mickey," Mike said.

"You're welcome!"

Mike shook Mickey's hand again. Then he turned to us. "I think he's going to do very well here."

"I hope so," Marc said. "But I'm still not sure about us."

In the weeks before camp, Mickey wavered between excitement and fear. "Camp is the best," Jonathan told him. "You'll like it a lot."

Mickey glared. "I won't! I'm *not* going!" He ran out of the den. *Slam!*

"He's going to break that door hinge yet," Marc said.

Ten minutes later, Mickey was back. "Can I bring my Eyewitness Flag Book to camp?"

Marc and I wavered too. Did Mickey really understand that he would be sleeping away from home for 19 nights? Would he worry we were leaving him there forever? Again and again we told him, "Jonathan went to camp and had fun with his friends, and then he came home again." Would Mickey be able to make friends? Behave appropriately, without us there to reinforce and remind him? What if they messed up his medications? I imagined Mickey lying awake all night, brooding and miserable and homesick. Could he stick it out? Could we? I'd felt bereft the first time Jonathan had left for camp; completely off kilter. Now I felt rubbed completely raw.

"Having children is like wearing your internal organs out in the open," I told Marc tearfully.

"You're too hard on yourself," he said. "You'll see, camp will be fine. He needs a break from all the sadness over losing his grandpa."

"I hope so."

"I know so."

We needed to defuse our own anxiety as much as we did Mickey's.

The hour and a half ride to Ramapo was difficult. "Turn around, I want to go home," Mickey repeated endlessly. As we pulled onto the dirt road into camp, we heard singing; cheering counselors lined the path. Mickey refused to get out of the car.

Marc looked at me anxiously. "It'll be fine," he told Mickey.

Mickey glowered. "It *won't* be fine."

Eventually we coaxed him out. "Remember the first day Jonathan went to day camp?" I whispered to Marc. Jonathan had been six; Marc and I had had to pry Jonathan's fingers from the doorframe.

"Right. Another fine moment in parenting."

We met Nadav, a young man from Israel who would be the head counselor for Mickey's section. We explained that Mickey had recently lost his grandfather. "My father is a rabbi, I can help him with that," Nadav said reassuringly. "It's better to keep the goodbyes short. We'll get him interested in an activity right away."

"Remember, keep it positive and upbeat," Marc whispered.

I turned to Mickey. "Give me a hug," I said. Mickey looked distracted, but dutifully inclined his head so I could kiss the top. "I love you," I told him. "You're going to have a great time. I put a calendar in your duffel so you can check off each day, and we'll see you again in three weeks."

On the way back to the car we saw Mike. "Well, *that* was a white knuckle experience," I told him.

"Oh, I've seen worse," Mike said cheerfully. "Mickey isn't even a contender for Hardest Car Extraction today." We laughed. "Please don't hesitate to get in touch with us any time. You can call whenever you need to."

We got into our car and each of us sighed deeply. Marc said, "It'll be *fine*."

"It *won't* be fine," I said. We laughed at our own nerves.

"Most kids are scared the first time," Marc said. "Remember Jonathan and Parents Weekend?"

Eight summers earlier we'd gone to visit Jonathan at camp. Initially he'd seemed happy and eager to show us around. Two hours later, he was sobbing. "I hate it here! It's horrible! You don't love me, or you'd take me home." He didn't let up all afternoon. By the time we'd checked into our motel that evening, our stomachs were churning. When we returned Sunday morning, Jonathan greeted us nonchalantly. "It's weird," he said, "But ten minutes after you left last night I felt fine."

∿

I fully expected to get a call from Mickey's camp saying, "It's not working. Come and get him." The call never came. I held out 48 hours before I finally phoned for an update.

"He's adjusting nicely," Mike told me.

"Any difficult behaviors?"

"There have been...a few moments of agitation," Mike conceded, "but overall, he's great. He's doing better than many first-time campers."

"Mike called them 'moments of agitation,'" I reported to Marc.

"I like that phrase," he said. "It's so non-judgmental."

We wrote to Mickey every day. He didn't write back; I hadn't expected him to. Jonathan hadn't either, even though I'd given him a stack of pre-addressed, stamped envelopes. Jonathan's camp had had a policy that you had to hand over a letter to the counselor every couple of days; Jonathan had outsmarted them and simply mailed home the empty envelopes.

On pick-up day three weeks later, Marc, Jonathan and I arrived early, waiting impatiently until they opened the camp gates. Mickey ran to meet us. He was tan; there was stubble on his cheeks.

"Mom, Dad! Jonnie! Come meet my counselors!" He took off down a wooded path strewn with pine needles, greeting everyone he passed by name.

∿

Mickey has gone to Ramapo every summer since. Each time, he returns to us a little more mature. And each summer, he has ventured closer to the horse. His second year, he told us, "I petted the horse." A year later, "I fed the horse an apple."

And then, finally, a call from the camp office: "Do we have your permission for Mickey to go horseback riding?"

Did they ever.

"I have your happy camper standing right here," the counselor said. It was our one allotted phone call with Mickey during his three-week stay; we'd been waiting eagerly all evening to hear his voice.

"Mom! Dad!" he said, vibrating with excitement. "I have a new best friend named Eddie in Tent Two!"

By the time we hung up, my face ached from beaming.

BEHAVIOR IS COMMUNICATION

Every family who has been through the public school's special education system can tell you at least one horror story.

Mickey's ninth-grade year was ours.

Education is the only industry in town in our affluent suburb north of New York City. Our nationally ranked high school is the town's crown jewel. When Marc had been nominated to the school board three years earlier, he learned quickly what he was in for. At a public meeting, the board discussed launching a pilot program to introduce foreign languages in the elementary schools. The district planned to offer it initially only to first-graders, then expand it year by year. An arm in the audience shot up. "What do you mean you won't be offering Spanish to my second-grader?" a woman sputtered. "You have to! Otherwise you are hurting his chances of getting into Harvard."

That is the culture of our town and school system. Middle school at that time was often referred to as the "dark hole" in the school system, its weakest link, yet Mickey had thrived in Dori's self-contained special education class. He had learned to advocate for himself, even in the face of being stalked and bullied by Brandon York. Now, as we prepared him for high school, we worried. Our high school was a college preparatory factory. What were they going to do for students like Mickey and others who were *not* college bound?

Students in special education are evaluated at the end of each school year. Every third year, they undergo a more comprehensive battery of psychological and educational tests known as the Triennial. Triennials are brutal for parents. The reports are filled with test scores, percentiles and a hefty dose of jargon, the *lingua franca* of special education. *Discrepancy formula. Dysfluency. Dysgraphia. Praxis-planning. Regression-recoupment.* They spelled out Mickey's test scores and percentiles, telling us where he "fell" (or was it failed?) in relation to "typical" children.

By the end of eighth grade, Mickey had been through many evaluations. We knew this one would contain nothing new or surprising. Knowing our child's weaknesses was one thing. Hearing the excruciating details was quite another. Annual reviews were gut twisters. They never got easier.

The spring before high school was to start, two members from the high school special education team, Karyn and Marie, joined us for Mickey's Triennial. They would be taking over Mickey's educational program. Dori, his middle school teacher, opened the meeting. "Mickey scores in the average to low average range. He does not do well with too much down time. He needs structure, and help with organizing his work."

Next, specialists in speech, psychology, occupational and physical therapy weighed in. Marc and I winced as we waded through their reports, trying to extract hopeful, meaningful nuggets. Mickey's learning was "greatly enhanced by repetition." He was "able to learn appropriate verbal responses to situations that become somewhat automatic with practice." His "weakness continues to revolve around sustained focus and attention, especially as relates to verbal processing." He was "a concrete learner who has difficulty generalizing and understanding inferences and subtleties in language."

The psychologist noted Mickey's strong rote and working memory skills, but overall, she said, his language skills were "moderately to severely delayed." But, she emphasized, "Mickey is a friendly, responsive and cooperative child whose inappropriate behaviors are self-corrected when brought to his attention."

That was true at home too. "Are you disappointed in me?" he'd often ask. Mickey liked to please people.

Finally, the psychologist said, "When Mickey is alert to the requirements of the tests, he can perform with an increased degree of success. However, as test items become more complex, he resorts to extraneous verbalizations and off-task behaviors, confirming his inability to persist and tendency to become overwhelmed when overly challenged."

Extraneous verbalizations and off-task behaviors, confirming his inability to persist and tendency to become overwhelmed when overly challenged.

Those were the words that would come back to haunt us in the months ahead, when everything fell apart.

"We're going to create a comprehensive program to support students with more complex needs," Marie from the high school assured us. She said they anticipated four to six students in the program who would be grouped in self-contained classes in each academic subject. They would move as a group from class to class throughout the building, spending several periods each week in the Learning Resource Center, where they would be tutored with other learning-disabled students. They would mainstream only for such non-academic classes as art, music and gym. Rather than take the Regents Exams, which were required by New York State in order to graduate with a state diploma, they would take a watered-down version known as the Regents Competency Tests, a safety net offered to special education students.

That might work for some of the students, but Mickey still read at an elementary school level. The RCTs were easier, but they were still rigorous twelfth-grade-level exams in five academic subjects. "Do you really think Mickey can do this?" I asked.

"We'll do our best," Karyn said.

I was glad to know they were committed to educating him in his own district, but I was still worried. The high school had never taught students quite like Mickey, opting until now to send them to programs in other school districts. Would they understand his learning style? Accept his quirks? Mickey was used to staying in one classroom, not changing class each period. Would he adapt to such a large, confusing high school building? We wanted to see him get a real diploma. Was that possible? Everyone seemed so confident. They sounded so upbeat. I tamped down my doubts. I wanted to believe it would all work out. We were about to be my-zulled big time.

Autumn brought new beginnings for both boys: high school for Mickey, college for Jonathan, who would be a freshman at Carleton College in Minnesota, Marc's alma mater. Jonathan had developed a passion for art history during high school. I often thought how delighted my mother would have been not only when the high school literary magazine published some of Jonathan's short stories, but also at the quirky, clever essay he wrote about Edward Hopper's painting "Nighthawks" that got him into college.

I felt torn. Guilty. I wanted to take Jonathan to college, but his orientation was the same week Mickey was starting high school. How did people manage with three children or more? Did they always feel they were short-changing one of them? It was all I could do to meet the needs of two. As we often had to, Marc and I split responsibilities. I would stay home to handle Mickey's transition. Marc would fly to Minnesota with Jonathan, rent a car and see him safely to school.

Sending my first child off to college was more than a bittersweet rite of passage. It felt like a rift in the family fabric. I dreaded it. Jonathan was nervous and excited. I was determined that he not see me cry the morning he left.

It was 4am and still dark when he and Marc left for the airport. I hugged Jonathan goodbye and stroked his hair. "I'm so proud of you, and I love you so much," I told him. "Safe travels, honey. I'll call you tonight." We hugged again.

"Love you too," he said, squeezing me so tightly that I could barely breathe.

Then he was gone.

Mickey was disconsolate. "My brother doesn't live here anymore? We're divorced?"

"Oh no, of course not!" I reassured him. "He'll be back for Thanksgiving."

But November felt a long way off, as the three of us settled into a quieter rhythm at home.

On the first day of high school, Mickey was vibrating with excitement and anxiety. "It'll be fine," I said.

"It won't be fine."

"Everyone feels nervous on the first day of school. I felt that way. Dad felt that way. And Jonnie was nervous about high school too. Everyone feels nervous. You'll be with all your friends from middle school," I reminded him. I handed him the new navy-blue backpack he'd picked out at Eastern Mountain Sports the week before.

"Will my cats miss me?"

"Yes, but they'll be here when you get home."

A short yellow school bus pulled into our driveway. Mickey's face lit up; he recognized the bus driver from middle school. "Hi, Barbara, I missed you!" he said and bounded happily on board.

Karyn called at the end of the day. "A little rocky but we had a good first day," she said.

But as the days wore on, Marc and I began to suspect that the high school staff had never taught a group of students quite like Mickey and his classmates. Mickey was on the tip of the spear, and we knew that many more such students would be coming up behind them in the next four years. All through September, Karyn called daily to catalog Mickey's many socially inappropriate behaviors. Refusing to work. Calling out. Yelling. "He was very uncooperative," she'd say. Or, "He ran out of the building this morning." She began and ended each call with the words, "I'm just reporting," as though she were merely conveying neutral information.

Transitions had always been fraught for Mickey; I assumed we were just having the usual adjustment pains.

"So, Mickey, tell me one thing you did today in high school," I'd say each afternoon.

"No, no, no. No talking."

Mickey had loved being in the middle school chorus, but in high school he lasted one week before the music director tossed him out. I asked Karyn what had happened.

"It's not appropriate for him."

Had he disrupted the class? Sung off key? All she would tell me was that the chorus teacher said he didn't belong because it was "a competitive chorus." What did that mean?

What I did know was that Mickey was anxious whenever I asked about school. "I'm not going!" he'd announce every morning. "I want middle school instead."

Every student at the high school is assigned a dean who, according to the district's website, serves as "an advisor, teacher, listener, and primary support person who works with students and parents, both separately and together, on developmental issues, course planning, college selection, and problem solving. They seek to understand the expectations and concerns parents have and advise accordingly. Counselors and teachers work together closely to make the high school experience a rich and rewarding one for each student."

Mickey was assigned a dean who was a well-respected, seasoned administrator, and also had a granddaughter with autism. I asked for a meeting with her and Karyn.

"If chorus won't work, what about an art class?" I asked them. "He loved art in middle school."

"Our art program is too academic. We don't have anything appropriate for him," the dean said. *How could that be?*

"I'm not asking for an art history class," I said. "But he enjoys painting. Is there a studio art class he could take?"

"Mrs. Carter," she said, "we have exhausted all the non-academic courses that this high school offers."

What? No drawing? No ceramics? No photography? Not even music appreciation? We'd "exhausted" them all?

Should I argue? But the dean didn't know me yet. I didn't want her to see me as yet another demanding parent. Our district was rife with them. I worried she'd suggest sending him out of district, away from his friends. So I held back.

Mickey had been in the high school only four weeks.

Behavior is communication. You hear that often in the autism community. What was Mickey's behavior telling us? I asked Karyn to touch base with Mickey's former teacher, Dori, about how to better manage Mickey's behavior. Yet each time I checked, Karyn told me she had been unable to reach Dori. I arranged to have Shana meet with the high school staff to share some ideas on creating a behavior plan for him. She visited the school and reported back that a mother of one of the students in Mickey's class had complained to Karyn about Mickey's disruptive behavior, saying, "He's interfering with my daughter's education." Another "Betsy." I flushed with anger, thinking of the many times through the years that I'd shown patience and understanding for the difficulties other people's children were having—including that woman's daughter.

By mid-November, I woke each morning with dread, knowing that I was going to struggle to get Mickey onto the school bus. My stomach clenched each time the phone rang. Just seeing the high school's phone number on caller ID made my heart hammer. I'd panic. Had he had a seizure? Gotten into a fight? Tried to run away?

I emailed the teachers daily, concerned that Mickey was struggling with the volume of material they expected him to know. The quizzes were covering more information than he could possibly absorb. Couldn't they test him more frequently, I asked, in smaller chunks? We were all for challenging Mickey, but couldn't they modify the material more appropriately? We wanted him to feel successful. Getting a 52 on the last science quiz did not make him feel good. Or us. It was a short leap from work that challenged him to work that frustrated him. The trick was figuring out how much pushing he could handle. I told the science teacher, "I had a stressed and angry kid on my hands last night. I think we need to dial back a little."

The science teacher was blunt. "The work is too hard for him."

"Could he take a different test than the one you give the other students?" I asked. "What about giving him multiple choice questions, or a word wall?" (A word wall is a list of commonly used words a student might need to answer specific questions.) "If you want him to explain something like the digestion process, for example, why not give him a phrase bank?" (Like a word wall, this is a list of phrases to choose from in order to answer questions.)

"No. Then Mickey would just be guessing."

"But if you give him a word bank with 20 words in it, and there are only ten questions, he still has to pick the correct words. The work bank worked for him in middle school."

I spoke to Karyn about it. She said, "We know how to teach. We deal with autistic students all the time." Had the staff been trained to work with autistic students specifically, I wondered, or did she mean they'd covered autism as part of their training in special education?

I emailed Dori for advice. She wrote back that when she read my email, her heart broke. "I entrusted them with a child I worked very hard with, and they haven't tried everything… He is very capable. He made tremendous growth from sixth to eighth grade. Giving him a word wall and multiple choice the way you're asking for isn't about 'letting him guess.' It's about the fact that he has word retrieval issues, so open-ended, fill-in-the-blank questions are tough for him."

She *got* it. I felt such relief. I typed: "They're telling us that Mickey isn't 'on par' with the other three kids. They say he isn't learning."

"He shouldn't be compared to the other three kids!" Dori wrote back. "He has an IEP-driven education. An *Individualized Education Plan*. Could he have modified grades? Yes, I know, the whole program is modified, but what about differentiating the work for him specifically? You have to teach to the child; the child shouldn't have to adjust to the curriculum."

She'd always been so positive. She understood him, knew his strengths, thought he was smart. She *liked* him. Was it possible that the staff at the high school didn't?

I typed: "They say he doesn't know the difference between a question and a statement."

The phone rang. Dori. "This is way too much to type, let's talk," she said. "Of course he knows the difference between a question and a statement. If you give him a visual to go with it, he knows it. I worked on it with him. So did the speech therapist."

"Has Karyn contacted you about Mickey?"

"Not since last spring."

Really? I could sense there was animosity between the two teachers; I had no idea what it was about. There was probably more to this than I was ever likely to know.

"I've asked for a full team meeting right after the Thanksgiving break," I said.

She offered immediately to come to the meeting on her lunch hour. I accepted gratefully. Shana asked to come too.

~☉

"Skill wise he's strong but he lacks independence," the math teacher said at the December meeting. "He doesn't want to do work on his own. He can't do negative and positive numbers."

"That's too abstract for him," I said.

The science teacher spoke up. "His behavior is pretty good, but he needs constant reinforcement. He did well on the last two quizzes, he got passing grades." I was relieved, until he added, "Mickey seems to be understanding, but then forgets the material by the next day."

Marie, who in addition to running the new Comprehensive Support Program with Karyn was also teaching social studies to Mickey and the other students, said, "His behaviors have gotten better, but he does not do well on tests."

The English teacher agreed. "He didn't do well on my test either. He gets very frustrated. He doesn't seem to know who the characters are in the book we are reading. He writes 'he' for 'she.'"

I saw Dori roll her eyes at Shana. I could practically read the thought bubble above their heads: *Of course he knows who the characters are! It's just pronoun confusion. Don't you know that's common with autism?*

The dean said, "Does he *want* to be here? I'm concerned about his emotional health. He can't sit through a 50-minute period. It's hard to see that degree of frustration."

Were they trying to get rid of him?

He wasn't the only one frustrated. By now I was seething.

Dori spoke up. "In middle school he could sit for 20 minutes and do a work sheet independently. He's a concrete visual thinker. He can't do why/how questions."

Marie said, "Mickey is warm and kind."

Karyn immediately added, "He's very anxious and nervous."

"Where do we ultimately want him to be?" the dean asked. "Maybe he'd be better off learning some vocational skills, like how to fold a pizza box."

I was furious. And terrified. *Was that the best they thought we could hope for?*

Karyn told the dean, "We're looking into other programs."

Was she looking for ways to better teach Mickey? Or for a program she might ship him off to?

The dean said, "Maybe you should consider a private vocational assessment."

Private. Did that mean the school didn't want to be involved? I asked what a vocational assessment was.

"They would try him out at a few different job sites to see what might be a good fit. For example, an office, a movie theater, a video store or a fast food restaurant."

I flinched. He was only 14. He wasn't ready to *work*. There was so much he needed to learn. Why couldn't they make his academics more practical? More in keeping with the ways in which he learned best?

"I understand what you're suggesting, but in the meantime, could we just modify some of his homework assignments?" I asked. I pulled out homework from a week earlier; the assignment had been to write a letter as if you had just visited ancient Sparta.

"Let's leave aside the history part for a moment," I said. "Mickey doesn't know how to write a letter. He hasn't been taught that skill." I'd had to format that homework assignment for him, and had created a list of questions for him to answer. I explained that in the end what he wrote and turned in read like a letter, but only because I'd enabled him to do the assignment. He hadn't learned anything from doing it. I pointed out that if we were expecting him to do homework, it would also be helpful for someone to actually check it and write down the correct answers—which wasn't being done consistently—so that he could use his homework to study for exams.

Marc added, "Also, could we have a copy of test questions, to use as a study guide? Could someone work with him on study skills during his periods in the Learning Resource Center?"

No.

"The Learning Center is 'too distracting' for him."

The LRC was for learning-disabled students. If he couldn't work there, where was he supposed to get the one-to-one instruction he needed?

Marc changed direction. "Mickey has 11 free periods a week. He doesn't do well with unstructured time. His IEP specifically says his down time is supposed to be limited. He has even more free time since he got kicked out of chorus. If Mickey were a math genius and completed calculus BC in eighth grade, would you say he'd exhausted all of the high school's resources and give him nothing for the next four years? Do you mean to tell us that a non-studio art program can't be developed for kids like Mickey and other students who don't plan to be art history majors? Besides, isn't there a state requirement that says he has to have a year of one or the other? Can't we create an art class that's appropriate for Mickey and his classmates?"

No.

I was tired of hearing about all the things the high school didn't have, or couldn't or wouldn't do. Wasn't it their responsibility to fill his day meaningfully?

"What about hiring an extra teacher to work with Mickey and all the other students in the program on pre-vocational skills?" Dori asked. "Could Mickey have access to a laptop? Could Shana come in for an hour a week and work on keyboarding skills with him in the Learning Center?"

No.

Later, Shana told me that at that point in the meeting, she saw Dori slide a note to the math teacher next to her, and was able to read it. It said, "We can make this work. Please don't kick him out."

Kick him out?

I was scared.

I emailed Karyn several days later with pointed questions. Were there any opportunities for social interaction with mainstream students? Would it be possible for the teachers to coordinate their class plans to avoid giving more than one test a day? Had any of the teachers specialized in teaching children on the spectrum?

"Here are answers to your questions," Karyn emailed back. "There are opportunities for social interaction and pragmatics in homeroom, freshman seminar, during lunch and in the Learning Resource Center. We will make every effort to avoid two tests on the same day. We have all taught students with autism and have attended workshops and conferences on pervasive developmental disorders. Have a nice holiday."

I felt angry. A few workshops didn't replace hands-on experience. I knew Karyn was trying. I imagined how frustrating and unpleasant it was to deal with critical, angry parents. But it didn't feel like school administrators were doing nearly enough. I knew we weren't the only special ed parents who'd been complaining about the new Comprehensive Support Program; I'd heard that several of them had already been to Karyn's office to yell at her. That wasn't my style. Even when I was seething, I managed to contain my anger. It was a balancing act: I struggled to control my temper, because I needed these people. I couldn't risk destroying relationships upon which I was so utterly dependent.

That afternoon, Mickey came home with a note from the school psychologist that said: "Dear student: I have been placed in charged [sic] of following up on students who have unexcused absences from classes. Please come and see me at 7:45am or during homeroom on Dec 20 because of the following cuts from classes: Dec 15, two periods. If I don't meet with you by Thursday, your cuts will be handed into the Vice Principal in charge of discipline. Sincerely, Dr. C."

Cutting class? Mickey had an aide assigned to him at all times, for health and safety reasons. She shadowed him everywhere. It was physically impossible for him to cut a class. Maybe this was merely a case of mistaken identity?

But it worried me that the school psychologist had no idea who my son was.

~♀

"I'm staying right here," Mickey said adamantly the first day that school resumed after the holidays. He stood on the front porch, arms crossed and glaring.

The bus driver Barbara crooked her finger at him. "Mickey, I've got something exciting to tell you," she said.

"What is it?"

"You have to get on the bus so I can tell you," she said. He clomped onto the bus and sat. "What is it?"

"I'll tell you once you get your seat belt on." She winked at me. I gave her a thumbs up.

Was this his usual resistance to going back to school after a vacation, or more?

Nothing had changed since December. The teachers continued to focus on academics. I continued to ask for more functional goals. Mickey wasn't the only student who needed to work on life skills. I was sure the other students in his class needed that too. I learned that many years earlier, the high school had dismantled all the vocational programming. They'd done away with Home Ec. Shop. Computer programming. There had even once been a car bay to teach auto mechanics. Couldn't they at least teach cooking? There was a full cafeteria kitchen on site. I suggested it, but I was shot down—something about legal liability and a potential conflict with the union. Other districts provided vocational and life skills training. Why didn't ours? Was it arrogance? Cultural elitism?

Karyn, whose background was in speech and language pathology, ran a communications group. Mickey said it was his favorite class. We were glad he was getting social skills instruction there. But who were Mickey and the students practicing those skills on? Each other? He wasn't interacting much with students in the mainstream.

In late January, several parents—some of us with children in Mickey's program, others with children who would be entering the self-contained class in the next two years—requested a meeting with the director of special education and high school staff to discuss the Comprehensive Support Program. We also invited a "mediator"—that year's chairperson of our special education PTA, a group I had co-founded with my friend Ellen ten years earlier—to mediate between the parents and the school staff. The night before the meeting, I exchanged emails with her. She'd already spoken with Karyn. "Would you consider sending Mickey to a program in a different school district?" she asked. Was she conveying a message that the school hoped we'd send him somewhere else?

"Let me give you some background," I wrote. "They shipped my child out of district for two years when he started elementary school. I don't want to send him away again. He doesn't handle transitions well. If he gets too anxious, he has seizures. There is no reason they can't create the program he needs. I think they don't want to. When your child is shipped out of his home district to another district's program, he's viewed as a visitor, and so are you, because you're not a tax payer in that other district. You have no voice. No leverage. It's not like sending a child to private school, where, because you're paying tuition, the private school staff listens to you. Also, if your child makes any friends in that other class, they don't live nearby so it's very hard to make play dates. It took Mickey years to get comfortable here. I don't think it's fair to ask him or other kids on the autism spectrum who already have significant social issues to start all over somewhere else. In fact, I think it's cruel."

"Got it," she emailed. "What would you like the high school to do?"

"I'd like them to incorporate more functional skills in the curriculum." I pointed out that at the middle school, Dori had arranged for her students to socialize weekly after school with the members of an Autism Awareness Club from the high school. The club was in the high school building; why couldn't the high school also take advantage of this perfect opportunity to work on social skills with Mickey's class?

"And here's another example," I emailed. "Dori's students worked at the school store. It teaches them about being responsible, and it incorporates money and social skills in a natural setting, as opposed to a classroom. I'd love to see something similar in the high school."

She wrote back: "But it sounds as if there are already other school districts running programs just like that. They have children working at the mall, shopping for groceries and cooking their meals, all those life skills you're asking for. It takes so much work to put a program like that in place. Why do it here? Why reinvent the wheel?"

Had Karyn said that to her? Whose side was she on? Was she really hearing what I was saying? Her son wasn't autistic. He had a reading disability. He was clearly college bound. Could she really understand how complicated the issues were for children with complex developmental problems?

"We're all on the same team," I wrote back, hoping it was true. "Everyone wants what's best for the kids. I just wanted to give you a heads up about how deeply frustrated and angry many of the parents are. Speaking just for myself, I feel as if they've already given up on my child and are looking for a way to ship him out and be done with him. We sat through a meeting a few weeks ago where his dean suggested we send Mickey somewhere to learn to fold pizza boxes. How would you feel if that were *your* child?"

She didn't email back. I barreled on. "Last spring at our Triennial they told us they'd be hiring someone to run this program. They haven't. They just shifted a teacher over from one of the elementary schools to teach the math class for Mickey's group. The rest of the time the math teacher works in the Learning Resource Center. She doesn't run the program. Karyn does. Which really isn't fair to anyone, because Karyn already had a full-time job teaching and running the LRC, before the director of special education decided to create this new program."

Finally she emailed back: "I'm sure everyone wants what's best for the children. I think you need to think about compromising."

And I think you need to listen better, I thought.

At our meeting the next morning, Karyn began by describing the newly created Comprehensive Support Program as a "highly modified program that hoped to provide enough supports for the students to pass the standardized statewide examinations in core high school subjects and receive their New York State Regents Diplomas.

"But we suspect that at least three of the five students currently in the program may not be able to pass," she said. I knew Mickey was one of them. She reported that she and Marie had visited two other schools' programs, to see how others "differentiated" their curriculum for students who would not be able to pass the Regents Competency Exams.

"Could we create a class like that here?" I asked.

The dean shook her head. "It takes a critical mass of students to run a program. You need three students just to break even financially."

"We have more than three," I said.

"Yes, but sometimes it's hard to share staff that are in one place. It's easier to share kids across districts, the way BOCES [New York State's Board of Cooperative Educational Services] does," the director of special education pointed out. "Economy of scale. Sometimes it makes more sense to send students out of district."

I knew from Marc's work on the board of education that it cost $45,000 to $50,000 per pupil to send a student out of district. Educating a student in district cost less than half that. Didn't it make fiscal sense to educate our kids in our own district? I must have let my mind wander, because suddenly I heard the director mention Willowbrook as some kind of model.

Willowbrook?

Willowbrook was a notorious state-run institution that had closed years ago.

I had no idea what point he was making; simply the word "Willowbook" was enough to set my brain racing. *Abuse. Neglect. Medical experimentation.* I fought to contain my agitation. Marc reached under the conference table and squeezed my hand.

"Okay, everyone, I'm putting on my board of education hat now," he said. "This district is fortunate enough to have tremendous resources. Even Harvard says we are in the educational vanguard of the country. We've invested so much time and effort and money in our revamped AP program, but we need to do the right thing for *all* our kids. We have to address the needs of everyone, not just the quote unquote 'gifted' students. Here's what it comes down to. You already have a well-established program with the Learning Center and remedial classes. Now you're throwing needier kids into the mix. How far can you stretch the rubber band? To do this class properly it needs its own administrative management. Last night I was at a teacher's union meeting. They talked about helping each kid reach his potential. Doesn't that include *all* the kids, not just the AP and college-bound kids? 'Differentiation' is the major buzzword in this district. So is 'instilling the love of learning.' So what are we doing to instill a love of learning for *our* kids? You haven't even developed an art or music class for them."

I stared at the woman who was supposed to be mediating. She looked away.

We'd resolved nothing. The meeting was adjourned.

Winter wore on. A spot of brightness: Marie gave Mickey a global history quiz that contained a word bank, as I'd suggested. He got an "A." He had answered 23 out of 26 questions correctly. Across the top of his paper, she wrote: "Wonderful!" I was proud of him, and grateful to Marie for modifying the test for him.

Yet over and over we heard from his other teachers, "He's not learning."

How were they measuring that? His language deficits made it hard to assess what he was actually taking in. It was like saying that a student with a physical disability wasn't learning because he couldn't tie his shoelaces—he "knew" how to do it, but his body couldn't execute it because of the nature of his disability. Couldn't you make a similar argument for Mickey? As his tutor Nikki had once said, "His output does not correspond to his input."

"What do you want for Mickey?" the dean kept throwing back at us.

We wanted the same things you want for any child. We wanted him to be happy. Mickey had been successful in elementary school.

He'd thrived in middle school. How could we make high school work for him too?

Shortly after that January meeting, Karyn sent home a questionnaire to everyone in the program, asking us to evaluate Mickey's program.

"Do we let them have it with both barrels?" I said to Marc.

"You know we can't."

He wrote, "We have always approached his situation as a glass half full and not half empty. It is very frustrating to be told by his dean that Mickey should consider a future of folding pizza boxes. We have no illusion about college, but we don't want to put a ceiling on Mickey's potential. He is continually surprising us."

"Oh, c'mon! 'Frustrating?' How about saying, 'infuriating?'"

"Because you catch more flies with honey than vinegar."

Q: Would you like to continue with an emphasis on academic skills or would you prefer that the major focus of the program change to address life skills, e.g. skills needed to enter the workforce after high school, independent living skills, etc.?

"How about writing, 'What use is it to be able to identify the mitochondria in a cell when you can't even address an envelope correctly?'" I said.

"Because it sounds too snarky."

Marc wrote, "While we want to engender a love of learning and provide the means to fulfill that love, in reality it is more important that Mickey learn how to carry on a conversation, work cooperatively, advocate for himself, write and address a letter, send an email, go to the bank and post office, learn to cook, make change in a store, or balance a check book... Recently he has been give the task of sorting the mail in the high school office. We think this is terrific as it teaches him discipline and responsibility for completing a task correctly, and how to interact appropriately with other people. We would like to encourage more activities such as filing books in the library, acting as messenger and so on.

Mickey is computer literate. Is there any way we can capitalize on this ability?"

"We're tiptoeing around the elephant in the room," I said.

"Because we have to."

We both knew we had years ahead of us at the high school; we needed these folks. We couldn't afford to alienate them. I remember we were seething as we filled out that questionnaire. Reading our responses years later, I am struck by how restrained we'd actually been.

Mickey's winter report card was dismal. He was making no progress in reading.

"It shouldn't take the completion of two marking periods to recognize that he isn't making adequate progress in a subject!" I said to Marc. "Did you know that there is a reading specialist from BOCES who works in the high school? I just found out about it from another parent. Once again we're in the miserable position of having to beg for services he should have been getting all along."

We asked Karyn if Mickey could meet with the reading specialist. "The teacher may not have the time. Her schedule is very full and other kids were unable to get services."

Was it really possible that they couldn't find a qualified reading specialist anywhere else in our district to assist kids like Mickey who needed extra help? I knew it wasn't a financial problem. As a board member, Marc knew all the ins and outs of the district's budget. Or as he put it, "knew where the line items were buried." The money for resources was there. Did they just have such diminished expectations for Mickey that they didn't think he was worth the extra effort?

I called Mickey's psychopharmacologist, and described the trouble Mickey was having at school. He suggested we increase Mickey's Concerta to see if that would at least help him to focus better. After two days on the new dose, Karyn called. "It's not helping. He's agitated. We haven't seen him like this before. He's acting as if he has Tourette's." We decreased the medication immediately.

Mickey wasn't talking about his feelings, but his wrath was evident in the stories he wrote when he was alone in his room:

> This is a story about the very angry caterpillar. The caterpillar does not want to be a butterfly. That's why the caterpillar is angry and his face is red. That's why the caterpillar is angry and doesn't want to make a cocoon and turn into a butterfly. The book is called the Very Angry Caterpillar.

Medically, something far worse was happening. His seizures were escalating. In middle school they'd occurred every six to eight weeks. Now they were happening weekly; sometimes he'd even have two in one day. Could that be why he was struggling so much academically? Was epilepsy impairing his ability to focus and retain new material? Or was his cognitive struggle the result of the brain-slowing medications we were forced to ratchet up to treat the seizures?

Each time he'd have a seizure at school, I'd pick him up from the nurse's office. "He looks fine, he doesn't have a temperature," the nurse would say. "But he seems to think he has to go home every time this happens." Was she suggesting that he was using it as an excuse to get out of school? She'd never even seen him in the throes of a seizure. By the time the aide got Mickey to the nurse's office, it was already over. He looked "fine" to her? I was livid.

"One eye is more dilated than the other," I said. "I know you think he's fine, but trust me, as soon as he gets home, he's going to fall into a deep postictal sleep for the next four hours."

I spoke with the neurologist after each episode. "No question, stress can provoke more seizure activity," he said. Slowly but inexorably, we kept having to increase the dosage for Lamictal, Mickey's anti-seizure medication. Eventually we were forced to add a second anti-epileptic drug, Keppra. The doctor warned us that one of the many possible side effects to this drug could be an "increase in agitation." Or, as I'd heard other parents call it, "Keppra rage."

Stress was wreaking havoc on me too. One morning in February I woke with back spasms and muscle tremors. Jolts of electric pain shot down my left leg. I had herniated two disks. The specialist shot me up with cortisone, handed me a fistful of medications and a prescription for physical therapy, and sent me out the door with these words: "You need to cut some stress out of your life."

Which was impossible. All it took was opening Mickey's daily planner to pump my adrenaline. He was still coming home with assignments such as:

SCIENCE: study for test on genetics Lessons 3 and 4 on dominant and recessive traits.

MATH: finish work sheets on improper fractions and mixed numbers.

SOCIAL STUDIES: write six sentences regarding the life of the clergy in medieval Europe, and note sources.

"Are you kidding me?" Marc said. "Does he have any idea what 'clergy' even means?"

Mickey was fearful. Frustrated. Angry. Sad. He'd get off the bus and refuse to talk about school. "What can I have for snack?" he'd ask in response to my questions. We wrestled over math and social studies work sheets.

"It's. Too. Hard."

"Come on, just one more question," I'd coax.

"I'm going back to middle school." He threw himself down on the floor next to our cat. "Tell Dizzy how I'm feeling," he said.

Not for the first time, I asked myself, *Why were we keeping him in a Regents track program?*

But if we didn't continue to ask that they modify the program, we'd be caving in to what we suspected they wanted—withdrawing our son from their Regents track program. Sending him away from their school.

Mickey continued to come home with "failing" grades. He didn't show any of the tests to me; I'd find the papers crumpled up in his backpack. I tried telling myself he hadn't really failed, because a grade of 50 meant he'd also retained half of the material. Which was 50 percent more than he'd known previously. Wasn't that a net gain?

I knew they were still measuring him against the other students, not just against himself and whether or not he was meeting his IEP goals. I rationalized that there was benefit just being in the classroom, because he was learning to work cooperatively in a group. But ultimately, we kept returning to the over-riding question: what was the value of an academic curriculum, when he had much more pressing needs? Mickey still read at a fourth-grade level. His stress level was stratospheric. We emailed the director of special ed about our frustrations.

The second quarter report card says he isn't "progressing satisfactorily." We have repeatedly heard excuses about Mickey "exhausting" all of the high school resources, but when push comes to shove additional resources such as a reading specialist are found. We want you to understand the context of our comments. We are not out to "get" anyone. Our concern is with program management and mindset and how our kids can get the best and most appropriate education possible. The new program's success will be measured by our kids' success. We would appreciate it if you would not share this email. We already have a sensitive situation as evidenced by the anger and defensiveness in our last meeting. Mickey will be in the high school for several more years and we cannot afford to alienate anyone.

On a final note, Karyn mentioned again last week that Mickey is "disruptive" in class. We would like formally to request an independent FBA [functional behavioral assessment] from someone outside the district. As you say, it is always good to get a new pair of eyes and fresh ideas.

Understanding why a child behaves the way he or she does is the most effective way to develop strategies to stop the behavior. An FBA looks beyond the assumption that a child's behavior is simply "bad" and asks, "What function does this behavior serve for the child?" Schools are required by law to use an FBA when dealing with challenging behavior in students with special needs, but frequently parents have to push to have it done, as it is a costly and time-consuming process. An FBA usually involves documenting the antecedent (what comes before the behavior), the behavior itself, and the consequence (what happens after the behavior occurs) over a number of weeks. It also entails interviewing teachers, parents and others who work with the child; evaluating how the child's disability may affect behavior; and manipulating the environment to see if a way can be found to avoid the behavior. An FBA should only be carried out by a behavior specialist.

The director assured us he would not share our email. He wrote:

I understand and respect your observations but do not necessarily agree with all of your conclusions. Sometimes, we can be blind to the obvious and it is only through discussion that possible solutions to problems become seen/recognized. For better or worse, I try to take each child in the program and examine his/her needs independently of the other students... as I think you will agree, there are many different types of resources available in this HS [high school] but most, if not all, are aimed at fostering the child's ability to meet high academic levels of attainment... Additionally, the culture of this HS and district as a whole is to promote high levels of academic achievement...Mickey does present the staff with some challenges that are not being demonstrated by the other kids. In particular he can be very resistant to new demands and looks quickly for a way out. He does not modulate his volume appropriately and will speak out of turn and make statements that have nothing to do with the subject or task at hand. This can happen frequently during a session and can become disruptive.

The questions that come to mind when evaluating his behaviors are interesting. Is he acting in this way because of an "impulse disorder" (not being used in a clinical manner) or does he lack interest in the subject as it is being presented? If the latter is true, how do we restructure the instruction so that it becomes interesting or motivating to Mickey while being presented at a level that is appropriate for the others? If it cannot be done with the current resources, what other resource configuration is doable? The questions go on and on. I can assure you that, despite the frustrations you might have heard from Karyn, no one is giving up or has given up on Mickey. They are looking for better ways to meet his unique levels of functioning and to prepare him for the next steps in his life... I will see if I can get an outside pair of eyes to view Mickey and help us feel and see the obvious. I don't know what the outcome will be but it would be a mistake not to continue the examination.

It was March before they finally found him a slot with the reading specialist. It was only one 45-minute period a week. They had still not brought in a consultant to do an FBA. They told us Mickey was still spending time in the Learning Resource Center. With so much free time, why was he coming home with any homework at all? The materials in his backpack were disorganized. Why couldn't someone work on organizational skills with him?

"What do you do in LRC?" I asked Mickey.

"Work with Elena." His aide. A lovely person, but not a teacher.

"What do you work on?" I expected—hoped—he'd say "homework."

"We play Hangman!" he said gleefully. "I do coloring on the newspaper, and I draw moustaches on the women!"

"What a colossal waste of time!" I raged to Marc. "And we'd better not get another email from the director blaming Mickey. '*Impulse disorder?*' That's just victim-blaming. I'm sick of hearing, 'yeah, but' as an excuse. Are they unable to help him, or just unwilling? Mickey is not presenting 'new challenges,' as he put it. Maybe they're new to people at the high school, but they're the same challenges Mickey's always had."

The math teacher emailed me:

He was difficult today. Tried running outside. He was pretending he was a chicken laying eggs. Then he asked, "Do brown cows make chocolate milk?" He wouldn't do any class work. I asked him to leave the room. He ran out. This was the most difficult day with him ever. He's disconnected. He's not attaining or retaining material. He's plateauing. He's having outbursts in class, so he was asked to leave and stand in the hall.

Wasn't that rewarding his bad behavior? Didn't they think that maybe he was playing class clown to get out of doing work, trying to deflect attention from the fact that the material was just too hard for him?

The notes kept coming. "Mrs. Carter, Mickey refused to do any work in math today. In addition, he was very rude."

Rude? I felt mortified. I confided it to Miriam.

"Since when is rudeness a DSM criterion for autism?" she said. "He's a teenager! Teenagers are rude."

I wrote to the director yet again to see where we stood with getting an FBA. To the math teacher, I wrote, "We are wondering if he is truly mastering one topic before moving to the next. His tutor feels he is still lacking a foundation in fractions, and the class has moved on to square roots and basic graphing. Your thoughts would be appreciated."

On April 1 we received a form letter from the dean. "Dear parent: enclosed is a list of courses your child has requested for next year. In planning this program we have taken into consideration graduation requirements, teachers' recommendations and college admission standards. If I do not hear from you by April 11, I will assume the proposed program meets with your approval."

It was a jab to the heart. Mickey hadn't "requested" any courses. "College admission standards?" It was bad enough seeing notices all year announcing visits to the high school from college reps. Couldn't she have asked her secretary to spare us that form letter?

In the middle of April, a nor'easter dropped nearly nine inches of rain in 24 hours. Our backyard filled like a basin, and water began to seep under the door sills. Early the next morning we opened the door to the basement. The water was three feet deep. It was a surreal sea of floating shoes, stuffed animals and tax statements. Mickey stood on the stairs behind me, staring in dismay. "My toys got flooded!" His entire beloved collection of Thomas the Tank Engine trains was gone. I felt as powerless trying to hold back the flood water as I did trying to advocate for him at school.

A contractor pumped out thousands of gallons of water. Mold bloomed up the walls. We tore out every inch of sheet rock, every scrap of wall-to-wall carpet and padding. We filled two entire dumpsters. While we were still cleaning and salvaging what we could, we got word that they had finally hired a consultant, Dr. Christine O'Rourke, to observe Mickey and perform a functional behavioral assessment.

I emailed Karyn to alert her to the house situation, and that we had just made more anti-seizure med changes. She answered, "I was out at a conference yesterday, however, I heard that M had a difficult day, was calling people names, and refused to do work in class. Fred and Kelley H [vice principals in charge of student behavior] discussed his behavior with him. Today he was impulsive and oppositional and it was very difficult to redirect him. In fact his behavior was identical to the behaviors we saw at the beginning of the year."

"He's distressed about the house flood and having workmen here all the time," I wrote back. "Has Christine O'Rourke been in yet to observe? I think it would be helpful to have her see him at his most difficult."

Dr. O'Rourke observed him at the end of April and into early May. In mid-May, Mickey was hospitalized for a week. I slept in a cot beside his bed. The Keppra had failed to control his escalating seizures; the doctor wanted to wean him off and introduce Topamax, another anti-epileptic drug. Keppra, true to its reputation, had caused a spike in Mickey's agitation; but Topamax scared us too. Parents often nickname it "Dope-a-max" because it can cause memory loss and aphasia. Or, as doctors euphemistically put it, "cognitive slowing." Seizures, as one neurologist once told us, were like getting punched in the brain. We agonized: getting off Keppra and switching to Topamax might lessen his distress, but at what cost?

It was May before we received Dr. O'Rourke's report. The school district scheduled our annual review. They had finished building their case to where we feared they had been heading all along: kicking our son out.

Mickey had lost an entire school year.

It was late May, nearly the end of the school year when Marc and I arrived for Mickey's annual review. "Which one's the power seat?" I whispered.

"Sit with your back to the wall," he whispered back.

As teachers, administrators and therapists handed out copies of their reports, I placed a framed photo of Mickey on the conference table. I wanted to remind everyone that there was a real, breathing boy behind all those test scores.

All their reports stated that Mickey's transition to the high school had been difficult. He was struggling in all academic areas. When he was unable to perform an academic task, he "shut down or used avoidance techniques." He became frustrated. He called out, or challenged people. They also noted that Mickey was "friendly and outgoing with students and faculty. He relates well to adults he knows and is usually polite and cooperative with them." That was the Mickey that Marc and I recognized. Warm. Social.

We turned to Dr. O'Rourke. She shared what she'd observed. Yes, he was acting out. Yes, there were behavioral techniques they could use to address it. However, she said, if they expected to maintain any positive behavior changes, then they needed to match the instruction to his current educational needs and functioning level. "Currently he does not demonstrate the prerequisite skills to access the curriculum presented within his educational program," she said.

I felt vindicated. Yes, her report read like behaviorist jargon, but it confirmed what Shana, Marc and I had been saying for months: the curriculum didn't match Mickey's abilities. The middle school psychologist had predicted a year earlier that if Mickey were frustrated by the material and pace of the demands being put on him, he'd get anxious and act out.

Because behavior is communication.

Dr. O'Rourke offered four pages of suggestions to decrease "undesirable behaviors." She told the staff they needed to implement instruction that would address Mickey's future transition goals *outside* the classroom setting. How had they expected a student reading below a fifth-grade level to comprehend ninth-grade reading materials? He needed more focus on the basics. How to write a sentence. A paragraph. How to use graphic organizers and other tools. She pointed out that even the math was too language based. Mickey didn't understand sectors, pie charts, per capita consumption, BTUs of measurement or take home pay, all of which were examples lifted directly from his homework. Nor were they teaching skills "to mastery"—making sure he'd mastered one step before moving on to the next.

"So how are we going to design a more appropriate curriculum?" Marc asked. It struck me that he sounded like a concerned board member. What a tricky place he occupied, I thought. Needing to balance the responsibilities of impartial board member versus passionate parent.

"We could possibly purchase a modified academic curriculum that's already available," the director of special education said. "What I'm more concerned about, though, is that Mickey would be the only one utilizing the curriculum. I don't think it's in his best interests to be a singleton." I bristled. Maybe it wasn't, but Mickey hadn't been able to learn their way. I thought of Albert Einstein's words: *insanity is doing the same thing over and over again and expecting different results.*

"We also don't have any precedent for this," the director said. "Life skills curriculum isn't academic."

I was exasperated, and I wasn't buying it. Why did we keep banging up against a wall of unwillingness? What difference did it make if they hadn't offered life skills before? Actually, they had— even if it had been at least 20 years ago. They'd deliberately made a choice to eliminate classes in Home Ec, Shop or auto mechanics.

"You teach units on sewing and cooking in middle school. And what about the health class everyone has to take in mainstream tenth grade? Those aren't academic either," I said. "But they're still part of the official curriculum."

The dean cut in. "I'm still concerned this school may not be the right place for Mickey."

Here it was. Out in the open. Was she going to mention folding those damned pizza boxes again?

"Where would you suggest?" Dr. O'Rourke asked.

The dean mentioned two autism-specific schools in the county. Shana shook her head; she'd worked in both places. "Many of the students are non-verbal, they wouldn't be appropriate peer models for Mickey."

Then the dean said, "Mickey has been unteachable here at the high school. I really feel you need to consider a different placement."

Unteachable? I swallowed hard. *Don't cry.*

Was I teary because I was angry at their blaming him? Or at the fear that it might be true?

"Bronxville High School runs one of the best," the director of special education said. "I can send Mickey's packet there. Once they approve him, you can go over to see the program."

I was furious. They *were* pushing Mickey out. Even though they'd promised a year earlier to create a workable program for Mickey. What about all the other kids coming up from the middle school in the next two years—were they going to ship them out too? They were only interested in creating a self-contained program for the most compliant, easy kids. They *could* do it. They just didn't *want* to.

How are we supposed to tell him he has to leave all his friends here? I thought. *He'll be heartbroken.* I didn't know anyone else from our district who went to school in Bronxville. He'd have to ride a school bus all by himself. He was already so anxious. Changing schools would just make it worse.

But what if there really was a better program for Mickey somewhere else? Were we so blinded by our anger that we were refusing even to consider what might actually be a good option?

"We'd be willing to take a look at another program," Marc said. "Let's reconvene this meeting after we've seen it and know what all our options are."

We were silent as we walked to our car. "Are you okay?" Marc asked.

"No, I'm seething. Aren't you?"

"Of course I am! But we have to let the process play out. We need to at least look at other programs before we reject the idea."

"Mr. and Mrs. Carter? Can you wait up a moment?" Dr. O'Rourke was behind us. We turned and shook hands.

"Thank you for your report," Marc said. "We thought your assessment was right on the money."

"I was glad to do it," she said. "I must tell you that when they first called me, they asked me to come observe a 'low-functioning child.' Then I met Mickey. He's verbal. He reads. He's very connected. He is not low functioning."

I didn't think so either.

But that was how they saw him.

For years experts told us that Mickey was "developmentally delayed." I'd heard "delay" as a promise: that with enough therapy he would eventually catch up. Then the seizures and the drugs he took to control them exacted a cognitive toll. In middle school he'd been able to multiply and divide fractions; now in high school he was struggling with basic addition. It was a wrenching choice: should we let go of the Regents Diploma track and choose a life skills-based program that would lead to an IEP diploma? Without that Regents Diploma, he wouldn't even be eligible for a civil service job. The decision we made now would limit his future options. But was that more about *us* than it was about Mickey? What was in Mickey's best interest? What did he need most?

Watching Mickey struggle all year, I'd come to realize— finally to admit—that maybe it wasn't just the town we lived in that was elitist. In our own ways, we too had been guilty of intellectual snobbism. I still remembered with shame the remark I'd made during Mickey's first evaluation at the teaching hospital in Manhattan when he'd been 20 months old. How in the moment before the blade fell and splayed me open, I had tried to diffuse the tension by making that thoughtless, stupid remark: *So long as he isn't going to vocational school.*

In those early, desperate years after the doctor said, "Don't expect higher education for your child," I had nurtured a fantasy of proving her wrong. I'd imagined that someday I'd send her an invitation to Mickey's graduation. From college. Hell, from medical school. Why not fantasize all the way?

In those soul-searching months of Mickey's first year in the high school, we finally had to face the excruciating truth. It was time to let go of our fantasy. It felt, said Marc, like "getting slugged in the face with the cold fish of reality."

Both Marc and I had majored in English literature in college. Marc got the first of his two Master's degrees in Medieval and Renaissance Literature. I had a Master's in journalism. I worked for ten years in book publishing. We were hyperliterary, and I'd assumed our children would be the same. Jonathan's first sentence had been "Read the book," and academics had come easily to him. It was deeply humbling to accept that Mickey had a severe, intractable language disorder. One we couldn't fix.

"You know, Mickey has more empathy than anyone I know," Dori once said. "In middle school, he was the mayor. He knew everyone, and he loved greeting everyone by name." I clung to that now. People delighted in him. He loved to be with people. Sociability was his strength. Not academics. He didn't need algebra or genetics or medieval history. He needed realistic, everyday skills. How to read a train schedule. Follow a recipe. Make change. Our high school wasn't offering that. But it was a long leap from letting go of academic aspirations for Mickey to hearing them say he was "unteachable."

No one is unteachable. Least of all Mickey.

They sent his packet to Bronxville. We heard nothing. Again and again we called the special education office. I was furious. Frantic. Sad. Didn't they feel the urgency for us and for Mickey?

They didn't let us visit the program until literally the last day of school in June. Marc and I arrived just as students and staff were packing up to leave for the summer. We watched as they dismantled bulletin boards, stowed away books and toys, and stripped the room bare in anticipation of moving to a different classroom in the fall. The teacher explained, "This room was temporary. Our regular classroom is in the basement. Or it was, until the April 15 flood."

We cringed with sympathy. It was the same flood that had decimated our own basement. I found myself wondering yet again, why were so many special ed classes housed in basements? Mickey's second-grade special education classroom had been tucked away next to a boiler room. It was emblematic of how many people viewed special education and children who needed it: as something lesser. Something to be hidden away. Out of sight, out of mind.

hiding away the special ed classes

We observed for 15 minutes before the students departed. Were any of them on the spectrum? I couldn't tell. Many of them had Down's syndrome. I tried to imagine Mickey fitting in there. It was impossible to tell. How can you assess any program in 15 minutes? It wasn't the teacher's fault; our school should have sent us to visit the program earlier. Once the room emptied, she sat with us and said, "Please tell me all about your son."

"He's a warm and loving boy with a great sense of humor who wants to fit in and doesn't know how," Marc said, and suddenly his eyes spilled over with tears. I put my arm around him. Usually I was the one who cried.

The teacher was sympathetic and kind. "I started this class myself many years ago," she said. "We've had several students with autism, although none right now. We have an eclectic approach. I'll try anything." Her students ranged in age from 14 to 21. Most, she told us, read below second-grade level. She spent more than an hour answering our questions. We realized that she *was* the program, and that made us nervous. What would happen if she retired? It was obvious that she was dedicated and energetic, clearly a gifted teacher. But there was no curriculum specifically geared to the needs of autistic students. Mickey needed to be in a more structured, one-on-one, behaviorally based program. Much as we liked the teacher, this class didn't feel right for Mickey.

We emailed the director of special education. "We want you to know that we have been sorely disappointed in the high school's failure to take a proactive approach in dealing with Mickey's education needs," we wrote. "We were placed in the awful position of having to evaluate a new placement for our child based on too little information and not enough time."

Mickey would need to stay at the high school. We *had* to make it work. We made a list of our concerns, outlined solutions we wanted to see implemented for the fall, and concluded our email, "We are sorry that it has come down to this but we have been driven to this point by the high school's failure in fact and in attitude. As Mickey's parents, *we will take any and all steps necessary to protect his interests.*"

We were threatening legal action. The director knew it. He replied that he was "dismayed" by our email's "tone and contents."

"Are we really going to sue the district to get them to buy an appropriate curriculum and hire an appropriate teacher?" I asked Marc.

He was grim. "I hope not. Can you imagine how bad that would look? A member of the board of education actually suing the school district? But it's time to hold their feet to the fire."

We were both heartsick. Mickey could never make up the year they had squandered.

~☉)

Marc made an appointment with the school superintendent.

"Are you as nervous as I am?" I asked.

"Yes," he said. "I'm 55 years old but I still feel like a little kid being called to the principal's office."

"I'll come with you."

"No. It isn't necessary. I have a good working relationship with him."

I suspected that was code for "and you'll get too emotional." Which was probably true. I knew the superintendent didn't react well to angry or weepy women.

Marc called me as soon as he left the administration office at the high school.

"I think it went well. I told him I was there as a parent, not a board member. A very angry, informed parent, who knows the inner workings of the district."

"And?"

"I told him how frustrated we are. I said, 'The elementary and middle school both had appropriate programs for my son.

Then we got to high school and it came to a dead stop. Why does the high school march to such a different drummer? They act like an elite prep school. Everyone talks a good game about "differentiating instruction," except when it comes to educating my kid. They've made it clear they'd like to get rid of him.' Then I told him he ought to go talk to parents from other school districts in the county, because he'd be shocked. The word on the street is that this town doesn't care about its special ed kids, only the students who are Ivy League material."

"And?"

"He was surprised. *Really* surprised. His jaw didn't visibly drop, but I could tell he was listening hard. He promised he would look into it immediately."

"Did you bring up legal action?"

"No. I kept it collegial. I'm sure as soon as I left he went to see the director of special education. Who is probably sharing our letter right this moment."

I had a metallic taste in my mouth. I realized I was trembling. Would we need to follow through on our threat?

"So now what?"

"I think we wait."

~◎~

Special education funding legislation is complicated. Many parents believe that federal and state governments provide all the monies; some assume special education is entirely funded by the federal government.

Far from it.

United States federal law IDEA (the Individuals with Disabilities Education Act) mandates states and public agencies to provide early intervention, special education and related services to children with disabilities. Under the IDEA, all children with disabilities are entitled to a Free Appropriate Public Education

(FAPE) in the Least-Restrictive Environment (LRE), and some are entitled to Early Intervention (EI) and Extended School Year (ESY).

IDEA is the most important piece of civil rights legislation for children with disabilities ever passed in this country. But IDEA only requires schools to do what they deem "appropriate." Not "optimal." Not "best." "Appropriate" means "good enough."

Part B of IDEA authorized Congress to contribute up to 40 percent of the cost of special education. In reality, the federal government has never actually paid more than 18.5 percent. On average, most states estimate that special education monies from the federal government make up less than 15 percent, which means that states and local school districts are forced to scramble for the rest.

According to the National Council on Disability, which advises Congress and the President on disability issues, "While public school doors are open to students with every type of disability in the United States, inadequate financial resources make it difficult for dedicated teachers to meet their needs."

To complicate it further, under IDEA the count of children with disabilities cannot exceed 12 percent of the state's total school population.

According to 2006–2008 figures from the Centers for Disease Control and Prevention (CDC), one in six children (approximately 16 percent) in the United States has a developmental disability, ranging from mild disabilities such as speech and language impairments to serious developmental disabilities, such as intellectual disabilities, cerebral palsy and autism. According to their most recent figures in 2014, one in 68 children has been identified with autism spectrum disorder (ASD). ASD is almost five times more common among boys (one in 42) than among girls (one in 189). The Autism Society of America says that in the next decade, we can expect four million people to be diagnosed with autism. No one can say with any certainty whether these autism numbers are based on improved or simply broader diagnostic criteria, more aggressive epidemiological methods, or a genuine increase. What may be called an "epidemic," says Roy Richard Grinker, Professor of Anthropology and Human Sciences at George Washington University, is "really a reflection of a change in the way a culture perceives a condition or disease." What does seem certain, however, is that as the numbers of diagnosed children rise, so will the demand for increasingly scarce resources.

Unfunded mandates create a huge burden on local schools. Given this economic reality, it isn't surprising that there is often friction between parents and school districts. Parents can be unrealistic or unreasonable in their requests; school administrators feel their resources are stretched too thin. They have to focus on the financial bottom line. I get that. It's their job.

But it's also understandable why so many families feel compelled to sue their school districts. It was just never the route I'd imagined we'd need to take.

Marc didn't tell anyone on the board about that conversation with the superintendent. Not then. Not ever. Nor did we tell anyone how close we were to suing, or that we had a special education attorney on retainer, a nationally known, go-to lawyer in the autism community who is respected and feared by school districts.

If this could happen to us, I wondered, in one of the finest school districts in the nation, how did other families who didn't have our knowledge or resources survive? I knew how exceptionally lucky we were to have the means and money to hire a good attorney.

Ultimately, we didn't need his services. A month after Marc met with the superintendent, the district hired a teacher to work one-on-one with Mickey. We shook hands with Alan Cantor for the first time in August, in the special education office. He was young, enthusiastic, and well over six feet. Someone Mickey could literally look up to. Alan had taught special education as well as mainstream. He'd also worked in several group homes for developmentally disabled adults.

"I like his background," I said to Marc.

"I like him too. I think Mickey may do better with a male teacher than a female."

We were relieved. Hopeful. Mickey would be in a class of one. A singleton, the special ed director had called him. A word I didn't like. I knew it was descriptive, but it sounded uncomfortably like "simpleton," which is how I imagined high school staff secretly saw my son. Alan would report to, and work with, Karyn and the other teachers in the Comprehensive Support Program. The high school assigned Alan a small windowless classroom the size of a walk-in closet.

We took Mickey to meet Alan just before school began. Mickey was apprehensive. "No Mr. Cantor," he kept saying all the way to the classroom. He hid outside the room, and I felt that familiar knot of tension in my gut. Alan came to the door and held out his hand. Mickey shook it, but looked away.

"Hey, buddy," Alan said. "Great to meet you. Do you like video games?"

"Yeah."

"We've got a PlayStation set up. Want to give it a try?" Then, as an aside to us: "Don't worry, we won't be using it much. It's just a positive reinforcer."

Oh good, he speaks ABA, I thought.

"We have a terrific behavioral therapist named Shana who works with him at home," I said. "I'd love it if you could meet with her to share ideas."

While Mickey played an NHL hockey game, Alan showed us lists of books and multi-sensory curricula he planned to use. He asked what we wanted him to work on. We talked a long time. He suggested we get Mickey a special programmable watch to help him structure his time. The watch would give him reminders: Time to pay attention. Time to take a break. "I'm going to encourage him to work in ten-minute intervals in the beginning. Eventually we'll stretch those out longer."

The first day of school, Mickey got on the bus without balking. That afternoon we got an email from Alan, telling us the high school had finally "found" an art class suitable for Mickey. Alan also reported that Mickey would continue to attend Karyn's communication skills class twice a week. I was glad: it was the one class Mickey had said he liked in ninth grade. Alan told us that he had scheduled Mickey for twice-weekly reading support from a specialist, and that Dr. O'Rourke would consult monthly with him on implementing the behavior plan she'd suggested at our meeting the past May.

We were elated. We'd gotten everything we had asked for.

When the weather was good that fall, Mickey and Alan took nature walks, discussing the fauna and flora by the stream behind the school. "I want him to be more curious about the world around him," Alan said. He encouraged Mickey to write his observations in a journal. Each afternoon, Alan emailed us with an update on what they'd done that day.

From Mickey's journal:

September 18: Today we relaxed at the pond. We didn't hear the fire alarm. Mr. Cantor took a picture of me.

September 27: Last night I played video games. I played Golden Eye. I killed people in Golden Eye. The people went to heaven. I had a good time. My best friend is Mr. Cantor. Me and my best friend work and play. We talk about making change. If my friend has a problem I'll make a phone call. I'll talk with my friend.

One day after school Alan came to our home. I put out a plate of cookies. "Coffee?" I asked.

"Any chance you have green tea? I'm trying to be more health conscious."

I sighed. "I wish that would rub off on Mickey."

"Yeah, I've noticed how much Mickey hates vegetables. You should try making him vegetable smoothies. Put kale in the blender, it's really delicious."

"And how do you intend to get him to drink that?" I asked, laughing, but thinking, *obviously you don't have children yet.* "Seriously, Shana spent a whole month once trying to get him to eat carrots. They made him gag. I'm glad you'll be meeting her soon, maybe we can all tackle the vegetables together." Shana had been the linchpin of our home program ever since the end of fifth grade, after the Joyce Wilkes debacle. Now with Alan on our side, I felt as if finally, everyone was on the same team: Team Mickey.

I asked Shana to call Alan. They met one afternoon after school. She shared Mickey's binder, which was filled with five years' worth of goals and data she'd been keeping on his progress. She'd charted every self-care goal they'd tackled. Swallowing pills. Tying shoes. Buttoning a shirt. Zipping a zipper. Toileting appropriately. Showering (having first to desensitize him because the sound of rushing water initially terrified him). Shaving with an electric razor.

After their meeting, she stopped by our house. "Alan is great!" she said. "He really wants to do what's best for Mickey. I think we'll work well together. He said something I probably shouldn't repeat, but of course I have to tell you because I tell you everything."

We laughed. Our friendship had gone beyond that of therapist and parent. We'd become close friends. She was only eight years older than Jonathan; we often joked that she could have been my daughter.

"So what aren't you supposed to tell me?"

"Alan said that when they first hired him, they warned him, 'The Carters are difficult and demanding.' But then he started working with you, and he didn't know what they were talking about because you're so lovely and easy to work with."

Difficult? Us? I was the mom who always baked brownies to bring to meetings. Even though I'd been seething by the end of ninth grade, I'd still given each teacher and administrator a token, end-of-year gift. Not because I'd felt generous; I hadn't wanted them to take out their anger on our child. Difficult? We'd never brought a lawyer to a meeting, as many parents did. I knew that scenario firsthand: as a district-appointed parent member trained to assist other parents, I'd sat in on scores of IEP meetings for other families. Marc and I hadn't sued. In fact, we'd never even raised our voices.

Demanding? Well, yes. If it's demanding to insist they teach our son appropriately.

"I love Mickey's quirky sense of humor," Alan said. "The way he loves Marx Brothers movies. He likes anything zany and subversive. And I like how social he is too. Very outgoing."

"Last year they told us he was the mayor of the cafeteria."

Alan stopped smiling. "That isn't true. He's not. They told me the same thing, but I've observed him. Maybe it looks that way on the surface, because he knows the names of every student who walks by, and he greets everyone by name, but he isn't having conversations with anyone. None of the mainstream students even sits with him. Mickey eats by himself. It's loud and crowded and overwhelming in there. He bolts his food and gets out as fast as he can."

I was startled. Sad. I'd wanted so badly to believe that Mickey was holding his own in the chaos of the cafeteria.

"I'm going to see if we can set up a lunch bunch. Mickey can purchase his food and bring it back to the conference room and eat with some of the students from the comprehensive support class," Alan said. "We can work on everyone's conversation skills."

Which meant he'd have even less time in the mainstream. Not what I'd hoped for. But I trusted Alan to do what was best.

"Let's also work on getting him out of sweat pants," he said. "The other students wear jeans. We want him to look like he fits in." A good point, but a challenge. Whenever we asked why he didn't want to wear jeans, Mickey said, "I don't like to." He couldn't articulate what it was he didn't like. We assumed it was sensory. Was the feel of denim on his skin too irritating? He hated heavy clothing. He would walk outside in January wearing sandals and shorts if we didn't stop him. Shana began to systematically desensitize Mickey to wearing jeans. During their work sessions, she'd have him put on jeans for two minutes. Five minutes. Fifteen. A half hour. They built up to wearing jeans for two hours.

In November, Marc and I planned a trip to DC with Mickey over the long Veteran's Day weekend. We hadn't travelled with Mickey in several years, and were ready to try again. Alan did a study project with Mickey to familiarize him with Washington landmarks. They looked at pictures of the White House. The Capitol. The Smithsonian. The Washington Monument. The Mint. Marc and I prepped him too.

We left after school on Friday, got stuck in Beltway traffic, and didn't arrive at our hotel till 9pm, too tired to look for a restaurant. Mickey was exuberant as he bounded out of the car. "Can we eat room service food? Can I push the elevator button?"

I suddenly remembered when Mickey had been two and we'd stayed in an Embassy Suites hotel. We couldn't coax Mickey to eat the breakfast they served in the lobby. All he'd wanted to do was ride the glass elevator. Again and again he pressed buttons, clasped his hands and chortled with glee as we rode up and down and up and down. A man who must have been watching us a while stepped into the elevator with us, pushed the lobby button, and said, "It doesn't get better than this, Mickey."

Mickey flipped TV channels while we waited for our food. "Good news! They have movies!" He chose a burger and "freedom fries" from the menu, then settled down happily to watch Pixar's computer-animated comedy *Ratatouille*, a story about an anthropomorphic rat who dreams of becoming a Parisian chef.

Unfortunately, that was all he wanted to do the rest of the weekend. Watch *Ratatouille* over and over, memorizing the dialogue. Push buttons in the elevator. Buy stick flags and stuffed animals in the gift shop. He balked at leaving the hotel. Once on the street, we couldn't coax him to set foot in even one museum or monument. He insisted on hamburgers at every meal. We were frustrated.

"I guess we're not taking that family trip to London anytime soon," Marc said.

"We can salvage this," I said. I handed Mickey a digital camera. "Mr. Cantor wants you to take pictures of all the interesting things you're seeing." I urged him to photograph famous landmarks, or the marching bands and veterans parading on Constitution Avenue. Instead, Mickey snapped pictures of flags. Squirrels. Street signs. Corners of buildings. Everything except monuments, or what most tourists photograph. Why those images? What was catching his imagination? What did these images that seemed so mysterious to me mean to him? He didn't have the words to explain. I was relieved to have found something he wanted to do, and grateful to Alan for suggesting it.

Back at school, Alan encouraged Mickey to write longer sentences and paragraphs in his journal, and to pay attention to grammar and logic. Frequently he'd give Mickey a photo and ask him to make up a story.

December 6: This is a story about a man and a lady. The lady is beautiful and she is wearing nice clothes. She is about to dance to the ball. The lady is wearing the jewels. The man is looking at her to see if she is nice or not. The lady and the man are about to dance.

In the week following our visit to Washington, Mickey had a seizure. Disoriented, he stumbled in the den, tangling in the curtains as he fell. *Why now?* I thought, stricken. I realized I had been holding my breath for months. Waiting. How long had it actually been?

I looked through my notes. The last seizure was in June. Seven months ago. I studied the record. Counted.

Twenty.

He'd had 20 seizures in ninth grade. In case I'd had any doubt. Needed any proof that stress had been the catalyst.

Now he'd gone months without a seizure, and it would be another nine months before we saw another.

Jonathan came home from college with a respiratory virus and an oversized duffel crammed with dirty laundry.

"Hey, Ma!" He lifted me off the floor.

"What, you ran out of quarters for the washing machine?" I asked. I wasn't really annoyed. I was thrilled to have him home for the next six weeks. I hugged him tight again.

My mother-in-law Beverly flew in to visit. The five of us traipsed down to the Metropolitan Museum. Mickey's knowledge of the museum was based on his beloved Sesame Street video

"Please Don't Eat the Pictures," when Big Bird, Cookie Monster and company are accidentally locked in overnight at the Metropolitan. "Let's see the broken statues!" he said, tugging on Marc to visit marble Aphrodite with a smashed-off nose and multi-armed Shiva in the South Asian gallery. While Marc chased after Mickey, Jonathan escorted his grandmother and me on his tour of his favorite paintings, talking to us about such techniques as focal points and foreshortening; impasto and glazing; chiaroscuro and sfumato. We all met up again in the Greek and Roman galleries, where Jonathan explained the symbology on a Minoan krater vase. Beverly was wowed. "He's better than a docent!" she said.

After the Christmas break, Jonathan returned to Minnesota for the rest of his sophomore year. Mickey resumed working with Alan.

January 9: My brother is at college. My brother loves me. I play Golden Eye with my brother and my dad. My brother sleeps in his room. My brother drives a car.

The other students in Comprehensive Support continued prepping for the Regents Competency Tests. At the end of January they took the Regents in Math. Just as Karyn had intimated the year before, several students did not pass. Mickey's close friend, Caitlin, simply shut down. Unlike Mickey, she didn't act out. She just put her head down on the desk and refused to speak. Alan was asked to come co-teach math and social studies, and to bring Mickey with him. I bristled. What about what *my* child needed? Alan was hired to be Mickey's teacher.

"This will be good for Mickey," Alan reassured me. "He needs to learn how to learn in a room with other students."

Mickey was happy and thriving, but over the next two months the rest of the class imploded. By April it was clear that the academic, Regents-driven curriculum wasn't working for any of the students in the Comprehensive Support Program. Mickey had been the canary in the coal mine, an early warning signaling trouble for everyone else. Administration decided that in the fall, Alan would teach the entire class of students from Comprehensive Support.

In May Dr. O'Rourke sent us her assessment of Mickey's tenth-grade year: "Overall marked progress has been observed across all domains including academic and social skills, as well as behavior management. Mickey has demonstrated substantial gains during the course of the school year."

Alan's written report echoed hers. "Mickey is better able to express himself and manage his emotions."

Karyn's report: "Mickey is focused and usually on task within the group setting. He expresses a desire to follow the norms of his fellow students. He has developed an awareness of the other students and is a valuable member of the group."

Vindication. Marc and I virtually hummed with relief.

The "unteachable" boy was eminently teachable.

Jonathan, who was majoring in economics in college, was still pursuing his passion for art history. "I'd love to run an art gallery someday," he said. That summer he secured an internship at Christie's Auction House in Manhattan. They assigned him to their contemporary art gallery with the unlikely name Haunch of Venison in Rockefeller Center, and we stopped in late one afternoon to visit. It was filled with multi-million-dollar art installations and a bevy of "gallerinas," beautiful, black-clad, impossibly chic young women. We studied a huge glass and stainless steel shallow cabinet whose shelves were lined with hundreds of colorful pills and capsules. "It's by Damien Hirst," Jonathan said.

"No kidding?" I said. "Well at least it's not one of his usual rotting animal displays. How much are they asking for this?"

Jonathan said, "Thirteen million."

"I think the emperor has no clothes," Marc said.

At the end of the summer, Jonathan told us, "Well, I got that out of my system. I realized that I don't want to sell art. I want to own art."

"Now we know what to get you for a graduation gift," Marc said.

From the local newspaper that autumn:

> Alan Cantor, a special education teacher, and his contained classroom were introduced as a pilot program in the district last fall. This school year, Cantor's classroom has grown into a fully established, in-district, community-integrated program for special needs students. Cantor's classroom replaces  the need to educate high functioning autistic high school students through out-of-district programs. Such outsourcing, Cantor explained, "was not only costly, but also a disservice to the students because it removed them from their immediate community." This year, Cantor's classroom consists of eight ninth-, tenth- and eleventh-graders, most of whom have high functioning autism or other developmental disabilities.
>
> "I think of it as a civil rights issue," Cantor said. The problem with someone who does not walk is not that he cannot walk. The real problem is that there is not a cut-out in the curbing to allow for his wheel chair."

The article featured a photo of Mickey with the caption: "A student in Alan Cantor's class learns kitchen skills at McMenamin's Grill."

Every Thursday afternoon, Mickey and the other students attended cooking class. Each had his own cutting board, apron and hand towel. They prepped food, set the table and sat down to eat what they'd cooked. At the end of the meal, they wiped down their areas, cleaned their cutting boards, placed dirty dishes on the cart, and swept the floor. Many of the meals they prepared were too sophisticated for Mickey. I doubted he'd eat *steak au poivre*. Peppercorns? Shallots? Dijon mustard? "Ketchup is my favorite vegetable," Mickey said. I hoped it really *was* a vegetable. It was the only one he'd eat.

Alan supplemented the cooking lessons with discussions about planning meals, making shopping lists and buying groceries. Mickey wrote in his journal:

> Today in cooking we went to the computer lab to research recipes for chicken cutlets.

Alan also took the class on field trips to local businesses to learn about different community jobs and services. They visited the supermarket, compared prices and learned how to check out and pay. They visited the bank and learned how to make deposits and withdrawals. These trips often ended with lunch in a restaurant, where the students practiced ordering independently from a menu, asking the waiter questions and calculating tips. As Alan told the newspaper reporter:

> I see life skills as the most important part of the curriculum because they maximize students' potential to live independent lives as fully functional social adults. Some of the life skills I teach—figuring out a bus schedule, doing the laundry, counting change so as not to get taken advantage of, and budgeting for expenses—are things we take for granted as normal parts of everyday life, but they might have to be explicitly taught and

reiterated for students with autism or other developmental disabilities. However, if they are taught and practiced, students are fully capable of managing these skills.

Mickey was thriving. Karyn arranged for him to work an hour a week at the town library, a venue they chose because Mickey was still easily overwhelmed by crowds and noise. He liked order. Predictability. The librarian put him to work alphabetizing and shelving DVDs. Once a week he interned at the local Red Cross office, collating information packets and stuffing envelopes. He also delivered mail and newspapers in the school building. "He loves it," Karyn told me. "He's very cute. Every time he drops off my mail he sings out, 'Speedy delivery.'"

Alan started a club called Spectrum of Friends. Every Friday afternoon for an hour after school, 15 students from the mainstream met with Mickey's class to socialize, play board games, do puzzles and talk. "I am the luckiest teacher in the world to be able to hang out with these kids every day," Alan told me. Mickey greeted me excitedly when I arrived to pick him up.

"These are my new friends! Hey kids, this is my mom." Slinging his backpack over a shoulder, he turned back and waved. "Goodbye you all, have a great weekend!"

Mickey still told us little about his days, but we were able to glean information from the journal entries that Alan helped him write.

During speech and language we made eye contact, did listening skills, and homonyms and solving problems.

Today in Living in the Community we learned how important it is to look clean and look good, taking care of ourselves makes us happier and healthier.

In health today we learned all about the digestive system. We also reviewed how to make healthy choices. We can never do that too much.

That December, the *Huffington Post* published one of my essays. I'd written about how I felt when people used Mickey for their community service projects. I sent a copy of it to Karyn, who wrote back, "Thanks for sharing this article. I continue to learn and understand through your guidance." Our cold relationship was starting to thaw.

That winter we attended a conference at the Arc of Westchester on helping young adult children transition from high school to adult disability services. "You need to take your son to the Department of Motor Vehicles," our workshop leader Ralph said. I was puzzled.

"But he's not going to drive. He has epilepsy."

"He still needs a non-driver photo ID. Otherwise he won't be able to get on a plane. You should also apply to Social Security for SSI—Supplemental Security Income—and Medicaid."

"But I thought those were poverty programs," I said. "We can pay for him."

"It doesn't matter how much money you have," Ralph said. "Even if you had one hundred million dollars, you'd still need to do this. He needs to qualify for those services or you won't be able to access government-funded programs."

And it wasn't enough to apply. We would have to make sure that Mickey didn't have more than $2000 in the bank. Ever. I was aghast.

"You mean we have to pauperize him?"

"Yes. Otherwise he'll be disqualified," Ralph said. "You need to go into deficiency mode. When you fill out those forms, describe your son on his worst day. That's how you ensure he'll get all the supports he will need."

I was appalled. "Everything we've done till now is to make him as independent as can be, and now we're supposed to focus on how disabled he is?"

"I know how you feel," he said. "But yes. You need to put on the Disability Cloak."

We hadn't even known how much we didn't know. No one at the high school had told us this information; I doubted they knew either. Clearly we all had a lot to learn, and quickly. I dropped off a package of conference materials for Karyn.

In February I sent her another piece I'd written. She emailed, "Thanks for sharing this. You are a very powerful and thought provoking writer."

I was surprised. Touched. Gratified that she no longer saw me as "difficult" and "demanding."

That spring Alan taught a unit on New York City. The students bought tickets and took the local commuter train into Grand Central Station.

We learned about Columbus Circle in Central Park. There's a statue of Columbus. We also learned about different animals in the zoo. My favorite animal at the zoo is the polar bear. When I was in Grand Central I saw the clock. I rode on the train. I went to the whispering gallery. I went up the elevator. I don't like when it's crowded. There was a couple of snowflakes on me. And I like seeing the clock.

Surprisingly, Alan was getting pushback on the curriculum from some parents who still held out hope their children could pass the Regents exams.

"I know there have been some questions for next year," he wrote in a group email. "What we decided to do in light of the addition of the health class and the continuation of the cooking class, as well as keeping all the other major features of the program intact, including band, chorus, art, gym, English, math, the internships and job activities was to create a class called life skills and fold the science and social studies into that class."

He outlined trips for the following year: the Bronx Botanical Garden, the New York Hall of Science. He described how he would prep the students, integrating history, culture and science. "I tried teaching US history this year and the students had a difficult time putting the material into any meaningful context," he said. "They remembered disconnected facts about the Civil War or the branches of government but it wasn't advancing any of the key skills that the program targets like language, communication, and problem solving. Remember, we have no curriculum that we are bound to follow... I am much more concerned about advancing students' language and problem solving skills than having them study WWII or the Lincoln–Douglas debates... It's not that we are not doing social studies and science next year, rather we are doing them in a way that we found to be far more meaningful and successful this year. I hope this clears up any questions."

"No questions here," I replied to Alan. "We're happy."

We wrote a letter of recommendation for Alan to the superintendent, urging that he receive tenure, and cc'ed Karyn, who was pleased. She emailed, "Marie went to the library with Mickey last week and she was impressed with his focus and work ethic."

Thanks to Alan, I thought. How grateful we were to him.

I wrote back to Karyn, "That really made my day! Any chance we could increase his time at the library next term?"

All year parents in our class had been expressing concern about the lack of transition planning at the high school. I'd visited other high schools in neighboring districts who employed transition coordinators, interviewing staff and taking notes. Then I'd helped put together a task force. Our meetings bore fruit: the district was hiring a part-time coordinator for the following school year.

"Our new job developer will meet with you, Mickey and me to come up with plans for next year," Karyn said. "I'm thinking maybe a different location for a little bit longer time."

At the end of eleventh grade Mickey wrote in his journal, "I love my classmates and the greatest teacher in the world—Mr. Cantor—who didn't make me write that. I'm looking forward to next year."

CONSUMED

I'd known twelfth grade would be a challenging, emotional year for Marc and for me. I don't think we anticipated just how painful it would be. While parents of typical eleventh-graders had been shepherding their children through SATs and college essays, our year had been filled with lawyers and estate planners, as we struggled to set up several supplemental special needs trusts.

A special needs trust (SNT), also referred to as a supplemental needs trust, is a legal vehicle enabling assets to be held on behalf of someone with disabilities without affecting his or her eligibility for means-tested public benefits such as Medicaid or Supplemental Security Income. Assets held by the trust are not "countable" for the purpose of qualifying for such programs, but there are strict regulations regarding disbursements of those assets. SNTs are meant to supplement the funds and services available through government programs.

Special needs attorneys specialize in handling these issues, which are largely unfamiliar to general lawyers. A special needs attorney can guide you through the intricacies of guardianship and trusts as well as such government programs as SSI, Medicaid and food stamps. We already had a personal attorney handling our wills. It was imperative we have him work closely with our special needs attorney, making sure everything meshed, in order not to jeopardize Mickey's eligibility for government programs.

Just as we had once learned the *lingua franca* of special education, we now became fluent in the language of eldercare and special needs law. Tax IDs. Government clawback. First party versus third party trust. Revocable versus irrevocable trust. Trust and estate distributions. Fiduciary accounting to the court. When our boys were born, we'd put money for each of their college educations into custodial accounts under the Uniform Gifts to Minor Act (UGMA). But Mickey wasn't college bound. We rolled his UGMA account into a first party trust.

We learned that every word in the trust is important. A judge couldn't read our minds to know our intent. We needed to spell everything out. We'd had to examine and project every possible scenario of our deaths and what it would mean for Mickey's future. It brought up feelings I hadn't fully anticipated. Not just the obvious one, the fear of one's own death. Instead, it evoked feelings I thought I'd dealt with already. Sadness at the diagnosis. Anger. Terror about Mickey's future. As the parent of an autistic child you think you've done your grieving. Then it smacks you in the face again. Guardianship was the last step in this painstaking process. It had to be done before Mickey's eighteenth birthday, the age of majority, when in the eyes of the law he became an adult. We filed papers asking the court to allow us to assume guardianship of all legal, medical and financial decisions on Mickey's behalf.

At the beginning of twelfth grade, Karyn sent out an email to all the parents in the program:

> I hope you are well rested and excited about the upcoming year. Alan and I have talked, planned and met throughout the summer…with our new transition coordinator…she will meet with each family individually during the fall…Alan and I met with her today and we are very excited to have her join our team. I think this will be a great year!

The coordinator was warm and knowledgeable. She gave us a transition checklist and time line. What to do, and when. Registering with New York State's Office for Persons with Developmental Disabilities. Applying for SSI. Obtaining a Medicaid service coordinator. Seeking guardianship. Creating a special needs trust. Applying to the DMV for a non-driver ID, and to the state for adult housing. Adult agency options, programs and recreational support services. Obtaining transportation services. Registering to vote. Selective Service. Explanation and forms for each. So much information it made our heads swim.

We already knew that in order to preserve Mickey's eligibility for government-funded benefits, we couldn't leave any money in his name. Instead, everything for him had been placed in a special needs trust. That trust would one day supplement Mickey's government benefits, and could be used for anything other than his food and shelter. Medicaid pays for a wide array of services; the trust would pay for things Medicaid wouldn't. Quality of life things, like hobbies, vacations and entertainment. But would that trust be enough to take care of Mickey for the rest of his life?

That fall we learned how imperative it was to play by the government's rules. SSI stipulates that anyone receiving money from them cannot have more than $2000 in his name. "If you go a penny over $2000 they will hunt you down," my friend Iris had warned. I'd thought she was exaggerating. The SSI payments had started arriving, but we forgot to monitor Mickey's bank account closely enough. We got a letter from SSI saying Mickey's account had gone over the allowed $2000, $100 over. Not a big sum, but no matter. They were halting his payments. They claimed that we now owed *them* $900—two months' worth of payments.

We panicked and called the special needs attorney. "Take all the bank statements and paperwork and sort it out in person," she advised.

We went to the local Social Security office to plead our case. I walked in and tried to ask a guard a quick question. He yelled at me to wait my turn. Cowed, we sat nervously till our name was called, and slunk into a cubicle. We fanned out all our paperwork, explained what had happened, and promised abjectly it would never, ever happen again. Because I had been the one to file the initial SSI paperwork, they would only talk to me. Not Marc.

"But my husband is our son's legal guardian too!" I said.

"Doesn't matter," the woman said.

"Can we put my husband's name on the account too?"

"Only one guardian allowed."

"What if I have our lawyer write a letter saying you have my permission to talk to my husband?" I asked.

"Doesn't matter," she said. "If you want us to talk to him, you'll have to come here with him."

"Every time?"

"Every time."

"The coordinator at the high school told us we're supposed to register our son for food stamps too," I said. "Do we do that here?"

"Can you afford to buy your son food?"

"Yes."

"Then let someone else who really needs it have it. You don't want to go down to that office anyway. Those folks are mean. It's miserable to go there."

More humiliating than crawling to SSI?

We went to our bank and arranged that as soon as Mickey's account got close to $2000, they would automatically sweep $1500 of his money into our account. In the eyes of SSI, we were Mickey's landlords. Mickey was paying us rent to live in our home.

The high school hired a large agency that serves children, teens and adults with developmental disabilities to run a job internship program for the students in Mickey's class. In late September, they sent Mickey and another student once a week to do office work at the American Cancer Society. They were supervised by two job coaches from the agency. It went well for a month. Then suddenly and mysteriously, the agency told Karyn that the internship was over and that they'd have to find another. We got word the next Friday that Mickey and the other student would start an internship at a T.J. Maxx department store the following Monday. That weekend, we drove Mickey past the store so that it would at least look familiar. "You're going to have a job there on Monday," we told him.

"I feel nervous," Mickey said.

"It's okay to feel nervous. Everybody feels that way about starting a new job," Marc said.

Monday morning, Mickey got on the school bus without fuss. Three hours later Alan called.

"Mickey is okay but there was a little incident at T.J. Maxx," Alan said. My heart started to pound.

"They sent him to the store with the job coach he doesn't particularly like," Alan said. "I don't think she's had much experience with this population." Alan told me they'd put Mickey in the middle of the store and asked him to fold and tag clothes. Something he'd never done, and didn't know how to do. "Mickey got upset, and the coach didn't know how to de-escalate him. He ripped up tags, and pushed her. She got scared and called the school. He's here now."

"How is he?"

"Contrite. Subdued."

I called Shana to relay what had happened.

"The job coach set him up for failure," she said flatly. "Was the store crowded? Was there music playing? Did she make it very clear what she expected him to do? Did she even test him first to see if he had the skills they expected?"

When Mickey got off the school bus that afternoon he refused to talk. He climbed into bed and napped till dinner time. He asked for a slice of pizza, but took only two bites. Again and again he asked, "Are my cats going to die? When are they going to die?" Fudge curled up next to him and meowed. When he asked, "Is Fudge coming over to me because I'm sad?" I felt teary.

That evening I got an email from Karyn.

I know Mickey had a rough day today. I will speak to [the agency] tomorrow about this placement. While this placement may not be great for him, he needs to understand he cannot disobey and push the "boss."

We wrote back:

We totally agree that Mickey cannot push or yell at the boss and has to learn to use words to express his upset. Mickey has been brooding since he came home. This is his first failure in the workplace and he feels it very keenly. That being said, we are very surprised that [the agency] placed Mickey in a sink-or-swim situation without any one-on-one skill assessment, task-specific preparation or training. We thought that Mickey would be doing office work at T.J. Maxx, not folding and tagging stock. He has never done those tasks before, and folding t-shirts is a skill he is just learning at home and hasn't mastered. If [the agency] looked at Mickey's past experience at American Cancer Society, or read the excellent report from his library internship, or referred back to our intake interview as to what environments work best for Mickey, they would have realized a busy department store is not the right place for Mickey. They need to give a lot more thought to each child's placement, taking into consideration past experiences, strengths and weakness and not make snap placement judgments.

We had noticed for years that whenever we took Mickey out to an unfamiliar place, he got agitated when strangers got near him. Just as he'd said "Chicken!" to Aretha Franklin when she made the home visit, he'd said it to the job coach at T.J. Maxx too. Now we heard it on line at the deli, or in the supermarket aisle. He seemed to use it whenever he was frustrated or anxious. Concerned, we mentioned it to Alan. "We've tried talking to him to stop, or at least keep it in his head," Marc said. "How do we break this habit?"

Alan wrote to us that at school he was using "token economy, differential reinforcement, verbal praise, scripting ('Where do you keep your thoughts?' 'In my head') and other standard behavioral interventions." He added, "If you really hold him accountable for any inappropriate behavior and follow through on the consequences you can expect pretty good results. At least that's been my experience."

Alan made it sound so easy. It wasn't. Maybe in a classroom, but what about the real world? Sometimes Mickey seemed uncomfortable in his own skin, and didn't have the words to tell us.

Karyn asked the job programmer from the agency to meet with us in her office. Mickey came too. We discussed finding another job site for him at a book store. He squirmed in his chair. "No more talking. I want to LEAVE."

A few days later we finally figured out why Mickey seemed to be so uncomfortable, when Jonathan alerted us. "There's blood in the bathroom, Mom," he said. "Something's up with Mick."

Indeed there was. He had an infected pilonidal cyst at the base of his tailbone. The pediatrician sent us to a surgeon. "We can treat this medically for the moment," the surgeon said. "But someday he'll need surgery."

Why hadn't Mickey told us he was in pain? Or bleeding? Had he been scared? Unable to find the words to explain what he was feeling? *People with autism don't always show typical pain behavior*, I reminded myself. I remembered a summer day long ago: Mickey, a sturdy three-year-old, had been running happily down a concrete path when he'd tripped. I'd run to pick him up; his legs and arms were scraped raw. Most kids would have been shrieking. Mickey merely brushed away the gravel embedded in his knees, and resumed running.

~⑤

Karyn emailed to let me know the agency had set up a work site at Barnes and Noble for Mickey after winter break. We told Mickey, who asked, "Can I take things home from the book store?"

"It's not a library," Marc said. "But if you see a book you want, tell us when you get home, and we can go back together to buy it."

Marc emailed Karyn:

> We can't stress how important it is that Mickey have a successful experience with this. We were shocked about how distraught he was after the T.J. Maxx incident. We will talk to Mickey and tell him how pleased we will be if we get an excellent report, and that he needs to follow directions and work hard. Is there some sort of reward mechanism in place? Will they be sure that he is given breaks? This all may sound unnecessary, but we really want to ensure that he has a positive and productive experience.

That month, we also received a letter from the District Health Coordinator letting us know that they would soon begin a series on sexuality in Health class. They would cover reproduction and pregnancy; sexually transmitted infections and contraception; sexual orientation and gender identification. One phrase leapt out at us.

Condom demonstration.

How were they going to present this information so that Mickey could understand it? Put a balloon on a banana? He was still naive about conception and sexual activity. Alan told us there had already been some internal conversation with staff about the appropriateness of the topics. We emailed the health curriculum teacher:

> Mickey has the social sophistication and understanding of a much younger child. We do not want to move forward with

the curriculum until we have had a chance to discuss it with you, Alan and Karyn.

She replied with sensitivity, assuring us she would wait until the team met to discuss the curriculum she was proposing. "We are proceeding slowly and cautiously, mindful of our students' needs and level of comfort."

Marc wrote back to reassure her that we had no problem with teaching sex education in the schools.

The district did an excellent job with our older son Jonathan when he was in elementary school, and the classroom sessions engendered a lot of excellent discussion at home. Mickey's needs are different. I am sure all of us will come up with a very satisfactory solution.

Which they did. Mickey noted in his journal, "Today in health we learned about girls and boys."

He did not attend the condom demonstration.

Mickey began working at Barnes and Noble, under the guidance of a job coach from the agency. After the first week, she sent Mickey home with a note to tell us that he was performing poorly and was uncooperative. She didn't know how to motivate him.

We knew Mickey wasn't always easy to work with, but wasn't she a trained coach?

We asked Shana to observe Mickey at the book store and meet the coach. Shana reported that the coach and the store manager weren't making it clear to Mickey what he was supposed to do. The manager didn't have a list of tasks. "Just have him neaten up the shelves," he'd suggested vaguely. Mickey didn't know what that meant, nor did the job coach make it clear. Did they want him to alphabetize? Organize? Put the books in size order? Make them face the same way? When they told him to put stickers on books, Mickey muttered, "Chicken. Go away, leave me alone."

Shana gave the job coach a two-page list of behavioral suggestions: Remind him to say good morning to the manager. Remind him not to talk to strangers. Use a timer or clock so he knew when to work, and when to take a break. Give him a visual schedule to lessen his anxiety about not knowing what was coming next. Praise him appropriately: *Good following directions. Good straightening the books. Nice work putting stickers on the books.* She reminded the coach that if she needed to communicate with us in the future, to email us instead of writing something on the form Mickey brought home. "Don't put anything negative in writing because Mickey will read it," Shana told her. Shouldn't that have been obvious to the coach?

Shana told us the job coach had confided that no one had given her any information on working with Mickey. She told Shana she'd never used a timer or a visual schedule with other students. Never worked with autistic children before. Shana also said that the job coach seemed more interested in talking about herself. She'd asked Shana for professional advice on handling her own teen daughter's problems. "She welled up with tears five times!" Shana said. "I had to keep refocusing her on Mickey. Now you know I have tons of sympathy, but c'mon! I was there to help Mickey."

Shana emailed the coach with further suggestions. The coach replied that before she could start sending us brief, positive reports, she'd have to discuss doing so with her supervisor. The next day she told Shana that the supervisor didn't want her to send any messages home to us at all.

Shana visited Mickey at the book store several more times. She thought Mickey was working more happily, but at the end of the internship, we received a performance evaluation. Under the question "Please check the grade of work which you feel this student trainee has done on the job," the job coach checked "Poor/Unsatisfactory."

I was livid. Why hadn't they trained their staff to work with autistic people? Why had we had to send our own private therapist—at our own expense—to train their job coach? The coach was learning on the job—on our dime—at Mickey's expense. They'd failed Mickey by letting him fail at every job site.

"How do we salvage this?" I asked Marc.

"He needs specific tasks, and more hours, with a job coach who knows what she's doing. Two hours once a week isn't enough time to master anything. It keeps coming back to equity, doesn't it?" Marc said. "Would the high school hire a dean with no knowledge of colleges? Of course not. So why would they hire an agency with no knowledge of autism?"

"I'm not blaming the high school folks for this one," I said. "I don't think they realized. They hired a nationally known agency, so they assumed. We did too."

I blamed myself. Why hadn't we asked questions at the beginning of the school term? Questions like: What kind of experience do your coaches have? Are they ABA trained? How do you handle behaviors? What kind of students do you work with? How do you measure a student's progress? Who is accountable if there is no progress?

At the same time, Alan reported there had been a change in Mickey's behavior in school. He asked if we'd made any medication changes. We hadn't.

Karyn wrote to Marc:

> I know Alan has mentioned that we are seeing an increase in inappropriate behaviors with Mickey—shouting out, talking back to Alan, running away and pacing in the classroom and hallways. We continue to be concerned.

So were we. Sometimes we'd seen behavioral changes like these after making adjustments in Mickey's medication, but there hadn't been any in a while. He'd been taking Claritin for his spring allergies, but we didn't think that had anything to do with what Alan and Karyn were reporting. In any case, we'd stopped giving it to him several days ago. His behavior was fine at home. What was setting him off in the classroom?

I knew what was setting *me* off.

That week a woman from our synagogue emailed us an invitation to dinner for a new social group she was forming for "Empty Nesters."

Empty Nesters. We'd been hearing that phrase a lot all year from parents of typical twelfth-graders.

I wrote back:

> Thanks so much for thinking of us, it sounds like fun. Unfortunately we're not available that evening. Actually, we're not empty nesters. But we appreciate the invitation anyway.

I knew she hadn't meant to hurt me, but it still stung. I understood how painful it is when children leave home. It had been hard for us when Jonathan left for college. But Marc and I were not empty nesters, and in all likelihood might never be. I don't think I fully appreciated just how different our family's situation was until that twelfth-grade year.

One morning I woke to the cheery sound of bird song, and discovered a bird's nest, nestled on the little ledge outside my bedroom window. It was perfect. Tightly woven, circular, six inches across, perhaps four inches high. A symmetrical marvel of avian engineering. A cradle ready to be filled. "Come look at this, Mickey!" I called.

Each morning we checked the nest. On the third morning Mickey summoned me, excited. "Mom! There's an egg!"

I peered in. One oval egg, an indescribably beautiful blue that made my heart soar. Chicks! I imagined the sight of baby birds with gaping gullets, clamoring and craning in hopeful, hungry need.

"Let's keep a journal about this," I suggested. I gave him my digital camera, and we took pictures. The next morning, we spied a plump, brown-gray robin with a warm orange underbelly sitting in the nest. She hunkered down low, laboring. Her head twitched, sensing our presence. Barely breathing, I angled the slats of the shutters. Her head cocked to the side, listening. At the click of the camera, she lifted off. In the nest: two perfect blue eggs.

I uploaded two of the pictures to Facebook with the caption: "The Joys of Spring." All day friends posted comments, charmed by the sweetness of those photos and our project. Again and again, I returned to the window, captivated by rhythmic bird song that sounded like "cheerily-cheerily-cheerily."

The next morning: three blue eggs! We snapped another picture. Hours later, I returned to check on them, wondering if there would be a fourth egg.

The nest was empty.

Distraught, I peered into the garden. "Look at that tree!" Marc yelped. On a nearby branch, a black crow sat squawking. Gleeful. Bits of blue shell hung from his beak.

Mickey looked stricken when I broke the news.

"Will the bird make more eggs?" he asked. "No, honey," I said. "She won't be coming back to that nest."

I shared the sad news on Facebook. "I was so looking forward to your daily updates," my high school friend posted wistfully. *Birds die every day*, I kept telling myself.

I thought about how when Jonathan was small and got sick, I'd say to him, "Let's build a bird's nest." I would cozy the couch with cushions and pillows and his beloved Peter Rabbit quilt and tuck him in. A bird's nest is such an obvious, perfect metaphor for security and nurturing that we don't even think about it. Mothers-to-be often talk about the overpowering urge to "nest." But for the first time I was struck viscerally: a nest is truly a harbinger of spring. Of incipient life.

I felt sad and shaken for days, but of course it was so much more than the loss of the nest. Going through Mickey's homework folder, I'd discovered yet another work sheet: an illustration of a bird. He was expected to label the parts.

"This isn't life skills! Why are they wasting time teaching academics like this? It's like ninth grade all over again!" I raged to Marc. "Does he really need to recognize an upper from a lower mandible? Why aren't they focusing on things like how to wait for change when he pays for his lunch sandwich?" Recently the class had begun reading an abridged version of Mary Shelley's *Frankenstein*, a book that scared and confused Mickey. He struggled with everyday language; what meaning could he make of a classic work of literature written nearly 200 years ago? As an English major I'd read the book in college; I couldn't imagine how it could be relevant or useful to him. I knew there was still pushback from some of the parents who wanted more academics; was this the result? I was scared. Was the teaching staff bending to that pressure, shifting from their focus on pre-vocational skills?

I was at lunch the next day when my cell phone trilled. Alan. "Mickey is having a terrible day. He's angry and agitated. I'm wondering if something medical is going on."

"We're not seeing those behaviors at home," I said. "Neither is Shana."

"I think he has a lot of complex psychological issues going on. I also think that the behavioral approach may be *causing* the problems."

"What do you mean?"

"He's been working for rewards so long, I think he sees them as a form of control over him. Work is supposed to be intrinsically rewarding, but for him, it's just something that stands between him and the reward. The rewards produce temporary compliance, but I don't think they make lasting changes in his attitude or his behavior."

I was taken aback. Alan had been such a proponent of behavioral techniques till now. *Intrinsically rewarding? Didn't we all work for rewards of one kind or another? As grownups we call them "paychecks."*

"Do we need to do a new functional behavioral assessment?"

"I really don't think that will help at this point,' he said. "He has issues. I think he needs a psychiatrist and some talk therapy."

Talk therapy? "Mickey's disability is language based," I said. "How is a doctor going to get him to talk?"

I was shocked. Hurt. Alan had been our ally for years. I knew he'd spoken out of frustration, but was he giving up on Mickey?

Marc and I felt lost. We didn't know what to do. Neither did Alan. Mickey became completely withdrawn in school. Angry. Refusing to participate. Several times Alan phoned to ask us to come pick up Mickey. "He's just not available for learning," Alan said.

"Aren't we just reinforcing the bad behavior?" I asked Marc. "What are we all teaching him? That if he behaves badly enough, he gets to go home?"

Behavior is communication. What was Mickey telling us? Why was he shutting down? We suspected it was too much of everything. Anxiety about the job internships. The painful pilonidal cyst. A curriculum on sexuality that made him uncomfortable. Homework sheets he couldn't do.

But most of all? We thought it was the social situation at school. We suspected he was feeling lonely. Rejected. Several of his more socially adept classmates had lately been getting together on weekends. They talked about it in class, in front of everyone. They talked about going to the school carnival. They talked about visiting Ethan's house to see his new puppy. They talked about eating out at the diner. Alan told us he had needed to intervene:

Ethan loudly invited three students to his party, and when Mickey said, "I want to come too," Ethan said, *"You're* not invited."

"I feel like slugging that kid," I fumed to Marc.

"Mickey's not the only one in that class with social challenges," he reminded me. "Let Alan handle it."

That afternoon we received two letters. The first was from the State of New York. It had taken seven months, but the court had finally granted us legal guardianship of Mickey.

The second letter was an invitation from the high school PTA to a workshop on "helping your child survive freshman year at college away from the safe nest of home."

Could the contrast be any starker?

Our nest wasn't going to be empty. Mickey was going to live with us for a long, long time, until the day we couldn't do this any longer. Then we would have to find a safe group home for him. A thought so painful I could not breathe.

Again I pictured that empty nest on the window ledge. "Stop it," I told myself sternly. "Nature is arbitrary. Cruel."

But here's what I wanted to know. Where was that mother robin? Why didn't she dive bomb that thieving crow? Why was she so helpless to protect her young?

Why was I?

~๑

I was in a clothing boutique with a childhood friend one morning when she said, "I don't know how to wear this. I'm such a fashion retard."

I was shocked. I said, "Please don't use that word."

She turned red. "You're right. I am so sorry," she said. And she was. Truly embarrassed.

She was about the last person I would ever have expected to hear it from. She was one of the smartest people I knew, and I didn't mean her Ivy League education. She was passionate about social justice. She thought long and deeply about everything. She treated Mickey with unfailing compassion and respect, and had taught her two children to do the same. So to hear the R word slip so automatically from her lips was as shocking as if she had suddenly taken off her clothes and danced naked in Times Square.

My mother-in-law had recently forwarded a joke that had obviously been making the rounds among her friends. It was a silly story about children who mistake words they hear, not worth repeating here. But the subject line of the email was "retarded grandparents." I took a deep breath. Then I clicked on "reply all" and wrote this message:

> For years I've received jokes like this and kept quiet, but one of my New Year's resolutions this year was to speak up, so here goes. As the parent of a developmentally disabled child, I find the use of the word "retarded" personally offensive. So-called jokes like these reinforce the discrimination and intolerance children like mine face daily. "Retarded" is not a synonym for "stupid." It's time to retire the "R" word from everyone's vocabulary.

I hoped I hadn't offended her. My mother-in-law immediately emailed back:

> Actually I didn't even notice the title of the joke. But you are right about this.

That was my point: no one noticed. Not even the people who knew and loved my son. That's how ingrained that word is in our culture. It's a knee-jerk reflex in people's vocabularies. No one else replied to my email. I imagined that many of her friends who received it probably felt sorry that my mother-in-law had a humorless prig for a daughter-in-law. And it's true. I *am* humorless when it comes to this.

People use the R word as an all-purpose putdown. It's hateful trash talk, the ultimate playground zinger. The Special Olympics has campaigned aggressively against the word since the film *Tropic Thunder* several years ago, which introduced the term "Full Retard" to the cultural conversation. Even President Obama had been guilty. Not of using the R word, but of viewing those with disabilities as something to joke about, when he told Jay Leno on *The Tonight Show* that his poor bowling performance was like "Special Olympics or something." (Obama later apologized for his remark.) Or Pulitzer Prize-winning author Thomas Friedman, during interviews on both CNN and *Charlie Rose*, who repeatedly said that our involvement in Afghanistan was "like adopting a special needs baby." Rahm Emanuel, who at the time was White House Chief of Staff, was quoted using the phrase "f—ing retarded," in the Wall Street Journal.

I wasn't trying to be the word police. I knew that if we banished this word from everyone's vocabulary, something equally noxious would probably take its place; I'd heard "autistic" used as a derogatory term too. The R word had been retired by medical and social service organizations; wasn't it time everyone else did too? People needed to understand that the R word was as offensive to persons with intellectual disabilities as the N word was to the African-American community. The malice behind the R word was so palpable and ugly and heart constricting. Did people think kids like Mickey with intellectual disabilities didn't know they were being put down when someone called them that word? That they didn't feel the insult and disdain?

That old saw "sticks and stones will break my bones but words will never harm me" was patently untrue. Words do wound. This wasn't about political correctness. I was asking for no less than a basic cultural shift.

The first weekend in June, we attended a special needs bat mitzvah for our friend Alison Singer's daughter in the Center for Jewish Life at our synagogue, where Mickey's service had been. Mickey sang the familiar songs, lifting and swaying his arms as if to conduct the band of Israeli musicians. He seemed happy and engaged. After the service, we stood in the lobby, talking to the director of special education from our school district, when Mickey suddenly said, "I need to go home."

I glanced at him. "Just one more minute," I said.

"I want to go *now*."

I looked at him again. His face had gone pale; his eyes were glassy and unfocused. My heart began to pound. "Mickey?"

No answer. I knew what was coming.

I caught him just as he slumped, and staggered against his dead weight. "Marc!" I yelled.

"Someone get a chair!" the director called.

We couldn't get his legs to fold. Couldn't get him into the chair. His body was too rigid.

Together Marc and I tried to lower Mickey to the floor, but he was a plank. Marc wrapped his arms under Mickey's, chest to chest, and clung to him.

The seizure lasted forever. Three minutes. Afterwards, the director helped us walk Mickey to our car. I felt perversely glad that he'd seen Mickey have a seizure. He'd been hearing about this for years; maybe now that he'd finally seen it himself, seen how sudden and devastating seizures could be, he would stop arguing whenever I insisted that Mickey needed to be accompanied by an aide.

We took Mickey home to sleep. In the early evening we had to leave to attend the annual Board of Education picnic dinner. I felt uneasy. "We'll only be five minutes away," I told Milagros.

Our hostess was bringing out dessert when Marc's cell phone buzzed. Mickey had just had another seizure.

Milagros met us at the door. "Everything's okay," she said again and again. She was trembling. She hugged me; I hugged her back, holding on a long moment.

She said Mickey had been taking a shower. She heard a loud bang, and ran into the bathroom. Found him up against the tiled wall. Rigid. Eyes rolled back. A miracle he hadn't fallen before she'd gotten to him. Somehow she'd managed to lift all 150 slippery pounds of him out of the tub. Wrapped him in a towel. Gotten him to his bed. How had she had the physical strength?

I reached the neurologist on call, who told me to give Mickey more Topamax that evening and the following morning. "It will make him sleep a lot, but that's okay," she said. "Two seizures in six hours? Has he been sick?"

"No. But very stressed." I described the behaviors Alan had observed the past few days.

"It's a well-documented phenomenon that up to a week before a seizure, some people will display subtle behavioral changes like irritability," she said. "It's called prodrome. Kind of like feeling achy and sick on and off the day before you actually come down with a virus. If he has another seizure tonight, take him to the hospital."

He didn't. I checked him hourly all that night to make sure he was still breathing.

A week later, Marc, Mickey and I flew out to Minnesota for Jonathan's college graduation weekend. Marc's mother Beverly joined us, as well as my brother Marty, my sister-in-law Susan, my niece and two nephews. We were proud of Jonathan, who was graduating with Departmental Honors on his Senior Thesis in Economics. He had lined up a job internship, and would be returning home to us for the summer. The weekend—filled with celebratory dinners, campus tours, concerts, a Minnesota Twins game—was thrilling and bittersweet. How had four years sped by so fast? Marc and I savored it, knowing it was the only time we'd see a child graduate college. As we posed for family photos after the graduation ceremony, I saw Jonathan look across the auditorium, to a group of his friends. His eyes welled up with tears. I rubbed his back. "You'll miss them," I said. He nodded hard, unable to speak. I'd felt the same way at my own college graduation 30 years earlier. Four years, living with and working alongside your best friends, an extraordinary time of freedom and growth. Nothing quite like those four years ever happens again.

We picked up the mail when we returned Sunday night. With sinking hearts, we read Mickey's fourth quarter IEP goal report from school. All but one of his social/emotional goals were checked as "not attained."

Mickey returned to school the next morning. That afternoon Alan emailed us:

Mickey had a bit of a rough day. We are doing a unit on the history of music so we learn about an artist, listen to their music, and write about it (I developed a music appreciation sheet that helps the students articulate their thoughts on the music). Mickey only sat for about five minutes with the group and wrote "angry," "broken," "it sounds bad," and "ugly." We were listening to "It happened in Monterrey" by Frank Sinatra. He sat on the couch for the next two hours and wouldn't return to work. At Friendly's he didn't want to sit with any of the students or staff so he sat alone. I was in the booth right next to him. When we returned he started to tease Justin and Ethan. I explained to him he would not earn his song [being allowed to perform a song during club was his weekly reward] tomorrow if he continued to tease students. He called me several names and ran out of the room. He waited for the bus by the bench and ripped the notices on the bulletin board. I asked him why he did that and he told me he wasn't coming to school tomorrow. He was very unhappy here today. Sorry the news isn't better.

I was crushed. We'd had such a successful weekend. Mickey had been so happy. I remembered how excited he'd been sitting in the student union watching sports on a big screen TV. He'd been surrounded by typical college students, and he'd actually seemed to blend in. He'd behaved completely appropriately.

"It's June, school's basically over," Marc said. "Let him decompress before he goes to camp."

He emailed Alan:

Liane and I have decided that Mickey will not return to school for the remaining days. It is just counterproductive at this point, he is too unhappy. We are not sure what is going on as we do not see these behaviors at home and we didn't see these behaviors during our trip to Minnesota. I think we all need a break and some time to think things out so we can make next year a success.

We had no idea how.

Mickey left for camp. I was at a fish restaurant a week later when suddenly a swell of nausea washed over me. The room got too bright, the clatter of glassware too loud. My heart pounded; my throat constricted. I couldn't breathe. Was it the smell of seafood? A panic attack?

I fled to the ladies' room. Eventually the sick feelings subsided.

But several days later it happened again. Nausea. Racing heart. Tightness. I went to see the cardiologist.

"Everything checks out okay," she said. "I don't think it's your heart. You should see the gastroenterologist."

I dreaded the idea of someone threading a camera down my throat. But the nausea became unrelenting. I felt systemically sick. After I awakened nauseated one night, teeth chattering, I scheduled the endoscopy. When I woke up from the anesthesia, the doctor told me, "The good news is that you don't have an ulcer. You have mild to moderate reflux. We'll have the biopsy back in a week. We'll start you on a proton pump inhibitor, but if you don't feel better, come back and we'll explore further."

The futuristic-sounding proton pump inhibitor, it turned out, was a fancy name for an acid-reducing medication. I was hopeful. And for a while I did feel better. Then the nausea and constriction came back. The doctor called it "non-specific gastritis." Was he suggesting it was all in my head? Anxiety gnawed at me. I dreaded eating. I found myself cancelling social appointments, because they all revolved around meals. I was consumed with feeling ill. I thought about the many meanings of that word *consumed*. Swallowed. Spent. Drained. Depleted. Devoured. Destroyed. I woke in the night with feelings of dread. *I can't be sick. Mothers of special needs children have to live forever.*

I returned to the doctor. He palpated my stomach and weighed me. I had lost 12 pounds. "I think the medication isn't helping as much because you have a hybrid form of gastric reflux and irritable bowel syndrome," he said. "Are you under stress?"

I told him that my younger son had autism and epilepsy. He nodded sympathetically. "Okay, let's just get an abdominal ultrasound to rule some things out."

On a sweltering day in early August I went to an over-air-conditioned radiology office in Manhattan. I shivered in the waiting room for nearly an hour, turning the greasy pages of a year-old copy of *People* magazine. Out of the corner of my eye I saw movement: something dark and small scurried across the soiled carpet.

"Liane Carter?" Someone called, and escorted me into an examination room, where I put on a flimsy paper gown and lay down on the table. I chatted with the technician, a pretty woman with an Eastern European accent and kind manner. She took a brief history. Then she pressed the transducer repeatedly over my stomach. She frowned at the screen. "See anything interesting?" I asked, feigning nonchalance.

"I'm only the technician, the radiologist has to read it," she replied quickly. She didn't look at me.

I hadn't been home more than ten minutes when the phone rang.

"The ultrasound showed something," the doctor said. "You have gall stones, which I'm not concerned about. They also saw a large mass in your liver. It measures about six centimeters."

The room spun.

"It might be a hemangioma," he said.

I heard "oma" and immediately assumed "cancer."

"What do we do next?" I asked, terrified.

"I'd like to get a CT scan."

"I'm leaving for vacation tomorrow," I said. "Should I cancel my trip?"

"You can wait till you get back," he said. "Unless you're the kind of person who's going to go crazy waiting."

"I'm exactly that kind of person," I said.

"In that case, call my office and ask them to fax you a referral. Then call the hospital's radiology department and tell them I said you need to be seen right away."

Then he added, "You can't eat for three hours before the test."

As if I could.

"What do you think it is?"

He was quiet. "I don't know," he said.

I hung up.

Bad things happen to people every day, I thought. Man plans, God laughs. No one gets out alive. What made me think I'd be any different? Once again, fear rushed through me. *I might never see Jonathan married. Never see grandchildren. Who will take care of Mickey?*

I raced to Mayoclinic.com to look up "hemangioma."

"An abnormal growth of blood vessels," I read. "Can cause nausea and vomiting. Sometimes requires surgery. In extreme cases, complete removal and a donor liver."

If that's even what I have.

I called the hospital, while Marc argued with our insurance company. "No she can't wait till tomorrow," I heard him say angrily. "The doctor said *today*. No, she is *not* going to your local radiology lab, the doctor wants her seen at the hospital."

"They say they'll only authorize it if you go through the emergency room first," Marc said. "Forget *that*. We'll put it on American Express and fight with Aetna later." We drove back to Manhattan. To the same hospital where our children were born. The same hospital where Mickey has spent endless days and nights tethered to EEG monitors. Recently he'd asked us why Puffin, the cat I'd had before I was married, had died. "Was she old?" I'd thought about how Puffin's bile ducts had grown torturously knotted. She'd been jaundiced. Cirrhotic. Then, finally, comatose. I'd told him, simply, "Her liver got too sick." He worried it over for days, finally asking, "But my other cats' livers are okay?"

How was I going to tell Mickey something was wrong with my liver?

At the hospital they made me swallow a gallon of ice water. I shook with cold as the nurse took my history. "What did the doctor say *exactly*?" he asked.

"He called it a large mass," I replied. It felt as if my words were coming out of someone else.

They positioned me in the scanner. I couldn't stop shivering. My breath was ragged each time they ordered me to hold it. The nurse told me that when they infused the contrast dye, I would feel warmth flush though my body, a taste of metal in the mouth, a damp heat in the groin. "Don't be alarmed, it's normal," he said. The procedure was over quickly. I dressed, went to the bathroom for the third time, and Marc and I tore out of the hospital.

By the time we were on the Bruckner Expressway I had to pee so badly I was groaning. "Is there a jar in the car? A bucket? *Anything?*" I pleaded. I was desperate. I imagined squatting by the side of the road. It was the South Bronx, where normally I'd be afraid to stop. We saw a yellow McDonald's sign off the road and aimed for it.

I rushed into the bathroom, and saw the bathroom wall was smeared brown. I tried not to touch anything. Back in the car, I emptied a bottle of Purell sanitizer over my hands. Then, from the Deagan Expressway, I called the doctor.

"When will you know something?" I asked frantically.

"I'm out of the office tomorrow. I generally send patients a letter. But you can log onto your account with us."

An account?

Jonathan came home early from his internship. I was grateful Mickey was away at camp. All evening, Jonathan couldn't stop hugging me.

I was locked in a private hell. I had never felt so alone. Mechanically, I tossed clothes into a suitcase. I didn't care what I took. New clothes or old, what did it matter? My desk was a mess. I'd meant to organize it before vacation. My drawers were disheveled. My closets needed cleaning. *I can't die yet, there's too much to do.* It grew late. Finally, I collapsed into bed. "I'll take care of you," Marc said, and I pressed myself tight against him. I bargained with God. *I'll take surgery. Chemo. Just let me keep going. I can't leave Marc to manage without me.* All night, I drifted in and out of sleep, waking periodically in sheer panic, thinking, feeling, *oh my God oh my God.*

The next morning Jonathan handed me a card and gift. "I'm sorry it's late," he said. My birthday had been two weeks ago. *Would I see the next one?*

The card said, "You probably thought I didn't notice everything you've done for me." I unfolded it. "The big things...the little things…and everything in between. But I did notice, and I've been keeping track. And guess what?"

The card opened wide. It was a yard long, filled with hundreds of hash marks. It said, "I'm still counting. Thanks for everything."

Beneath it, Jonathan had written, "Love you so much."

Till then I'd held it together. No tears. Now I choked up. I put my arms around him, and he lifted me off the ground in a bear hug. Milagros handed me a book about angels. Though I was unlikely to read the book, I realized she wanted to comfort me, so I thanked her and tucked it in the pocket behind my car seat. Once more, I went over with her how to care for the cats while we were away.

Marc and I got into the car, set the GPS for Montreal. Two hours on the thruway passed. We stopped, took turns using the restroom. While I waited in the car, my BlackBerry buzzed with an incoming message: the doctor's office. I clicked. My BlackBerry was maddeningly slow; the hourglass icon spun endlessly, refilling and emptying its virtual sand. The email refused to open. In frustration I yanked out the battery, replaced it, and rebooted.

The email finally opened; there was an attachment. I couldn't open it. I needed a computer. There was one in the trunk under the luggage but where would I find WiFi? Marc returned, I showed him the message; he couldn't open it either. "Just call them!" he said. We pulled onto the highway. I called unsuccessfully three times, only to hear "If you know your party's extension…" I didn't. I pressed option four, and left a message. No one called back.

I vacillated from chilled to sweating to chilled. Again, I called. Finally someone picked up. I asked for the doctor. We couldn't hear the speaker phone over the roar of highway traffic, so Marc pulled onto the embankment. "He's not in," the operator said. "Please," I begged. "Isn't there anyone else there who can read me the report?"

"I'll have to have the nurse practitioner call you back," she said, her voice neutral.

We pulled back on the highway. Long minutes later, the phone finally rang.

"Hold on, hold on," we yelled over the highway rumble, and again Marc veered off the road. We stopped on the grass shoulder. Trucks whipped by; our small car rocked and shimmied in their wake. I huddled, fingernails digging into my arms.

"Dear Ms. Carter," she read. "This letter is a follow-up to your recent abdominal and pelvic CT scan. I have reviewed the test results that were obtained. Your CT scan reveals benign liver hemangiomas. No other abnormalities are identified on this exam. If you would like to schedule a follow-up appointment..."

I didn't hear the rest.

"Benign?" we chorused.

"Benign."

"So we'll schedule surgery when we get back?" Marc asked.

"No," the nurse said. We'll just monitor you. Have a good vacation."

Marc terminated the call, and we turned to each other.

We were both sobbing.

Reprieved.

ZONES OF COMFORT

As soon as we returned home from vacation, I checked in with the camp director to see how Mickey was doing.

"I saw Mickey around camp several times yesterday and spoke to him at lunch," Mike emailed me. "To me, he seems calmer, more relaxed and more comfortable here than I remember him being in past summers. He also seems more related and less given to speaking (to me) with a silly, joking tone. Camp got off to a great start for him. It looks like he has had a good year."

If he only knew, I thought.

At camp pickup, staff told us again and again that this summer had been Mickey's best experience there ever. Mickey was glowing. We watched with delight as Mickey proudly introduced his big brother Jonathan to all the campers and counselors, then showed us his cabin, his bunk bed, and what he'd made in arts and crafts. Best of all, a boy in the bunk came over to us, shook our hands, and said, "I'm Billy. I'm Mickey's best friend."

How could we make this camp success carry over to school this fall?

Earlier that summer, high school administrators had explored the possibility of partnering with the Devereux Foundation for transition services. Devereux is one of the oldest and largest non-profit providers of behavioral health care in the country. Their Millwood Learning Center provides intensive educational and behavioral interventions based on Applied Behavioral Analysis to children with autism and other pervasive developmental disorders. Millwood was one of the autism schools that had been suggested years earlier when everything had fallen apart for Mickey in ninth grade. At the time the program hadn't been appropriate.

But recently I'd attended a transition workshop run by Neil, their director of vocational and transitional services, as well as Cindy, the school's principal. I'd been impressed with their "can do" attitude. Neil had told me, "All of our transitioning students have jobs out in the community. Everyone is capable of doing something."

It was a relief to hear him say that. I knew that the great wave of children and teens diagnosed with ASD—half a million and counting—would be aging out of the educational and support system provided by the federal Individuals with Disabilities Education Act (IDEA) over the next decade. When a child reaches 21 in New York State (age varies by state) all the educational supports and services they have been receiving under IDEA will vanish, even though a child isn't going to magically stop needing support after reaching a cut-off chronological age. This forced transition is called "aging out." In the language of the system, your child hasn't graduated; he has "aged out" and "exited" the school system—into a woefully ill-prepared and underfunded adult service system charged with meeting his needs. As one parent told me, "They spent 16 years educating my kid to the best of his ability so that he could spend the next 60 years stuck at home watching TV."

Young adults with an autism spectrum disorder were far less likely to continue their education or get a job after high school when compared to young adults with other disabilities. According to a 2012 study in the journal *Pediatrics,* which was the largest and most definitive to date, two years after graduation, half of ASD young adults had no paid job experience, technical education or college. Seven years after high school, the numbers improved, but were still bleak: an estimated one in three young adults with autism had no paid job experience, college or technical school. That was a higher percentage shut out of the work world than for other disabilities. It was a problem policymakers urgently needed to address.

My friend Marjorie Madfis was tackling her concern about employment for her autistic daughter Isabelle head on—and innovatively.

After a 30-year career in corporate marketing, Marjorie plunged into entrepreneurship. She founded Yes She Can Inc., a non-profit that aims to develop job skills and job opportunities for young women with autism. Its first effort was Girl AGain, a small resale boutique for American Girl dolls and accessories in Hartsdale, New York.

"I had been thinking about Girl AGain for many years but after you and I attended the Autism Speaks town hall on autism employment entrepreneurship in New York City I was motivated to start Yes She Can Inc.," she told me over lunch. "Isabelle's career ambition has always been to work at the American Girl store to do doll hair. There are many other girls and women on the spectrum who are very passionate about American Girl and very knowledgeable."

Isabelle and a half dozen other young women ranging in age from 18 to 25 work as interns in the small shop. The store serves as an incubator for them to learn skills in a supportive, non-competitive setting. "It's not that they can't do the actual work tasks, it's the whole social engagement part of what happens in the workspace that's so baffling to them," Marjorie said. "Here they can use their expertise as the basis to learn new skills." She hoped the experience would help them get mainstream jobs someday.

"Employment is a huge, huge issue," my friend Peter Bell, CEO of Eden Autism Services in New Jersey, agrees. "Within the next ten years, more than 500,000 kids with autism will reach adulthood."

So much of the media attention focuses on children. People don't seem to realize that autism doesn't disappear in adolescence. Mickey will be an autistic adult for far longer than he has been an autistic child.

I still worried that Mickey needed to be surrounded with more typically behaved peers, because he tended to imitate whatever behavior he saw in the classroom. "Maybe we could ease him into Millwood with just a few hours a week, and keep him at the high school the rest of the time," Marc said. We agreed we couldn't switch Mickey abruptly. His social hub was still at the high school. But our backs were to the wall. We needed to try something different. I made an appointment to visit Millwood.

We liked what we saw. Our school district arranged that Mickey and his friend Jake would attend the Millwood transition program two mornings a week to work on pre-vocational skills. Neil asked us to bring Mickey in to meet with Cezanne, the teacher who'd be working with the boys. We liked her immediately. She had clearly worked with kids like Mickey. She was firm, kind and calm. She told us she'd like to assess the skills he would need to live in a group home environment—laundry, cooking and cleaning tasks. She would also assess his social skills and pre-vocational tasks, and come up with a set of program goals.

Cezanne emailed us after their first day together:

Hi! Mickey did a terrific job today! He set the table, made a sandwich and some oatmeal in the microwave for me, cleaned up, put the dishes in the dishwasher, hand washed some dishes, put the dry dishes away in the cabinets, and we talked about spoiled food. He and Jake are going to make a really nice team.

Mickey seemed happy about working with Cezanne and Jake two mornings a week. He was also excited to be back at the high school. "Can I have a party?" he asked.

"You mean a Welcome Back to School party? Sure. Who do you want to invite?"

"Everyone."

That made me happy. He wasn't holding a grudge against the kids who'd excluded him a few months earlier. In fact, I realized, he'd never held grudges. As soon as anyone said, "I'm sorry," Mickey forgave everything. I wished I could let go of anger as easily as he did.

"Today I made breakfast all by myself!" he told me. "Eggs, toast and turkey bacon. Can we buy some?"

Cezanne wrote us a note in the communication notebook after every session. I was grateful that she was always careful to write only positive things in the book, unlike the job coach the previous year. If problems or concerns came up, Cezanne emailed or called. She was always upbeat.

In October, the principal Cindy told me that Mickey was doing so well at Millwood that they wanted to add a third morning a week to his schedule. "There hasn't been enough time in the two mornings to complete everything we assessed on his first few visits," she said. "We'd like to break it down into a shopping/cooking/kitchen day, a vocational day, and a home living/self-help day."

At the beginning of November, Jonathan began working as the operations manager at the Autism Science Foundation, reviewing grant applications, running the back office and organizing fund-raising events. The same week, Neil let us know that Mickey and Jake would start working at the American Red Cross several hours a week.

"The transition will be fairly simple," he wrote. "We always spend day one just meeting people and familiarizing him with the people and the task he will be working on. I will be there with Cezanne in the beginning. Mickey will be entering information from the volunteer files into a database. The college interns usually do this job but after Cezanne assessed his computer literacy, he can definitely do this."

He could?

We were delighted.

Jonathan was still living at home until he could find an apartment, and I was enjoying having him near. One weekend we watched *Saturday Night Live* air a fake ad for the "Damn It! My Mom's on Facebook Filter." I thought it was a hoot. I loved Facebook. Like millions of people, I used it for socializing (and yes, I'll cop to watching cat videos), but more importantly, I'd connected to hundreds of other special needs parents, bloggers, disability rights advocates and professional women writers. I was active in more than a dozen autism-related Facebook groups, and belonged to a local and lively "Special Moms of Westchester" group with more than 1000 members. I'd even gotten professional writing assignments through editors I'd "met" on Facebook. Every time I shared a link to a new article I'd written, I got emails and Facebook messages from parents desperate for resources or advice.

Jonathan cornered me. "You're all over Facebook," he said. "You've been clicking 'Like' on too many things lately."

"It's not okay to 'Like' things?" I asked. The "Like" button is a "thumbs up" feature that lets you say that, well, you like what someone posted.

"It's okay sometimes, but not for so many things. You don't have to Like it every time I breathe."

I was confused. "You can see everything I Like?"

"Yeah, of course I can, it's all over Facebook."

"You mean if I say I Like the picture of Monty Python you posted, it comes through on your News Feed?" I asked.

"Yes."

"And that bothers you?" I was still confused. "What difference does it make to you if I click 'Like' on things that I like?"

"When it's my stuff you're clicking, all my friends can see it."

"They can see everything I Like?"

I know I click Like a lot, but how would his friends know? I wasn't Facebook friends with them.

"Yeah, if you Like stuff on my Wall, they do see it."

"So it's just your posts that I'm not supposed to Like?"

"Exactly."

Oh. I thought I was the cool mom because I tweet and Instagram. Here I'd been cruising the information superhighway feeling like a Formula One driver, and now my kid was telling me I was in the breakdown lane. I did a mental count. I'd Liked exactly six items he'd posted.

"You can Like some stuff, but not everything," he said. "Like, it's okay if you want to Like that I tell people to wear purple to show support as a straight ally of National Coming Out Day."

"So it's a judgment call. Well, I Liked your Dancing Parrot video."

"It's slippery," he allowed. "Like when I posted that I got a job, that was okay to Like."

"What about Liking the pictures of your girlfriend's kittens?"

"Dubious. That's a gray area. The boundaries are fluid. Don't cross any boundaries."

I didn't realize I had. I thought I was being supportive. I liked keeping in touch this way; it was a window into his world, especially because boys don't tend to open up easily to their moms. It's hard to know what those boundaries are today; we're living in a culture of over-sharing. Should we be interacting online? How much? Using social media made me feel hip, at a point in life where I was worrying about feeling old, left behind and irrelevant. I hoped I hadn't embarrassed him. But Jonathan frequently posted my articles on his Facebook wall. Recently he'd surprised me by creating a Writer Fan Page about me on Facebook.

"So when you posted that photo of the guy holding the sign saying 'Sasquatch is Real,' it wasn't okay to Like that?" I asked.

"Well, yeah," he conceded. "That was a good photo. But you need to stop Liking everything."

"You know, you friended me, not the other way around," I felt compelled to point out. But I was laughing. "Jonnie, I love you," I said.

"Yeah, me too," he said.

"Okay, let me be sure I've got this," I said. "If someone posts 'Save the Whales,' is it okay to Like that?"

"Mom," he said, surprisingly patient, "I love that you love whales. Just don't love *my* whales."

I nodded. "Got it," I said, even though I didn't entirely. I resolved to leave his whales alone.

"This would make a good essay," Marc said.

Jonathan rolled his eyes. "Mom can write her own essays just fine, Dad," he said.

I Liked that.

Along with the saying "If you've met one person with autism, you've met one person with autism," there's another paradigm in the autism community: "Presume competence."

We were so appreciative that Neil and Cezanne were doing exactly that. To presume competence means that you acknowledge that a child has an intellectual ability, while providing opportunities for him to be exposed to learning. You assume that child wants to learn and assert him or herself in the world. Presuming competence didn't mean we thought that Mickey automatically got everything. We did, however, believe that he was taking it all in, storing it and processing it on his own timetable. I always told parents of newly diagnosed children not to talk about the child in front of him, because he might very well understand what they were saying, even if he didn't appear to.

That fall I was thinking a lot about what it meant to presume competence, especially after Alan gave us a voter registration form for Mickey. "He's 18 now," Alan said.

"Are you kidding?" Marc said. "He doesn't know Dick Nixon from Dick Tracy."

Legally Mickey was entitled to vote, but without being able to weigh and consider the issues and candidates, what would his vote mean? I wondered. We had the legal authority to make medical and life decisions for him, but that certainly didn't give us the right to tell him who to vote for. But if he did vote, wouldn't he just be voting for whomever we told him to vote for? Yes, Mickey *could* vote. But *should* he? How do you know when—or even if—it's time to encourage a cognitively disabled adult child to vote?

There was a lawsuit in Minnesota that had set off alarms that year—as well it should have—about whether disabled people who could not handle their own affairs and were under the care of a legal guardian should retain the right to vote. It grew out of a 2010 incident in which a Minnesota voter claimed he saw mentally disabled adults being coerced by their caregivers to vote for certain candidates. I understood that someone with a disability could be taken advantage of—it was one of the worries that kept me awake nights. But how could you penalize all disabled people, just because they *could* be victimized? How could you take away a person's right to vote on the grounds of mental illness or intellectual disability? That violated a person's civil rights under the 1990 federal Americans with Disabilities Act, the nation's first comprehensive law to address the needs of people with disabilities.

ADA prohibits discrimination in employment, public services, public accommodations and telecommunications.

I thought about how when our nation was founded, only white men could vote. After the Civil War, Jim Crow laws, literacy tests and poll taxes barred many African-Americans from voting. The right to vote was hard won for women too. Today voting is a fundamental right protected by federal law. As long as you're a citizen and over 18, you can vote. It isn't based on educational level. No one administers a test. We don't ask voters if they understand the issues, or assess their knowledge of the Constitution. What if an IQ test (controversial in itself) for non-disabled citizens were required? What would that cut-off be? Who would make that decision?

"Mickey, do you know there's an election this year?" I asked him. He didn't. I asked him who our president was.

"Barack Obama."

I explained how the following year we would be voting for who would be president for the next four years, and asked, "Would you want to vote?"

"Can I vote for George Washington?" he asked.

I turned this over and over in my mind. For the rest of his life Mickey would be relying on federal and state programs such as Medicaid and Supplemental Security Income. Mickey could literally read a ballot. He was 18. A citizen. Entitled to vote. Shouldn't he be voting on candidates and issues that would affect his own life? We worried we were stripping him of this basic civil right.

There's a chasm between having the *right* to vote and the actual ability to understand the issues and voting process. Mickey didn't understand those issues yet. We hoped someday he would. We presumed competence. But we didn't think he should be voting until he understood that Election Day meant more than a day off from school.

⟨swirl ornament⟩

It was nearly Thanksgiving, our favorite holiday. I've always loved that it isn't a religious holiday. There's no obligatory gift giving. It's simply a celebration with food, friends and family, and this fall it felt as if we had much to celebrate. Jonathan's first job. Mickey's new program. Usually I started cooking and freezing food two weeks in advance, but this year would be different: for the first time in 15 years, we would not be hosting the holiday.

When Marc's mother Beverly had met us in Minneapolis for Jonathan's college graduation months earlier, Marc and I had noticed she was less steady on her feet. We began to wonder if the five-hour flight from her home in Scottsdale, Arizona to us in New York might be too much. "I think we should go out to her," Marc said. "I'm sorry. I know how much you love making Thanksgiving."

He loves it as much as I do—he clips stuffing recipes all year, and sends out invitations before Labor Day. But knowing how much he wanted to see his family, I swallowed my disappointment. "We'll make it a family vacation!" I said gamely. Jonathan balked. "What if I can't take time off from work? I just started a new job. And I already made plans to see friends that weekend!" he protested.

"We can fly back Saturday," Marc assured him.

I thought of the last time we'd spent Thanksgiving in Arizona with my sister-in-law Jill and her family 17 years ago, a time when we'd still believed we were a typical happy family. Mickey had been 16 months old, Jonathan six. I remembered how when their Labrador retriever Rocky bounded into the room, Mickey had exclaimed, "Dog!" and my fear about his lack of language had temporarily lifted.

We knew, of course, that Thanksgiving was the mother of all travel days. I'm a white-knuckle flyer at the best of times, but it was the new TSA screening regulations I was dreading most.

I imagined them ordering Mickey to walk through the full-body scanner. What if he refused? What if they tried to do the enhanced pat-down I'd been hearing about on the news? Autistic people are often averse to touch. We'd spent years teaching Mickey about the difference between good touch and bad touch. "What are we supposed to tell him now?" I said to Marc. "That no one can touch him intimately—except strangers in airports?" I hyperventilated as I imagined Mickey having a meltdown on the security line. Trying to explain to the TSA agents. Getting angry. Making a scene. None of us allowed to board.

But as usual the news coverage had overblown the issue. Relieved, we got through the security line at Newark without incident. Mickey asked to visit the gift shop, as he always does in airports. He likes stuffed animals. We know he's found what he wants when he clutches a tiny toy kitty or chimp to his chest and says, "Hey there, little fella." Sometimes he kisses it. He walked through the airport, an 18-year-old man-child, clutching a small blue bear. Boarding the plane, he said to the cheerful woman who greeted him, "Are you the flight attendant? You have a beautiful plane." Marc and I smiled at each other.

We gave Mickey the window seat. In order to get him settled, I unpacked his neck pillow, his fleece blanket, his iPod, and a cinnamon raisin bagel, creating a zone of comfort around him. He insisted on keeping the little window shade shut, to Marc's chagrin. "It drives me nuts when he does that," Marc confided. "I feel claustrophobic." I knew how Marc loved to watch the unfurling topography, the ribbons of rivers unspooling below. We both love flying into Sky Harbor Airport in Phoenix, turning and wheeling above the geological outcroppings that ring the Valley of the Sun. The palm trees, the beds of transplanted, tropical flowers blooming in the desert, the terracotta roofs and adobe homes... the landscape looks endless. There's so much sky in Scottsdale.

The flight was fine. As soon as we landed I texted our arrival to my sister-in-law Jill. "Sorry for the crappy weather!" she texted back. "No worries," I told her. We checked into the hotel's guest casita. Mickey unpacked a backpack bulging with a battalion of beanie babies. We inspected the boys' room; there was a bidet in their bathroom. We laughed. Had Mickey's twelfth-grade health and sexuality class covered *that*?

"Jonnie, if Mickey asks you what that is, just tell him it's a foot bath," Marc suggested.

We met Marc's family for dinner at Relish, a fancy hamburger joint with a blazing hearth and winter ski lodge vibe, till you noticed full picture windows that faced foreign-looking fields of cacti and red mountains in the distance. "Look, Grandma!" Mickey exclaimed. "I have an iPod, wanna listen?"

My mother-in-law returned the bear hug I gave her with a squeeze. "You look beautiful!" I told her. She preened, then pirouetted for me. "I've lost 20 pounds on my diet," she told me. Marc settled Mickey in with a pad and paper and sat beside him. While Jonathan talked to Grandma at one end of the table, Jill sat next to me at the other end. "We're in the middle of a really rough patch with one of the kids but I can't talk to my mother about it," Jill whispered.

"I think it's hard for her," I said, remembering how when Mickey's autism was first diagnosed, my mother-in-law had found it too painful to talk about.

After breakfast the next morning, the four of us drove to Grandma Bev's spacious apartment. Excitedly, she pulled me into her closet. "I'm de-acquisitioning and these shoes don't fit Jill," she announced. "Oh, but I just *love* these!" She sighed wistfully. "They're hardly worn at all." Feeling like one of Cinderella's stepsisters, I forced my feet into sky-high ankle boots. I modeled them for Marc, who rolled his eyes. "Having fun, Imelda Marcos? They'll never fit in the suitcase." But I wanted to please my mother-in-law, so I enthusiastically agreed to take six pairs.

"Can we just go already?" Jonathan asked.

"Yeah, Jonnie!" Mickey agreed. "Where are we going?"

Our destination was the newly built Museum of Music, where we all donned wireless headsets. Except Mickey. He refused, suddenly belligerent. He was tired; the two-hour time change wasn't agreeing with him. He insisted on listening to his iPod instead, and threw himself onto a bench. He wouldn't budge. I felt the familiar knot of frustration.

"I've got him," Jonathan said. "C'mon, Mick." He held the wireless headset to his brother's ear, and coaxed him along. Together they listened to Balinese gamelans; Mexican mariachi; Arabian ouds. I watched them, enjoying the fact that they were both enjoying the music and each other. Jonathan has always been able to get Mickey to do the things we can't.

All of us met up again at the gift shop, where Jonathan secretly bought Mickey an ocarina as a Chanukah gift. "I'll teach him how to play it," he assured us. While Mickey eyed a pile of plush bears, Grandma bought him a t-shirt that said, "Music is the language of the soul."

"Thank you, you know how he loves music," I told her, hoping the cotton would be soft enough for his sensitive skin and that I'd be able to convince him to wear it.

"What am I thinking?" Marc asked me as we exited the museum. Our eyes met.

"You're thinking why we have never tried a family vacation to Europe," I said.

He took my hand. "Two bodies, one mind," he said. "Do you think we'll get any time alone together this vacation?" He leaned over and quickly kissed me.

"Highly unlikely," I said. Still, I had to admit to myself that I was loving this. We were vacationing as a family.

Thanksgiving Day was sunny but still cold. We piled into Jill's den for finger food and football, then moved to the dinner table. Mickey ate one slice of turkey dipped in ketchup and half a corn muffin. Then he stood up. "Can I be excused?" Sitting at the table was hard; he had no small talk in him. He went to sit in the den.

Everyone else took turns around the table, sharing what each of us was thankful for. My brother-in-law said he was thankful to have his entire family at one table. One of my nieces was grateful for her "awesome new job in Los Angeles and amazing condo." Another was thankful she got into the college sorority she wanted. I listened to all the gratitude being expressed around the table, straining to think of something appropriate to offer. *I'm thankful to be here. I'm thankful for this delicious meal. I'm thankful for good health.* I was thankful that Mickey hadn't had a seizure, as he frequently did at these holiday events. But I was also thinking about the fact that Mickey was the same age as my niece who'd just gotten into that college sorority, and that not only would he never go to college, he'd never live alone in his own condo or anywhere else. He wouldn't have an awesome new job or maybe even any job at all, and at that moment he was sitting all alone in another room while everyone else was feasting at the table. Normally I felt thankful for both my boys, my loving husband, a strong marriage and caring friends, but just at that moment, I was feeling sorry for myself and hating that I felt this way. *Stop licking your wounds*, I thought.

After dinner Jill's father-in-law joined Mickey in the den. "Who are you?" Mickey asked.

"I'm Harold. I'm Uncle Stu's dad."

"Harold, do you like Snoopy?" Mickey asked. I paused, wondering how Harold would respond. It's hard to be with people who don't know my son. But Harold smiled kindly, so Mickey showed him a YouTube video clip on his iPad, and they both watched. Suddenly Peetie, a sweet black-and-white mop of a mutt, sprang onto the couch. Mickey was terrified of dogs who bark. But Peetie just snuffled, and cuddled beside Mickey on the couch. Mickey stretched out a tentative hand; Peetie licked it. I felt myself relax.

Friday morning I was happy to spend some girl time with Jill. We sat in the hotel's Wellness Center, clad in white spa bathrobes and sipping chamomile tea. Listening to her talk about her mother, I found myself remembering the last Thanksgiving I ever spent with my own mother. She'd been tied to the oxygen tank. I'd cooked an entire Thanksgiving meal at my house, packed it all up and brought it to her, but she could only manage a few mouthfuls. "Everything is delicious," she'd apologized, "but it's just too hard to eat and breathe at the same time." I thought how much Jill would miss her mother one day when she was gone. How much I would miss her too. She is the only parent I have left in my life.

That afternoon, Jill urged Marc and me to take some time for ourselves. We ran off, hand in hand, giddy with freedom. We dined outdoors at a sidewalk café in Old Town, strolled through art galleries, bought Native American turquoise bracelets and beaded belts to bring back as gifts.

When we returned, Jill pulled me aside. She told me that while Jonathan and her daughters played tennis, Mickey had wandered off. I pictured Mickey stepping heedlessly into traffic; horns blaring; the screech and sickening thud of impact. I flinched.

"Don't worry, it turned out okay," Jill hastened to add. "Jonathan ran out and found him. I have to tell you, I was really impressed with your son. He's amazing with Mickey."

Again I felt a rush of love and gratitude for Jonathan. "He's the best," I said.

~◎~

Flying home to New York the next day turned into a 12-hour ordeal. By the time we hit turbulence over Newark, we were all scared and cranky. Jonathan was clearly itching to get away from us. It was nearly two more hours before our taxi finally deposited the three of us in our driveway. As we unlocked the door, Dizzy meowed plaintively. "I'm home! Did you miss me?" Mickey called to her. Although Mickey was clearly exhausted, he was suddenly gleeful, overjoyed to return to the comfort of home.

Jetlagged but too jazzed up to sleep, Marc and I opened the fridge. No Thanksgiving leftovers. No spiced yam pudding. No cranberries simmered in maple syrup and orange marmalade. No meaty-rich mushroom tarts. Most of all, no plump, moist turkey. Suddenly I felt bereft. But what I was longing for was so much more than Thanksgiving leftovers.

I missed my parents so.

Marc stood behind me and wrapped his arms around me. "You have the boys and me," he said softly.

Yes.

We settled on the couch with some sandwiches, switched on the TV and watched a movie about a divorced couple who found themselves rekindling their romantic relationship while attending their son's college graduation. "What's this movie called?" I asked.

"*It's Complicated*," he said.

"Isn't everything?"

"Not us. Don't you know I'm crazy about you?"

"Ditto," I said, leaning my head on his shoulder. He took my hand, and we watched the rest of the movie in companionable silence.

We had known before Thanksgiving that something was amiss with Dizzy. The vet called the Monday morning after we returned from Arizona. "I'm afraid the news on the biopsy isn't good," she said. Dizzy had an aggressive cancer.

"Can we treat it?"

I could tell she was choosing her words carefully. "This kind of cancer doesn't respond to chemo. We could try a course of radiation, but it's not a cure. It might give her a few more weeks. Think about it, and we'll talk more."

We never had time to talk about it, though. Dizzy stopped eating. She crawled under my desk, and stopped responding to any of us. Jonathan spent the night sleeping on the floor beside her. She had been his cat for 12 years; we had to let him make the final hard choice.

"I want to go with you," he said resolutely.

"You don't have to," I said.

"How can you bear it?" he asked through tears.

I sighed. "Because we're the designated grownups around here."

Marc and I drove to the vet's office. We placed Dizzy's tattered old towel on the stainless steel table and laid her down. The vet was infinitely gentle and kind to Marc, to me, most of all to Dizzy. We listened to Dizzy's rasping breaths, petting and crooning to her until she was still.

We returned home with the empty cat carrier. Mickey was distraught. "Where is she?" he demanded. "I want her back. Make her alive again."

I let Alan, Karyn and Cezanne know that Mickey was sad and angry, and would probably be asking difficult questions.

Cezanne emailed to say how sorry she was. She offered to lend us a copy of a book called *The Tenth Good Thing About Barney*, a book for children about the death of a family cat.

By the next day Mickey seemed chipper and upbeat about going to the Red Cross and seeing Cezanne, but later we got word from Alan that Mickey had a meltdown when he got to high school for lunch. Alan said he'd he gotten off the bus angry and non-compliant. Was it Dizzy's death? Something else? Marc emailed

Cezanne to see if anything had happened that morning at the job site. As usual, she had a positive spin.

> He was tired and irritable when he got to the Red Cross. He said he wanted to take a snooze in the lobby, but came into the work area without a problem. Once at the work area he put his head in his hands and banged on the desk once with his elbows. I validated his emotions and told him that it was okay to have an off day once in a while. I gave him the choice of either sitting with his head down/sleeping or doing some work, but if he wasn't going to do work then he wouldn't be able to buy a snack afterwards. He said he was going to put his head down. I went to help Jake get started on some filing and Mickey came to me and said he decided to do some work. He did fine after that. He was his cheerful, polite self. I told him that it was very grown up of him to do his work even though he was having a rough day. I was so proud of him.

Cezanne seemed to have a knack for motivating Mickey. I'd told her that he'd never shown any interest in earning money for doing chores at home. He would empty the dishwasher, take the quarter we gave him, and leave it lying on a shelf. Cezanne talked to him about how much people enjoy earning money, and what he could do with his "wages." "Would you like to try that?" she asked him. He told her, "Maybe."

The next day Mickey hopped off the bus and burst into the house. "I did great at the Red Cross!" he said, and handed Marc a note from Cezanne. Marc read it and grinned.

"Go read this to Mom."

"It says I earned money today!" Mickey said. I handed him a dollar bill, which he immediately placed in his wallet.

Marc emailed Cezanne, "Who knew? This is the first time he ever expressed interest in earning money. Thanks for the great idea!"

"Mickey, what do you think you'd like to be when you grow up?" I asked him.

"A Pokémon Master."

I smiled. There weren't too many jobs for a crackerjack Nintendo player, but Mickey was clearly learning other skills at Millwood.

Cezanne emailed:

> I am enjoying working with Mickey and Jake so much. They really are quite the pair and lucky to have each other as friends. Mickey has grown so much since we started and I can see so much potential in him. His ability to tolerate difficult or tedious tasks has improved exponentially. At the Red Cross for example, he has learned to ask for a break to walk around for a minute (maybe to get a drink) to refresh his brain so he can continue his data entry. I am so proud of him! And I genuinely enjoy his company.

Mickey continued to work on such tasks as making a grocery list and going food shopping; speaking appropriately in a store, bank or restaurant; waiting in line; giving the cashier the correct amount of money and waiting for change. At home we practiced answering the phone and taking a message; doing laundry and unloading the dishwasher; following a recipe and measuring ingredients. Again and again, I tried to discuss making healthful food choices. I got nowhere with that last task.

"Is chocolate a protein?" Mickey asked.

"I wish," I said.

Mickey was building a résumé of work experiences. Clearly he enjoyed it. Some mornings we'd find him up and fully dressed an hour before his usual wake-up time. He'd bound onto the bus.

But his biggest challenge, we realized, wasn't acquiring basic work skills. It was learning the so-called "hidden curriculum": suitable social behaviors in the community and in the workplace.

Greeting others appropriately. Modulating his voice. Knowing that if a task got too challenging, he couldn't say, "I'm out of here!" and make a run for it.

He was still speaking out of context, referring to TV shows or books or events unspooling on the private screen of his mind. We were adept at decoding what he said, but others were not. How could they be? "Honey," I told him, "You have to explain where your thoughts come from. You can't just say 'Count Olaf' without explaining that he's the bad guy from *A Series of Unfortunate Events*. Do you think people can read your mind?"

"It takes a lot of practice," he said.

It did. Often we still got it wrong. Much of Mickey remained a mystery. It was like tuning in a radio; sometimes we heard his signal clearly; other times, we felt lost. "I wish we could clear the static," Marc said. He continued to fixate on his favorite movies, books and video clips on YouTube. We had to banish certain movies—*Airplane, Home Alone*—because he still always picked the most inappropriate dialogue or behavior to imitate. Often he still chose to sequester himself in his room, retreating to an electronic universe. "Can I play till the cows come home?" he'd ask. *He's a teenager*, I'd remind myself. He enjoyed searching the internet for pictures of favorite movie and TV characters, which he'd print out and tape to his walls. Other boys his age filled their walls with rock stars, sexy starlets, political slogans; Mickey populated his with purely imaginary people from Pixar cartoons or Nickelodeon sitcoms like Drake & Josh, or iCarly. He referred to them as his friends. *Friends*. It made my heart twist. But was that for me, or for him? Mickey was just being himself.

I thought about how when Mickey had been diagnosed in the pre-internet days, we'd had no road map to tell us what lay ahead. We'd had to create our own. We were still doing it. Yes, we relied on the few parents we knew who had already forged ahead of us to send back warnings and guidance: "Watch out for the bend in this road that will send you seeking false cures." "Brace for the mud slide of adolescence." "Pace yourselves so you avoid the speed trap of burn-out." Often we stumbled. But sometimes we got it right. Mickey's thirteenth grade year turned out to be one of those times.

At our annual review that spring, Cezanne wrote a formal summary of all that Mickey had accomplished with her.

In life skills, she said, he'd mastered all the tasks involved with doing laundry. In the kitchen, she said, "his strength is noticing when something needs to be done and taking the initiative to do it. He always asks to wash off counter tops and the table and attempts to wash items we've used during cooking or eating. He can read a recipe and understands most of the vocabulary…he is able to create a shopping list…he is consistent with money exchange, using the 'dollar over' rule (where if the price of something is $4.01, for instance, you give the cashier $5 so you don't have to figure out which coins to use) out in the community, shows understanding of kitchen safety, and operates the microwave independently."

Vocationally, she told us, he had mastered steps for using Microsoft Excel, Microsoft Word and the database at the Red Cross, although he needed prompting to continue working and to complete work accurately. His ability to maintain focus on a single task had greatly improved from the beginning of the year. He was now able to tolerate working on a task for up to 30 minutes.

Karyn reported that Mickey's listening skills had also improved. "In fact," she wrote in her report, "when he is called on to recall and relate what others have said, he is able to repeat accurate information, indicating that he has in fact been listening well. He likes the challenge of remembering information and enjoys the positive feedback he gets when his memory for information is accurate. He enjoys the role plays and can often come up with solutions during problem-solving activities. He can be a very positive member of the group when he is engaged."

Everyone agreed that Millwood had been a success.

Mickey had two more years of school remaining before he turned 21. We decided that for the following school year, he would attend Millwood five mornings a week.

We'd been fighting for equal rights and access for years. We'd dealt with the mechanics of protecting Mickey's future. Special needs trust. Guardianship. SSI. The next two years would go by in a heartbeat, we knew. What would happen when Mickey finally turned 21 and that little yellow school bus stopped coming to our front door? I felt as if we were standing at the foot of yet another new mountain. Was it surmountable? How would we muster enough traction for the climb? He had decades of adult life ahead. How could we help build a full life for him after high school? Where and how would he live? Would his seizures impede his desire for greater independence?

And our ultimate dread: who would love him when we were gone?

All parents want the same things for their children: loving friends, good health and work that is meaningful to them. I thought often of the saying, "There are two lasting bequests we can give our children. One is roots. The other is wings."

We were giving Mickey all the grounding and love we had. But what would "wings" mean for him?

always worried about the future. Scared of what would happen to Mickey

BROTHERS' BONDS

"Wings" for Jonathan had been entirely different.

One night when he was still in college, we'd listened to the weekend radio show he hosted on campus as it streamed over the internet.

"And this is a shout out to my parents, who I know are hearing this, which is a little strange. Why aren't you out partying across the street with the neighbors?" he said.

I smiled. He was probably a bit unnerved to think of us listening.

To tell the truth, I was a little unnerved listening to *him*. I wondered: who was that smooth-talking, self-assured radio personality? He sounded so urbane. So manly. And as his mother, dare I say—sexy? He was infinitely cooler than I ever was.

Could this really be the same radiant, skinny little boy I used to take for speech therapy, who liked to watch the video "Cinder-wewa" or told us the sky was "cwoudy"? When he was not quite two and we started a "Mommy and Me" class at the Y, he was the only child who wasn't ready to separate. He'd wrapped himself around my thigh, tight as a tourniquet. He wouldn't let me leave the room; even when he finally decided to play on the floor, it was only at my feet, one hand patting my leg to reassure himself. Once I left briefly to go to the bathroom, and through the cubicled walls of the ladies' room I could hear the heart-wrenching sound of his sobbing. It was embarrassing. Frustrating. All the other mothers were able to leave the room. One morning I tried standing outside the classroom window, wincing as I watched him wail. Another mother named Lynette turned on me. "How do you think he's ever going to separate when you still let him have a bottle?" she said accusingly. I flinched. Lynette was one of those moms who knew everything about raising everyone else's children because she had a career dressing up in a clown suit and running birthday parties for kids. Two weeks later, I felt a gleeful, guilty pleasure when Lynette's perfect little Noah bit another child.

Jonathan had been precocious and quirky. He could always make us laugh. "No Chopin, Daddy!" he said, turning off the stereo when he was two. "Raffi!" One day when he was three, he came home from picture day at nursery school and told me how Eric had arrived at school wearing a jacket and tie and sporting a miniature briefcase. Jonathan said wistfully, "Maybe someday I will grow a tie." He asked 437 questions a day.

Not that we hadn't had our moments. One particularly trying day he came home from nursery school, lost his temper and walloped me. I called a cooling-off period, after which I said calmly, "In this family, we use words, not our hands. Hitting hurts. How would you feel if I hit you?"

"Pretty bad," he allowed.

"Then how do you think Mommy feels?"

Silence.

"Did you hear me?" I asked.

He nodded.

"What did Mommy just say?"

"I dunno."

All the parenting books I read advised me to censure the behavior, not the child. I struggled not to say anything that might permanently damage his self-esteem, such as, "Why can't you ever listen?" I opted for, "I feel bad when you don't listen to me."

A pause. "Mom?" he said. "You're aggra-mating me."

But the delicious moments always outweighed the "aggra-mations." One night at bed time, he confided, "Mom, there really is magic in this world."

"How do you know?" I asked.

"Because there's God," he said. "And the Tooth Fairy, and the Sandman."

"And because there's *you!*" I'd said, squeezing him.

Jonathan was four when I got pregnant with Mickey. Though I was thrilled that he would have a sibling, I felt a twinge of disloyalty. Why would I want another child, when I already had such a smart and engagingly funny one?

I bled in the first trimester of that rocky pregnancy. The amnio was complicated; I developed an infection and heart palpitations. Jonathan sensed it. Anxious about me, he would cover me with his beloved blue blanket, snuggle next to me and pat my head. For the first (and possibly last) time he even offered to make his bed. One day my obstetrician said to Jonathan, "Do you know there's a baby in your mommy's tummy?"

"No, there isn't," he replied. "It's in her uterus."

We brought Mickey home three days after he was born. Jonathan patted him like a puppy. He liked his baby brother. Mostly. "I think Mickey doesn't like our house," he observed after a few weeks. "I think he wants to move."

"Where does he want to move?"

Jonathan didn't hesitate. "Australia."

But Mickey's first smiles were for his brother; he'd giggle and reach his arms, entreating Jonathan to pick him up. As Mickey grew, Jonathan became increasingly protective of his brother.

One weekend when Jonathan was eight and Mickey three, Marc and I took them to lunch in the food court at the mall. I sat at a table with them, and watched as Marc headed back to us with a tray. "Here comes Dad," I said, turning to the boys.

Mickey was gone. He had wiggled right out through the opening in the back of his chair and silently taken off.

"Mickey!" I shrieked.

"He went that way!" someone pointed.

Panicky moments later Marc and I found him standing with his face pressed to a glass wall, mesmerized by the motion of moving water in the fountain below.

Jonathan was an avenging Fury. "You don't watch him carefully enough!" he yelled. Did he really believe we would lose his brother? Or lose him? Did a secret—or not so secret—part of him wish his brother lost? Suddenly I remembered my six-year-old self, a little girl who loved-hated her new baby brother so much that one day I told him to put his finger in the electric socket, just so I could slap his hand when he reached out to touch it. I tried to reassure myself that all siblings feel these things. Jonathan's reactions were normal.

A few weeks later my cousin Marcia offered to stay with the boys one evening so that Marc and I could have a much-needed evening out. I watched from the car window as Mickey, distraught, flung himself against the glass storm door.

"What if this makes him regress?" I said, ready to leap from the car. Marc laid a restraining hand on my arm. "Wait," he said. We watched as Jonathan came up behind Mickey. Mickey whirled around, wrapped his chubby, dimpled arms around his big brother's waist, and pressed his tear-streaked face into Jonathan's stomach. They held tightly to each other. Slowly I let out my breath. "It'll be okay," Marc said.

~☺

But for a long time it hadn't been. In middle school Jonathan told me angrily, "I'm *never* bringing friends home." I asked why.

"Why do you think?"

"Mickey?" I asked, feeling that familiar knot inside me.

"Well, duh," he said, glaring.

That stung. But I understood. Nothing matters more to a 13-year-old than fitting in. Jonathan was often embarrassed by his brother's too loud voice and odd mannerisms—laughing inappropriately, shoving too much food in his mouth, humming as he ate. One night we took the boys out to dinner. Jonathan sat facing me, but his eyes kept darting to another booth across the aisle. The Look. "That man is staring at Mickey!" he hissed. "You should say something. Make him stop."

"Just ignore him," Marc said wearily.

Jonathan glared at the stranger across the aisle until the man averted his gaze. "I'm never eating out with this family again," he said fiercely.

Jonathan was studying genetics in his tenth-grade biology class when he walked in the front door one afternoon and without preamble asked, "How do you know I won't have a child with autism too?"

I cringed. The truth? We didn't—and still don't—know. I offered the only reassurance I could. "That's why I work hard to raise money for autism research. So that by the time you have kids of your own, we'll have better answers."

Sometimes Jonathan was impatient with Mickey, or with us. Angry at the disciplinary double standard. Critical of how we parented his brother. "You just have to be firm with him," Jonathan would say, annoyed. "You're not firm enough. Don't ask him. Just tell him what to do."

"Right. Because that works so well when I tell you what to do," I retorted. I felt defensive and frustrated.

But it was true that Jonathan could get Mickey to do many things we couldn't. Basic things. Wash his face. Chew with his mouth closed. Finish his homework. Mickey might mutter, "Shut up, Jonnie," but he listened to his brother when he refused to listen to anyone else. Mickey idolized him. When Jonathan left for college, Mickey had been bereft, asking if they were divorced.

During Jonathan's freshman year at Carleton, he told me that he was volunteering once a week at a group home near school to spend time with a developmentally disabled young man. The summer he graduated, Jonathan worked as an intern at Autism Speaks. Then he accepted a job as the operations manager at the Autism Science Foundation. "We hired him over all the other candidates because he really gets it," his boss Alison told me.

But I worried aloud to Marc. "He has lived most of his life with autism. Is it a good idea for him to embrace it in his work life as well?"

"He's working out his demons," my husband said simply.

In his early twenties, Jonathan appeared more comfortable in his own skin than I remember feeling at that age. He was close to his cousins, and for that I was grateful. But a mother's worry is never done. I still blame myself for not giving him the brother he wanted. His closest relative will never be a peer. A companion. A confidant. I cannot shield him from that pain. Nor can Marc and I shield ourselves from the pain of that knowledge.

Jonathan knows his brother will never be a financial burden; we have seen to that. But what of the emotional toll? Has he set unrealistic expectations for himself, trying to compensate for what his brother cannot do? Does he feel a survivor's guilt for his own good fortune? Does he realize how much we want him to live his own life? Certainly we've told him. We hope he has heard us.

I have never liked the expression "special needs." When we say children with disabilities are "special," what are we implying about our other children? That they are "ordinary"?

(handwritten margin note: always blame herself maybe more positivity don't blame yourself so much)

Because the so-called typical siblings are anything but typical. They carry their own private, potent payload. Resentment. Shame. Isolation. Fear. Obligation.

Love binds us.

Jonathan has many friends. He is smart and charming and funny and handsome. He was emailing me daily from his job at the Autism Science Foundation. We were sharing resources; he asked advice; he invited me to attend autism conferences with him. His Facebook wall had a category called "People Who Inspire Jonathan."

And next to it?

My photo and name.

Siblings are the profoundly unsung heroes of autism. They are the children who grow up in therapists' waiting rooms, learning lessons in self-sacrifice far too soon.

Jonathan is our hero.

This is a praise song. For him.

LEARNING TO SOAR

During the Presidents' Week vacation earlier that year of thirteenth grade, I'd accompanied my sister-in-law Susan, a cousin, and their teenage daughters on a girls' trip to Paris. All week long I'd sent Marc excited text messages and photos: Notre Dame, dazzling against a dusky night sky; a polychromatic pasta display at Bon Marché; a bateau mouche, slipping beneath a floodlit bridge. And chocolate. Chocolate shops seemingly everywhere. I was mesmerized by the exquisite windows jammed with cunning coffrets, petite pastel macarons and tempting trays of truffles. In the States we call this, rather prosaically, "window shopping." In France, they call it "lèche-vitrine." Licking the windows.

"Food porn!" I labeled the photos I sent Marc. He was hooked.

"Do you think we could ever do this?" he said wistfully on the phone. The connection sounded as close as if he were calling from across the street, not the Atlantic Ocean.

He had never been to Paris. He had never said this before. I felt a flutter of excitement. Could we?

I'm not impulsive (except for agreeing to marry Marc after dating him only two weeks), but I was no sooner off the plane from Paris than I was phoning the travel agent. In a burst of euphoria, I made arrangements quickly. Separate flights, so that in the event of a disaster the boys wouldn't lose both of us. Airport transfers. Travel insurance. I knew if we stopped to think too long about it we would talk ourselves out of it.

Then sobering reality set in.

Marc sent an email to our special needs lawyer. "This is a major leap of faith for us," he wrote to her. "We have never left Mickey at home with caregivers for a week and flown so far away. We are still hyperventilating thinking about it. That being said, we would like to make sure our new wills are fully executed before we leave."

All parents think of these things, but when you have a developmentally disabled young adult son, it's critical. When Marc and I were first married and too poor to travel, I had assumed that there would be time later, once we'd had children and they were old enough to travel with us. But in those early years, the only travel I did was racing with Mickey from occupational therapy to speech therapy to play therapy to therapeutic nursery school and back again. Over the years we attempted trial—and trying—family trips: a condo on Cape Cod, where Mickey wandered away into the road; Washington, DC, where he refused to enter any museums or monuments. Finally, a successful trip to Arizona.

"Why Paris again?" my neighbor Nancy asked.

"Because Marc's never been," I said. But it was more than that. Paris makes me happy. At home, I am the all-consumed mother of a disabled child. In Paris, I become an art and history lover. A *bon vivant*. A *flâneur*—one who saunters. In Paris, I feel young.

We had never left Mickey for a week. He had left us, of course, to go to summer camp. But now he would be the one being left. I shuddered, thinking how often he asked me, "Do people come back when they die?"

"We'll call him every night," Marc and I kept reassuring each other. "We'll Skype. Jonathan will spend lots of time with him. We'll make a big calendar the way we do for camp, so Mickey can cross off the days."

"Will it be too much for Milagros?" I worried aloud. She had been his sitter since he was a baby. They adored each other, but a week was a long time.

"It's time to call in some chips with the neighbors," Marc said.

I thought of the bundles of mail and newspapers and packages and dry cleaning we had taken in for vacationing neighbors in the 12 years we had lived on this street. All the plants we had watered, the fish we had fed, the snowy steps we had shoveled. We were good neighbors. Good sports, too. We'd watched everyone else come and go on their Caribbean cruises and their ski trips to Vail and Vermont. Watched and envied and romanticized the flurry of normal family life, even though I knew that often family travel is more about balky toddlers and sulky teens than spectacular sunsets and strolling on silken sand.

"What about his meds?" I fretted.

"We can set up one of those weekly pill planner trays."

"What if someone drops the tray?"

"We'll set up a back-up tray."

"Like wearing suspenders *and* a belt?"

"Exactly," Marc said.

We were covering all the contingencies we could imagine. But what of the things we couldn't control?

We'd revised our wills, but still needed to write a Letter of Intent. All the books on special needs planning say it's one of the most important documents a parent can produce. I opened one of those books and read, "Imagine if you went away and never came back. Certainly you have a picture of what you would like his life to look like after your death. However, the next caretaker may not have the same ideas and insight as you."

My stomach clenched. "Stop it, "I told myself sternly. I found myself remembering how when I was small, I loved to listen to my mother read aloud from one of my favorite books, *The Emerald City of Oz*. The Wizard takes Dorothy, Aunt Em and Uncle Henry to visit a remote corner of the kingdom called Flutterbudget Center, a town where people worry. Constantly. Obsessively. They begin every statement with "if." When Dorothy hears a woman scream, "Look out or you'll run over my child!" she asks, "Where is your child?" The woman bursts into tears and says, "In the house. But if it should happen to be in the road, and you ran over it, those great wheels would crush my darling to jelly. Oh dear! Oh dear!" Flutterbudget Center is filled with people who have foolish fears and worries over nothing. They let their nerves and the "what ifs" run away with them.

But were my fears foolish? The seizures were real. Autism was real. The guilt *felt* real. How dared I be so self-indulgent? Trips were frivolous. And costly. We should put that money into the special needs trust instead. And trumping everything: my certainty that no one could possibly love or take as good care of our son as we did.

But didn't we count? Any therapist would tell us so. Friends were forever advising me to take time for myself. "It's good for him to see he can be fine without you." "Everyone needs to recharge sometimes." "You'll be an even better parent." "It's important for a marriage." But Marc and I already had a strong marriage. As he frequently said, "We're two bodies with one mind."

"Are we really doing this?" we kept asking each other. Saturday night Marc and I went to dinner at our favorite French bistro. We talked about what we would see and do. "I've been on the website for the Louvre," he said, excited. "I think I finally understand how it's laid out." "Trust me, you don't," I said, laughing. This was the guy I once saw get lost in Bloomingdale's.

As usual, he knew what I was thinking. "I'd be lost without you," he said.

"That's what GPS is for," I joked. Giddy, we clinked our wine glasses. "To Paris," we said.

The next morning I went to get Mickey's meds. I saw a little plastic cup on the counter filled with pills. "Did you put these out in the cup?"

"No," Marc said. "Why?"

I looked closely. They were the night-time meds, not the morning ones. Milagros forgot. She hadn't given him his meds last night. The queasy feeling I'd been living with since booking the trip bloomed into full-blown fear. Epilepsy medication needs to be kept at a constant blood level. If that level falls too much, too fast, he could have horrific seizures. Marc and I stared at each other.

"How can we do this?" I asked.

Later I related this to my neighbor Amy. "You're going!" she said flatly. "If I have to come over here every morning and night and make sure he gets the right pills, I will. I'll even sleep here if it makes you feel better. You're going."

The next day, heavy rains closed the local parkway. I thought, what if there's a nor'easter while we're away? With tree-toppling winds and flooding? A year earlier, we'd lost power for five full days. What if there was an earthquake? The Hudson Valley was full of fault lines. The Kensico Dam might burst. I imagined streams sluicing through the village. A volcanic plume from Iceland had shut down all air travel to Europe. My cousins had been stranded in Germany. What if I couldn't fly home? I thought of planes. Bombs. Terrorism. The Indian Point nuclear reactor was only 20.77 miles away from our house. If it exploded, would Milagros know where to go? I imagined her unable to start the car, fleeing on foot with Mickey and our cats, then pictured coyotes prowling our suburban yards and picking off stray pets and small children.

Someone shake me. Stop it. Just. Stop. Breathe.

Thirty years earlier, right after we got engaged, Marc had asked my mother, "There's just one thing I have to ask. Is your daughter the kind of person who's only happy when she has something to worry about?"

"Oh yes," my mother had said cheerfully. "Why? Are you changing your mind?"

The great regret of my mother's life was that she never travelled to Europe. The reasons were varied and complicated, but I always sensed that what underlay all of them was fear. "Each time I go to Florida and say goodbye to your father, it's like a little death," she once confided.

Yes. Travelling felt like going toe to toe with my own mortality.

But I didn't want to look back later on, as she did, and regret the roads—or planes, trains and buses—not taken. My flutterbudgets needed a tighter leash.

If worrying was an Olympic sport, I'd be a gold medalist. I knew I'd be dithering until the moment I stepped on that plane. But I chose to trust that the plans and backstops we were putting in place would be enough. I wanted to introduce my husband to the place that made me so happy. That would make him rejoice as well. We would picnic in the Bois de Boulogne, and binge on brioches from the best boulangerie on the Rue de Bac. I wanted to wander those wondrous streets together, and watch him fall in love with Paris too. For our thirtieth wedding anniversary, we were going to *lèchons* those *vitrines*. Together.

So we did. And it was perfect.

For all my Hamlet routine—to go or not to go?—I was thrilled to see Paris seduce Marc as surely as it had me. We strolled. We sauntered. We savored Paris and each other. I remembered why I married him in the first place.

From the Marais to Montmartre, from the Left Bank to the Louvre, we walked until we dropped. We tasted our way through vibrant food markets, nibbling wild asparagus and raw milk cheeses; promenaded through the Palais Royal; meandered on Avenue Montaigne; window shopped along Place Vendôme. Best of all, we took an afternoon trip out to Giverny, Claude Monet's country home. It was an Impressionist painting come to life: the wisteria, the weeping willows, the pond filled with flowering lily pads and the synchronized sound of frog song. "I am in raptures," Monet wrote about his garden. We were, too.

The evening of our anniversary, we dined at the Bristol, in a sumptuous, candlelit circular room filled with flowers. As we waited for dessert, Marc whisked out a jeweler's gift case. The soundtrack of *Gigi* was running through my head as I opened the box. "How did you know pearls are traditional for the thirtieth?" I said, my eyes welling up. The waiter suddenly appeared, scattering handfuls of red rose petals across the white tablecloth. Marc and I started laughing.

"It's hokey, and I love it," I said.

Eventually Marc asked for the check. "Your dinner has already been taken care of," the waiter told him. He said something that sounded like "Claret."

Was he offering us more wine? *"Je ne comprends pas,"* I said to the waiter. "I don't understand."

"Your neighbors at home have taken care of dinner. Madame Clarvit? Madame Bauman? They say to wish you *un joyeux anniversaire de mariage.*"

Our jaws dropped in tandem. Yes—those selfsame wonderful neighbors whose papers and packages we've collected, whose plants we've watered and whose fish we've fed over the years, had secretly arranged to treat us to the most lavish meal of our lives.

And on top of all this?

Mickey thrived.

"He's happy," Milagros told us when we checked in each night. "He says he's on vacation and that he's the boss of the house."

"I pushed my neighbor Sam in the pool!" Mickey told us gleefully. The Clarvits took him swimming, out for ice cream, to a barbecue. Everyone checked in with Milagros daily. There were no seizures. For all my worrying, the worst thing to happen was that the school bus driver forgot to pick him up one morning.

We came back rested and restored, feeling ten years younger, a few pounds heavier, and exultant in our hard-won decision to celebrate ourselves.

Marc's cousin Larry emailed me: "Paris. You'll always have it." And we do.

Two days before Mickey left for sleep-away camp, he asked to get a haircut.

No big deal, right? But 15 years earlier it would have been unthinkable.

Back then, the barber shop had been the scene of some of our worst parenting moments. By eight in the morning of the Dreaded Haircut Day, Marc would already be muttering, "I need a scotch before I can do this"—and he doesn't even drink scotch. Bracing himself in the barber chair, Marc would clench Mickey in a bear hug and scissor-lock him with his legs. Mickey would flail frantically, head butting his father and screaming as customers gawked. Marc sweated through his shirt. When the barber declared he was done, I'd take Mickey into my arms. Sobbing and spent, he'd collapse against my shoulder, smearing us both with snot and hair. We tipped big. Very big.

Unable to face a repeat performance, we'd let long months go between haircuts. Mickey's great-uncle Jack liked to tease him. "You look like a girl, buddy!" he'd say. Some days when we'd walk by that barber shop on our way to the deli, I could swear that as soon as the barbers saw us passing, they'd quickly pull down the white shade in the window that said "Closed for Lunch."

I remembered how we used to sneak into his bedroom at night with a pair of shears to give him a trim as he slept. I thought of the time he was five and we took him to a local performance by the Paperbag Players; we hadn't known that they were going to perform a new skit called the "The Horrible, Horrendous, Hideous Haircut."

"NO!" Mickey had shrieked, and every head in the audience swiveled our way.

But now as we entered the barber shop Mickey sang out a cheery "Hi, Dom!" as he plopped into the chair. Dom draped him in a maroon cape, and picked up a clipper. A screen split in my head: I could still picture that terrified little boy, even as I watched my son, nearly a man, sitting solemnly watching his reflection in the mirror.

I waited quietly, soaking in the sounds of barber shop banter, the sports talk, the sharing of summer plans. It was all so completely ordinary. A radio was tuned to a Lite FM station; the song playing was Journey's "Don't Stop Believin." I reflected how anyone who'd seen my son all those years ago would never have believed that Mickey would one day request—*insist*—we take him for a haircut. Yet here we were.

"How's this?" Dom asked. I stood beside Mickey and glanced down; the cape was feathered in a field of light-brown hairs, as covered as a forest floor.

"Let's take it down a bit more," I suggested. "Is that okay with you, Mick?"

"Yeah, Mom," he said, and Dom resumed clipping.

"This feels better," Mickey told me. His hair was crew-cut short; I could see scalp. I think he's more handsome with a little more hair. But Mickey was happy with how he looked, and that was all that mattered.

"Thanks, Dom,' Mickey said softly. Dom dusted a brush with talcum powder, swept it across the back of Mickey's neck. Mickey stood, turned to me and asked, "Can I have a dollar?"

I gave him a $20 bill. He handed it to Dom. "Keep the change," he said breezily. A man of the world.

"Is Dom proud of me?" Mickey asked on the way out.

"Very proud," I said. "You know what? We're all very proud of you."

The whole visit to the barber shop had lasted 15 minutes.

But it took us 15 years to get here.

Later that summer, as he had each year, Mickey gleefully insisted on packing his plastic Groucho glasses—the ones with eyebrows, nose and bushy mustache attached—to take to camp. "I'll make the counselors laugh!" he told me. He put banana slices on his pizza, and then asked, "Was that Mickey's big mistake?" Alan called it "attention-seeking behavior." Maybe it was that too, but mostly, I thought, being funny was just one of Mickey's best ways of connecting.

He was 19, but still as mischievous as he'd been at nine months, when I'd first realized he had an impish streak. He'd been cruising around the couch, and stopped suddenly to pick up a speck of lint. "Don't put that in your mouth!" I'd warned. Quickly he pretended to pop it right in. Our eyes met; he chortled.

I knew that he needed to function more typically to fit in, and being a jokester wasn't always the best way. In public people still stared at him, and I still hated it. But often now, I questioned whether this was for his sake or for mine. I didn't want to suppress what was best in him: his joking, playful, unfiltered, fanciful self. But how to balance the need to fit in against the need to be himself?

Thousands of hours of therapy later, Mickey still struggled to regulate his anxiety. What was it like to have teachers and therapists and family members always correcting his behavior? Did it feel like having an insatiable itch that people forever prevented you—shamed you—from scratching? All those constant nagging reminders: *Chew with your mouth closed. No skipping in stores. Sit up straight. Stop burping. Don't talk to yourself on the street. Big boys don't carry Muppet toys in public.* Mickey was so attuned to others' feelings; what message was he absorbing if everyone he loved and trusted most seemed to level a constant barrage of criticism and disapproval his way? Had he learned to play class clown as a way of deflecting so much unwanted attention?

For years therapists had urged us to encourage more "age-appropriate" interests. We did. But he was still drawn to Sesame Street characters. His bed was piled with so many plush toys there was no room to roll over. He slept with a large SpongeBob pillow.

I'd come to wonder if wanting him to be more age-appropriate said more about our comfort level than about Mickey's development.

Professionals continually told us he had a "spiky" profile: test scores showed an uneven scatter of strengths and challenges. His interests were spiky too. He did have what would be considered interests suitable to his age: he loved watching sports. He enjoyed hanging out at the mall, eating at the food court and buying t-shirts at Banana Republic (which he called "The Gentleman's Store"). He wore Beats headphones to listen to music—Raffi as well as rock. We encouraged his interest in championships, players, team rankings and game rules, which gave him conversational currency with peers.

But if carrying a small Sesame Street Grover beanie in his pocket made him feel safe, why shouldn't he? Don't we all have our transitional objects, or habits and rituals that reassure? How many adults panic at the idea of leaving home without a smart phone? Why did we expect our children on the spectrum to be paragons of age-appropriate maturity, when we ourselves frequently chose age *inappropriate* activities or interests? One of Marc's favorite movies (sorry, hon, I'm outing you here) is the animated Pixar flick *The Incredibles*.

Instead of focusing on having age-appropriate interests, wouldn't we all be better off focusing on teaching our kids the appropriate times and places to pursue those interests? Listening to Muppet music on an iPod with ear buds was fine; carrying a Muppets backpack was not. I didn't want anyone bullying him.

Our role as Mickey's parents, I'd come to realize, was to help him contain some of his impulses by giving him socially approved outlets for those behaviors. "In public, you need to keep your thoughts in your head," we told him. "But you can talk out loud to yourself in your room or your bathroom as much as you want."

Years earlier, Dr. Stanley Greenspan had taught us to enter into Mickey's interests. "Those passions are the window to your son's emotional life," he'd said. I thought about that often. One night when I poked my head in his room, Mickey was engrossed with his iPad. "I'm watching Snoopy," he told me. "He's for everyone. Come see."

I sat beside him. "Looks like Snoopy is doing his happy dance."

"Yes!" he said. "I'm getting ready for my play date with Jake this weekend. Jake *loves* Snoopy."

I shared that with Lauren. "Aw," she said. "I struggled for years to come to terms with him skipping down the halls and singing Barney songs."

The bottom line was this: Mickey worked hard all day to meet other people's expectations of suitable behavior. If he wanted to watch blooper reels from *Reading Rainbow* and outtakes from *The Muppets Movie* when he got home, that was fine. Why shouldn't he seek out things that comforted or amused him? We all do. Marc and I have watched so many *Seinfeld* reruns we could do a responsive reading of the dialogue. (*Not that there's anything wrong with that.*)

It was Mickey's leisure time, not ours. Mickey got to choose. I respected his choices because I respected him. I'd stopped caring if his interests didn't fit someone else's idea of appropriate.

As long as they were appropriate for him.

One of Mickey's best coping mechanisms had always been his sense of humor. It worked. People always commented on it. They engaged, and responded to him. "That absurd Marx Brothers thing," Alan called it. I thought of that when I opened my address book one day and discovered that Mickey had filled it with fake names and numbers. Under "S" he had helpfully included contact information for "SpongeBob." He had also added phone numbers for James Bond, Ronald McDonald, Harry Potter, Fred Rogers, Martin Sheen, Willy Wonka and Sam I Am. All alphabetized correctly.

His comments and questions might be ones you expected from a six-year-old child. Maybe they sometimes sounded quirky, coming from a 19-year-old young man. But they were often insightful, and offered a window into the way his mind worked: *Do sheep wear cowbells? Will you feel better if I get chocolate? How do I have a dream? If farm animals sleep in a barn, who tucks them in?* When I found him poring over the dictionary one day, he explained, "I'm in love with the letter 'U.'" He read aloud: "Unbelievable… unseen…unselfish…" One day when I told him he was staying home from school because he had a cold, he asked, "Am I in for repairs?" Later, when I asked him if he'd napped, he responded, "Yes, before I woke up." Then he came into the kitchen to ask me, "Can I watch Carter Masterpiece Theater downstairs? I'm Alistair Mickey!" Singing "Heigh-Ho, Heigh-Ho" from *Snow White*, he hurtled down the playroom steps.

We savored those Mickey-isms. He was still so literal. He didn't quite recognize sarcasm, although in fact he would ask me on occasion, "Is that a sar-tastic tone of voice?" We loved watching him think. Once Marc asked him, "Mickey, what language do you think they speak in Canada?"

Mickey didn't know the answer, but furrowed his forehead, then guessed, "Connecticut?"

Marc and I smiled. "Actually, they speak English and French," I told him. "Have you ever seen what Canadian money looks like?" Marc handed him a Canadian $20 bill. "Who does that picture look like?"

Mickey studied the image of Queen Elizabeth, and said, "Aunt Harriet."

Mickey still worked with his sports coach Todd on weekends. I'd often get emails from him like this: "I'll be around this weekend if Mick's free. Love that guy. My mood always gets better when we're doing stuff." Todd was a former All State sports champion and minor league ball player, as well as a musician, DJ and radio show host. My neighbor Amy first found Todd to work on good sportsmanship with one of her sons. "You need Todd in your life," Amy said firmly. As usual, Amy was spot on. Todd has worked with Mickey once a week for the past eight years. Despite Mickey's gross motor challenges, Todd taught him how to ride a two-wheeler. Together they rode bikes, shot hoops, roller bladed, played street hockey and lobbed tennis balls. They studied scores and standings in the newspaper. Todd taught Mickey skills and good sportsmanship. Thanks to him, Mickey was literate in sports small talk. Todd had no background in special education, but had unerring instinct, finding fun, visual ways to teach. When a neighbor spoke to Mickey and Mickey didn't respond, Todd would prompt him: "Mrs. Zambetti just asked you a question, Mick, you need to look at her and answer." Todd has given Mickey so much, yet amazingly, he always tells me how much Mickey has given *him*. He worried about Mickey's seizures; often tried to think of ways the school could better work with Mickey, suggesting ways to capitalize on what he recognized as Mickey's many strengths—his prodigious memory; his affinity and skill with computers. Todd and Mickey laughed a lot. "He may be the funniest guy I know," Todd told me. "Thinks funny all the time."

Even when his lines were scripted, Mickey used them appropriately. "You have your mother's eyes," he told me one day. I recognized it as a line from *Harry Potter*. Then he put his hand on my shoulder and asked, "Do you feel the love?"

Mickey saw Harry as a hero. He often said he wanted to be a wizard too. It gave us a way to teach Mickey lessons on friendship. We stressed how Harry was a loyal friend to Hermione and Ron; we pointed out examples of how Harry was helpful, kind and polite. If he wanted to have good friends the way Harry did, he needed to act like Harry. "Even friends sometimes feel angry with each other," Marc told him. "But you always need to make up and say you're sorry."

Friday night before he left for camp, we took Mickey to synagogue. Rapt, he watched the woman who stood in front of the rabbi translating the service into sign language. Mickey lifted and circled his hands in the air in imitation. "Would you like to meet her?" I asked.

"Correctamundo!" he said.

I introduced him to Melissa, the woman who was signing. She laughed when Mickey told her, "I know what 'Shalom' means! It's 'hello,' 'goodbye,' 'peace,' and 'why are you so late?'"

I emailed her the next day to thank her for her kindness with him. I told her, "Mickey is now referring to last night as 'The Service of Hands.'"

She wrote back: "I think he's quite funny and charming, and I had a wonderful time meeting him too."

He continued to surprise and captivate. Waiting for Shana the next afternoon, he called me into his room to tell me, "I have a headache."

"Is that a real headache, or an I-don't-want-to-work-with-Shana headache?"

He grinned impishly. "An I-don't-want-to-work-with-Shana headache."

"You shouldn't say you have a headache if you don't. Do you know why?"

"Because it upsets you?"

"Yes, but why does it upset me?"

"I don't know."

"It upsets me because a headache might mean you're going to have a seizure. I get scared. So why shouldn't you say it?"

"Because you're worried I'll have a seizure."

"That's right."

"Mom?"

"Yes?"

"I have a broken leg."

I stifled a smile. "In that case, we need to take you to Hogwarts and get you some Skele-Gro."

Later that evening I walked by Mickey's room. He was on a break with Shana; they were playing a round of "Go Fish." They loved to be silly together; I heard Shana singing her requests for cards. Suddenly, a deep voice pulsated back, "GO...FIIIIISH..." The sound was rich. Resonant. His voice had vibrato. I was thunderstruck.

"Mickey! Where did you learn to do that?"

"It's my Opera Voice," he announced.

"Can I listen?"

"Sure!"

I called Marc. Mickey glowed with accomplishment. Making grand, sweeping arm movements, he theatrically sang out all the names of all the animals pictured on the entire deck of cards. I felt proud and delighted nearly to the point of tears. Who knew? Marc squeezed my arm.

"My beamish boy," he said.

Mickey came home energized after his first afternoon back in Alan's class the following September. "This is my last year in high school!" he announced. "I'm going to go to college next year."

Where had that come from? Were students in his class talking about college?

Mickey and Jake were now spending five mornings a week at Millwood with Cezanne. Each afternoon they returned to the high school for lunch and classroom time. Jake's mom Lauren arranged an internship for the boys at our synagogue one morning a week, with Cezanne's supervision. They would stuff envelopes, help with mailing, put stickers on books in the temple library and perform other clerical tasks. We were delighted. It felt good. Comfortable. This was the same synagogue that had done such a stellar job years earlier with Mickey's bar mitzvah, and I knew he would feel at home. "Mickey did a wonderful job there today," Cezanne wrote me. "I was so proud of him. We helped the temple set up for Yom Kippur services. Mickey worked for 45 minutes straight putting labels on bags, and another 40 minutes placing the bags on hundreds of seats in the sanctuary. He was very comfortable there."

"He was a little silly and loud today," she reported the following week. "But *very* happy! He actually sang for me today—'The Candy Man.'"

All fall we continued to get her upbeat reports:

October 3: He was attentive and participated the whole time. We did Excel and Word projects, social skills group, and vacuuming.

October 4: Nice day! We went grocery shopping and made chocolate zucchini bread. He loved it! Sending him home with the recipe.

October 12: Super day today! The boys are going to run the school store. Learning to use the cash register.

October 17: He ran the school store with me today. A few more weeks of practice and he will be able to do it by himself.

October 20: We went grocery shopping today and bought apples and butternut squash. Mickey told me he hates squash.

October 21: Mickey gagged when he saw the squash. He was able to put some in a bowl for Jake without throwing up. It's a step. He did a wonderful job today. Worked quickly and quietly and was very focused.

Obviously we were still making no inroads in his food sensitivities. But we were heartened at all the other tasks he was mastering.

November 9: Great day for Mickey! He was happy and productive. We made banana pancakes, did the laundry and ran the school store.

November 11: Mickey did an amazing job at the temple library! We continued stamping the books and we also put brochures into binders. Mickey is naturally efficient. He comes up with the quickest way to complete a task.

"You made my day with that one!" I wrote back that day.

Every day that fall was "great," "terrific" or "excellent." They used Microsoft Word to write stories, went grocery shopping and practiced Cezanne's "dollar over" rule.

November 30: Mickey taught Jake how to make grilled cheese! He didn't need any prompting. Then we practiced sending email.

We were happy to hear he was working on email, and even happier when we started receiving them.

Dear Jonnie,
I'm Hanging clothes at Millwood.
Love Mickey

That's awesome! What kind of clothes?
See you later today,
Jonnie

I'm Hanging Shirts and pants on the hangers today we're making potato pancakes.
Love Mickey

Hey Mick! What are you going to do at work tomorrow?
Jonnie

Dear Jonnie,
Yesterday we played the money game. I made cezanne buy liver milkshake, and earwax apple, and rotten pumpkins. I bought mud muffins, black bananas socks, and sticky chesse shoes.
Love Mickey

GROSS.
Jonnie

We loved it. It was opening and closing those circles of communication that Stanley Greenspan had taught us about years earlier.

Dear Dad
Cezanne And I exchange gifts this morning. I got the disguise Kit
Love
Mickey

Wow, Mickey that is terrific. I know how much you like disguises. Can you show me when you come home? Have a great day at Millwood and the High School. I love you!!
Dad

Dear Mom,
Today we played the money game. Cezanne Bought a button jacket with a ripped sleeve. I bought Gross Gorilla Green Gum
Love
Mickey

Dear Mickey,

You are very funny!

Love,

Mom

After the Christmas break, Cezanne added another job at the County Health Department to the boys' schedule. "Another outstanding day," she wrote. "Mickey was in a wonderful mood and did everything that I asked him to do without complaint. He has also been a really good friend to Jake these past couple of days. I'm so proud of him. He helped Jake tell a story to the students in Classroom One. He did the pantomime and helped with the repetitive parts. I could tell he was a little nervous sitting in front of five kids and five of the staff but he did a perfect job."

Then we started to get more mixed reports. He was still doing well, Cezanne said, but some days he was "silly" or "grouchy." Alan had been reporting some "off behaviors" at school too. Mickey complained that his head hurt, and had walked out of the high school building one day. Luckily Arthur, the class aide, had intercepted him.

"What's going on?" I asked Mickey.

"I'm nervous about going back to high school next year," he said.

Indeed, graduation fever was spreading through Mickey's class. Suddenly, it felt, both parents and students alike were itching to leave the security—and the restriction—of the high school's self-contained class. Many parents were opting to send their children to residential programs far away the following fall. It made me feel coerced into making decisions I wasn't yet ready to make. I roiled with fear, uncertainty and sadness.

I thought how when Jonathan was preparing to go to college, there'd been so many resources available. We'd had a whole shelf of books to guide our family. But for Mickey and us, there was no *Fiske's Guide to Colleges*. No *Barron's*. There is no book for an autistic child turning 20. No *US News and World Report* ranking best vocational opportunities; no handbook rating residential programs for developmentally disabled young adults. We were making it up as we went.

Petitioning the state for legal guardianship had been wrenching. Getting him Supplemental Security Income and entering the labyrinth of federal bureaucracy had been nightmarish. But this step—preparing to leave high school, and the world of what the government promises every disabled child, a "free and appropriate public education," wasn't just unnerving. We were terrified.

Mickey had caught graduation fever too. He had been a twelfth-grader for three years now, and he was asking to leave. Loud and clear. "I'm *not* going back to high school next year. I don't want another yearbook. I'm graduating."

He'd always loved his yearbooks, memorizing the name and face of every person in the building so that when he walked down the hall he could greet everyone by name. Secretly I ordered a yearbook for him. Just in case he changed his mind.

"Everyone is ready to go to college at a different time," Marc and I told him.

"I'm going to college!" he insisted.

Did he know what college meant? He knew that his brother and cousins had gone; he'd seen classmates leaving. He understood that college was the step that came after high school. Alan was telling us that Mickey had reached his academic limits.

"What do you think you do at college?" I asked Mickey.

"I don't know."

"Do you go to class?" I persisted.

"I. Don't. *Know.*"

Did he think it consisted of eating out, hanging with friends and watching televised sports in the student union, as he'd done during Jonathan's graduation weekend? Or perhaps he viewed it as extended sleep-away camp?

"Can we look at colleges this week, Dad?" he persisted.

"Sure, Mick," Marc said. Later he told me, "What do you think he's expecting to see?"

"I don't know that it's anything specific," I said. "I think this is his way of telling us he wants more freedom."

We were saying "college." But it wouldn't be. He was too cognitively challenged for that. "College" would be what we called whatever it was he did next.

Many parents of older children with disabilities advised us to keep him in school as long as we could. "Take whatever the public school system can still give you and hold them accountable," one parent told us. Mickey was legally entitled to one more year. Everyone warned us that once a child turned 21 in New York State and exited school, services for disabled adults were abysmal. "In school you're used to having people with Master's degrees working with your kid," cautioned another parent. "Once you leave high school for day hab, you're getting people making $10 an hour, barely above minimum wage" (day habilitation refers to a range of day programs available to individuals with developmental disabilities).

"But they have high school degrees, right?" I asked.

She laughed ruefully. "If you're lucky."

We couldn't imagine sending him to one of the residential programs other parents were choosing. Who else but us could manage Mickey's complex medical needs? Give him the sniff test to make sure he had showered?

"Do you want to go away the way Jonathan did?" I asked.

Mickey was firm. "No, no, no. I have to sleep at home." I thought about how our cat Fudge slept on his pillow; Moxie slept at the foot of his bed. "Fudge has a kissy head," he told me. Sometimes I overheard him talking to them in the dark: "I love you guys so much," he'd say. He wasn't ready to go. *I* wasn't ready for him to go.

"Residential placement seems so permanent," Marc said, and his eyes glistened with unshed tears. "Camp is one thing. Kids get really grubby there, but we always know we're going to pick him up and clean him up again." His voice cracked as he asked, "Would you pack a six-year-old off to boarding school?"

But day hab sounded like a dismal option. I knew the programs were funded by Medicaid. I'd heard parents describe it as "glorified babysitting." I thought about the first special needs preschool class we ever visited at the Alcott School. Seventeen years ago, and I can still see that impassive teacher who never left her chair or looked at us. How bored she'd seemed. We'd chosen another school. Is that what day hab offered? I pictured a warehouse. Indifferent, untrained staff. Keep-busy activities. Coloring. Stringing beads. A room full of disabled adults, parked in front of a TV for hours.

Not our child.

We had one more year to figure this out. One more year to teach our too-trusting son survival skills he desperately needed. Adolescence and the onset of epilepsy had made him emotionally labile. He could be belligerent when thwarted. Were these normal adolescent mood swings, or the harbinger of a seizure? Often we were still unsure. Anger and irritability could occur hours or even days before one struck, like the hissing whistle of a sky rocket before it exploded. We'd learned how to manage him. How to phrase our requests, how to modulate our voices. We knew how quickly he could flare up and spin out to that angry place, how difficult it was to reel him back. But the world wasn't going to tiptoe around Mickey. It was he who must learn to control his temper. I couldn't imagine that any effective residential life program would agree to take him until he could.

To that end, we enlisted the aid of Mark Krauss, the school psychologist. When we met with him for the first time, he told us, "Mickey is intelligent. He really has some insight into his behavior." It made me teary. In the six years that our son had been in that school building, no one else had ever said our child was intelligent.

Intelligent despite the terrible standardized test scores; despite profound language deficits that even now caused him to mix up his verb tenses or use scripted speech; despite three sedating anti-epileptic drugs that dulled him down. We no longer questioned whether he was innately intelligent. We *knew* he was. We heard it in the observations he made, in the questions he asked, in the way he cut to the emotional core of things. After the death of his great-aunt earlier that year, he'd told me, "I feel so sad. All our people are disappearing."

Still, we had felt cushioned and cocooned by school the past 16 years. Being in school had meant that we'd known where he was every day and that he was safe. We hadn't always been happy. In fact, we'd been so profoundly angry that terrible ninth-grade year that we'd put a prominent special education lawyer on retainer. We'd known what Mickey was entitled to by law. We'd been determined to see he received those services, and he had.

And there lay the crux of our fears: we couldn't keep him safe anymore. We knew our son needed to be stretched and challenged. But the world wasn't safe. How would we protect him, when we were no longer there to absorb the blows? Marc choked up talking about it. "How can we rely on the kindness of strangers?" he asked.

Did Mickey realize that he would never be able to go out into the world unattended? Never ride a bus or train alone? He would never drive a car; epilepsy had seen to that. Living with seizures was like living with the threat of terrorism. You had to stay vigilant, because you could be struck anywhere, any time. Even though he hadn't had a *grand mal* in seven years, the possibility always loomed. His complex partial seizures looked less dramatic, but were no less dangerous. Even if he didn't drop or convulse, even if it was so brief that someone who didn't know him might miss it entirely, a seizure still left him so profoundly disoriented that he would walk into oncoming traffic. More than once I'd cradled him in my arms after one of those episodes, only to have him ask me, "When are my parents coming to pick me up?"

One night that winter, we'd been watching TV in the den when we heard him open the front door. He was wearing nothing but shorts. I grabbed him just as he stepped onto the icy front step. "Where are you going?" I cried.

"I have to go to bed..." he'd murmured vaguely. I knew instantly he'd had a seizure because he had no idea where he was.

What if it had been the middle of the night? He might have wandered barefoot through the dark, snowy streets and we wouldn't have known. That very night Marc activated a chime in the alarm system for every single door in our house.

No one else would watch him that vigilantly. How could we send him away?

Other parents looked forward to their empty nests, to reconnecting as a couple. We had micromanaged every hour of Mickey's life for nearly 20 years. How would we ever shut off our dependency on his dependency?

Would we ever feel free? Or unmoored?

Marc, Jonathan and I agreed that high school was done. But where should Mickey spend his last year of formal schooling? We agonized for months.

Then we got lucky.

In March, a space suddenly opened at Millwood. Someone was graduating early from the transition classroom. They wanted Mickey, and they wanted him immediately.

"Shouldn't we phase him in more slowly?" I asked. "Maybe not make the complete break from Alan's class until the fall semester?"

"You could," the principal Cindy told me gently. "But I can't guarantee we'll still have the slot for him."

We described the program to Jonathan. A full day class. In addition to working on such life skills as cooking, cleaning and laundry, it would give him more time to work on social and workplace skills. Money management. Travel training. Our school district would pay for it. They would bus him there.

"Is this a marriage of convenience?" Jonathan asked.

"This is a very good placement," Marc assured him. "And it buys us breathing room." We would have one more year to figure out what came next.

Mickey glowed when we told him he had done such a good job at high school that he was graduating early and moving up into an advanced program that helped kids get ready for college. That he wouldn't be going to high school anymore. That he would continue to work with Cezanne every morning, and would be in Jackie's classroom at Millwood every afternoon. We told him how proud everyone was with his accomplishments and that this was a very big step up.

He told Cezanne that he was excited to start full time at Millwood, but was also a little sad and nervous because he would miss Jake.

"Jake's been your buddy since you were four," we reassured him. "You'll still see lots of him."

On his last day that week, Mickey's class at the high school gave him a going-away party. Karyn emailed me at the end of the day. He'd been so touched by their send-off, she said, that he'd told her, "I feel loved."

Which he was. Even when he hadn't been easy to be with, he was still lovable.

We crossed our collective fingers, and made the switch.

After his first week in Jackie's class at the new program, Mickey wrote Marc an email.

Dear dad

Yesterday I went to gym and do volleyball. Then I went for a walk. Then I played on the computer. I feel great about my new class.

Love

Mickey

A month later, Cezanne told me, "Mickey has been in such a great mood, really polite and respectful. I think this change has been good for him."

His new teacher Jackie wrote me, "Mickey can be so funny! We continue to learn about and get to know Mickey; he's a great kid. He will be a great addition to the class. Andy, the student you met who likes to go to museums, has already begun to ask Mickey to go on vacations around the world with him (it's his dream to travel) and will ask Mickey questions about his likes and dislikes; it seems to be a good working relationship for Mickey even though he sometimes tells Andy, 'I don't want to talk right now.'"

In May, we had our last triennial. Cezanne summed up everything Mickey had accomplished with her, adding, "Mickey sometimes gets bored with repetitive activities and needs assistance to remain focused and complete tasks."

"Who doesn't?" I said. Everyone laughed.

Mark Krauss, the psychologist who had tested Mickey that winter, had written, "Mickey is a cooperative and kind-hearted person who displayed good focus and motivation on the evaluation. Mickey is well liked by teachers and peers."

Alan noted, "This was the fifth year that Mickey had been a student at the high school. His academic progress had been delayed because of his disability but he has an acute spatial intelligence that is reflected by his vivid imagination and great sense of humor... The area where Mickey has shown the most growth is social skills… He has shown remarkable growth and maturation as a student and a person. He has great potential and with the proper supports can lead a very independent life."

At the end of June, Cezanne emailed me to say goodbye.

> These last two years have been like a dream job for me. I truly enjoyed working with Mickey. I am really going to miss him. Please keep in touch, I couldn't bear it if you didn't.

I wrote back:

> Thank you so much for your email, it made me a little teary! I guess Mickey's not the only one who doesn't like change :-) Of course I will keep in touch, and I hope you will too. We will truly miss you. Mickey has learned and gained so much from you. Thank you for everything.

The following Monday, Jonathan started an exciting new job as a strategy analyst at a cutting edge global marketing and technology agency. Later that week, our neighbor Amy invited us to a backyard barbecue to celebrate her son's graduation from high school. I felt a flush of anxiety. It wasn't about having to tamp down my residual sadness about Mickey and college. Well, okay, maybe it was just a little. Mostly I was worried because there would be 50 or so people there, many of them teenagers who'd never met our son. Would he stand out? Would people stare? Or try not to stare? I didn't know if Mickey noticed, but I always did. It could still pierce my armor and slice straight to the heart.

Mickey, however, was eager to go. He was so keyed up with excitement he didn't even balk when Marc told him he couldn't wear a t-shirt. He pulled on a pale blue polo shirt without protest. "Can I bring my Muppet album?"

"No, hon, not appropriate."

"Okay," he said agreeably. "Next time."

Without even waiting for us, he strode confidently across the street. He greeted people happily, working the crowd. I shadowed him; even as I stopped to chat, I kept my eyes on him. He walked out to the deck; I was right on his heels. He walked back into the kitchen; I stood close behind.

"Can I have some water?" he asked the caterer.

"*Please*," I prompted him.

"Don't follow me, Mom," he said, irritated.

I was startled. But really, who could blame him? I got it. He hated my hovering.

Of course I wasn't only monitoring his behavior. Mickey was excited to be here. Maybe too excited. I worried it could trigger a seizure. I remembered a Shabbat dinner in this same house two years earlier. Mickey beside me at the table. How his head had pivoted toward me, and his eyes had rolled back. The room went eerily still as I cradled him. "I've got you, you're safe," I'd whispered to him over and over until the seizure subsided. He'd been completely disoriented, and had climbed under the table. "I'm going to bed…" he said. Marc took him home. Though shaken, I'd tried to be mordant, saying, "That's one way to clear a room fast."

No young adult wants his mother policing him. Maybe I was being too vigilant. I took a deep breath.

"Okay, Mick," I said. "I won't follow you."

Mickey plunked down at a table filled with teenage boys I didn't recognize; one of them slid over to make room. I thought back to the time Shana had observed him in the elementary school cafeteria. Her report had been gut-wrenching. Each time Mickey sat down at a lunch table, all the other kids got up and moved. Mickey still didn't have much small talk in him. He still struggled to sustain a complex conversation. But I watched as he listened intently and hung in there. No one stared; no one pointed; no one moved away. Later I saw him in the backyard with the other boys, somewhat awkwardly whirling a Frisbee back and forth. I felt a rush of gratitude. The other kids had absorbed him into their group without question.

I wasn't kidding myself; I knew there were many times he still stood out. I found myself wondering, as I often did now, whether this bothered me more for his sake, or mine. Wasn't it really about my own abiding discomfort when it felt as if people were judging him—and by him, I meant us—so critically?

I longed for him to fit in. I always would. But I also wanted him to be exactly who he was: his playful, endearing, unfiltered self. How did I reconcile those contradictory wishes? Was it even up to me any longer?

Our neighbor Nancy's daughter Ali joined me. "I had a great conversation with Mick," she told me. Ali was studying to be a special education teacher, inspired, she has said, by growing up across the street from Mickey.

"Was he talking about the Muppets?"

"Not at all," she assured me. "He told me he's been working out at Planet Fitness with his friends at school. He asked if I wanted to go with him."

I loved that he'd mustered up appropriate conversation. Yes, he could only sustain it for brief periods. But how far he had come, since that day 18 years ago when his first speech therapist told me he might never speak at all.

Marc joined me on the deck. Together we watched three handsome young men tossing a football in the twilight. Our son was one of them. He was holding his own.

"Look at him," Marc said softly. He took my hand, and squeezed. "You know what's remarkable? How unremarkable this looks."

In July Mickey left for three weeks of camp. Happy and healthy. Eight days later the phone rang.

"Something's wrong," the camp nurse said.

For the past two days he'd been lethargic. Not eating. Throwing up. Telling them his side hurt. She thought he was constipated. Or that he might even have a blockage. She wanted permission to give him an enema. I immediately vetoed that idea.

"We'll meet you at the hospital," I said. Marc and I flew up the highway. "Did you bring a copy of the guardianship papers?" I asked. I didn't want anyone challenging us about our right to make medical decisions for our adult son.

"Where they always are. In my wallet."

Mickey must be so scared, I thought. I pictured raucous scenes from television medical dramas. Screeching ambulances. Crash carts. People shouting. Emergency rooms can be frightening for anyone, let alone someone with sensory and communication issues. We burst through the hospital doors, and found Mickey on a gurney, a camp counselor by his side. "Hey, Mom. Hey, Dad." He sounded surprisingly chipper. "I was throwing up."

The doctor on call introduced himself and motioned us down the hall. "The good news is that it's not an intestinal blockage." He pointed to a round blob on the computer screen. "But *that* is a kidney stone."

"Wow," I breathed. "That's supposed to be incredibly painful."

"Yes," he agreed. "I'm surprised he's not writhing in pain. If I had a stone that size I'd be doubled over."

The nurse appeared. I liked that she spoke directly to Mickey instead of us. "I need to run an IV line for you," she told him. "It won't hurt, just one little stick and it's done."

Mickey balked. "No stick!"

I tensed, remembering how Mickey had once slugged the pediatrician who'd tried to give him a shot.

"Honey, this way they only have to stick you once," I told him. "Then they can do a blood test and give you medicine to take the hurt away. Here, squeeze my hand. Don't look."

Still, he yowled, watching the needle penetrate his arm. "The faster we do this, the sooner we take you home," Marc reminded him.

He could handle a kidney stone but not a small, quick needle. His sensory system was still a puzzle to us, but we respected it.

Testing showed he was dehydrated. The nurse set up a saline drip, adding a pain killer and anti-nausea medication. Two saline bags and several hours later, the doctor said he felt comfortable discharging him. "But it's not over," he cautioned. "You'll need to follow up with your doctor tomorrow."

At home that night between bouts of nausea and heaving, Mickey asked plaintively, "Am I going to die?"

The next day our pediatrician sent us to a urologist. We sat in a crowded waiting room nearly two hours as Mickey grew increasingly belligerent: "No doctor! I'm out of here!" But when a pretty nurse appeared, Mickey perked up. "What's your name?" he asked her. She directed us into the doctor's office; finally, a tall man strode in. Mickey lit up with excitement. "Hey! You look like my rabbi!"

"Actually, you do look like Rabbi Jacobs," I said.

The doctor smiled. "I've heard that before. I give shorter sermons." He bent over a microscope. "There's blood in his urine and he's still dehydrated. Mickey, how are you feeling?"

"Great!" Mickey said cheerfully.

Great?

People with autism don't always show typical pain behavior, I reminded myself yet again, thinking how well he'd handled the painful pilonidal cyst. He'd seemed stoic even when he had three wisdom teeth extracted. EEGs and blood draws still frightened him, but when he said something hurt, we knew it must be bad.

And this was very bad. Despite heating pads and medications to ease the pain and help the stone pass. All week he was rocked by waves of nausea and retching. Yet only once did he say plaintively, "Make the hurt go away." Is there anything worse than seeing your child in pain and feeling helpless to relieve it?

"The more water you drink, the faster the kidney stone will come out," we told him repeatedly. One evening I heard him in the bathroom, forcing himself to burp again and again.

"What are you doing?"

He put a hand to his throat. "Getting rid of the stone."

"It can't come out that way," I said. "It will come out when you pee."

"Be on the lookout for that stone," the urologist's nurse reminded us. "It could be the size of a grain of sand. Or even a tiny pebble."

Finally, two days before he was due to have a procedure to blast the stone with shock waves, we caught a fragment that looked like a flax seed in the mesh strainer they'd given us. We brought it to the doctor. He sent us for another X-ray. The stone in the ureter was no longer visible.

"This could have been so much worse," Marc and I reassured each other. Mickey had been a trooper through the ordeal; as always, he was resilient. It was over—for now.

There was another small stone floating in his kidney that we would need to monitor.

But lurking beneath our brave fronts was the fear that never goes away. Someday he would live apart from us; who else would ever watch him as vigilantly? Recognize when he was in pain? Know how best to reassure and comfort him? Advocate for him?

Who would love him that way, when we were gone?

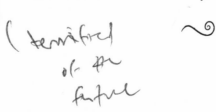

(terrified
of the
future

"Does it feel like we just dodged a bullet with that one?" Marc asked. "I'm exhausted. We could use a break." We'd intended to spend a week in the Berkshires while Mickey was at camp; obviously we'd cancelled those plans.

"We need a day just for us. Want to visit the county fair?" Marc asked.

"Sure. Will there be funnel cake?"

"What's funnel cake?"

"No idea," I said cheerily.

It was a sunny, no-humidity, not-a-cloud-in-the-sky day in late August; Marc and I headed upstate to the Dutchess County Fair. I was looking forward to "just us" time. A day away where by tacit agreement we weren't going to talk about autism. Or kidney stones.

I consulted the brochure. "Horseshoeing…weaving…chicken clucking and rooster crowing contests…husband calling? I think that means yelling, 'Soo-weee' to the hogs, not 'Ralph, pick up your dirty socks.'"

We held hands as we passed through the gates onto the midway, stopping to gape at the food concessions. Fried Oreos. Fried pickles. Chocolate-covered bacon. "And this is why America has an obesity problem," Marc said. Virtuously, we split a Greek salad.

After lunch we strolled through livestock pavilions. *Mickey would have liked seeing the animals,* I thought. But I knew that the music, the crowds, the rides and games would have driven him into sensory overload. I could imagine him fearfully eyeing the oversized stuffed animals and asking, "Do they move? Do they talk? I've had enough!" I remembered the time we'd taken him to the Northern Vermont State Fair when he'd been so terrified of a policeman on horseback that he'd bolted.

We were standing by a pen filled with goats when suddenly a tall boy shoved in front of us. He hung over the fence and thrust out a handful of hay.

A man grabbed him, and hissed, "Stop it! Say 'Excuse me!'"

"No problem, it's fine," Marc said amiably. Autism Radar: both of us recognized immediately that this boy was on the spectrum.

"Really, it's *fine*," I repeated.

I don't know if the man—I assumed he was the father—heard us; he was still reprimanding the boy. I heard exasperation. Anger. Shame.

I wanted to offer reassurance. To tell him how we of all people understood. *Please don't apologize, we're not like all those strangers who roll their eyes*, I wanted to say. *He's not misbehaving, he can't help it. Our son used to do the same thing.* But I couldn't find the right words. I didn't *know* the right words. I was afraid that instead of offering support I'd embarrass him. Or worse, make him angry. I looked around; a woman—the boy's mother?—stood nearby, eyes averted.

I suddenly remembered a time I'd taken Mickey to see Jonathan play clarinet in a school concert. Initially, Mickey had sat quietly. I'd felt relieved, believing he was actually blending in. That no one was staring. Then Mickey began to squirm and talk to himself. I'd handed him a picture book. A beanie baby. A bag of pretzels. He kept squirming. I started to panic. If I couldn't pull something out of my bag of tricks fast, Mickey was going to disrupt his brother's concert. I knew the woman beside Mickey was watching, and inwardly I shriveled. I saw her reach into her purse; then she handed Mickey a loop of string to play with.

"Thank you," I whispered. I wondered if I should say more.

But I didn't have to.

"I have a son with PDD too," she said.

Autism radar.

Later that day at the fair, I saw the boy and his parents again. They were walking between exhibition halls; the father was holding the boy's hand. So familiar, it made my throat ache.

I wanted so much to tell them, "It gets better. It will be okay." But I didn't know that, did I? How could I? That was my family's truth, but every family's journey is different.

Marc reached for my hand and squeezed hard. We didn't say a word.

~⊙

Summer was ending. Mickey returned happily to Jackie's transition class a few weeks later. Fall was uneventful until late October, when Superstorm Sandy barreled up the coast.

The chicken had almost finished roasting by the time the hurricane made landfall. Our lights flickered and went out. I lined up candles on the kitchen counter and called Mickey to come eat dinner.

"Are we having an adventure?" he asked. He sounded nervous.

"We certainly are!" I said cheerily.

All night I lay in bed listening to the wind howl, praying none of our massive oak trees would fall on our house.

We woke the next morning to news of devastating destruction. Enormous trees had toppled throughout the region. Telephone poles had sheared off; electrical wires littered the streets. People had drowned. Entire communities had washed away. NYU Medical Center in Manhattan—a facility we knew so well from our many stays on the epilepsy floor—had flooded. Nurses and doctors had managed to maneuver every single patient, even ones on ventilators, down dark stairways to safety.

We called Jonathan in Manhattan. He'd lost power too. We urged him to take refuge uptown with my brother and his family.

I found Mickey flipping light switches back and forth. "I'm making the power come back," he explained. Magical thinking.

"It doesn't work that way," I told him, "but we can still cook." Luckily we had a gas range. I filled a pan with water, struck a match, and opened a box of macaroni and cheese.

"This is the adventure?" he asked.

"Oh, yes!" I said cheerfully. We had a gas-fired water tank. As long as the hot showers held up, we could hold out.

Day Three after the storm: Halloween was cancelled. I started eyeing all the unopened bags of fun-size candy bars. I distracted myself by making strong coffee, and listened to news on the radio. It was gut-wrenching. A mother's two children had been ripped from her arms by raging flood waters. As soon as Mickey walked in I switched off the radio.

All our food had thawed. We tossed everything into four large trash bags. It was 41 degrees outside, yet Mickey still insisted on wearing nothing but shorts. He hated the feeling of clothes. He seemed impervious to cold.

"Put on sweat pants and a shirt," I insisted.

"No, I need to nap." He climbed back into bed. He resisted all efforts to get him out of the house. Finally we lured him to an early dinner at the deli with the promise of burgers and fries. We were walking through the parking lot when Mickey suddenly said, "Oh, no. I forgot to put on underwear."

Day Four: The eerie silence was broken only by the steady thrum of a neighbor's generator. The power company was saying it would be another week. *Just shoot me now,* I thought.

But I knew I had no business complaining when others were in so much worse shape. We'd been lucky; the house was standing, and we'd had no property damage. I was thankful I didn't live on the Jersey shore, where houses had been swept off their foundations. Or Breezy Point, Queens, so ravaged by fires it looked like London after the Blitz.

Our synagogue had power. They invited families to come share the warmth and WiFi, so we packed Mickey's electronic toys, our phones, the laptop, a power strip and a shopping bag's worth of chargers.

"We're still having the adventure?" Mickey asked dubiously.

"Absolutely," I said, determined to stay upbeat. Marc went online to order 40 D cell batteries for our lanterns. At the dinner table that night I snapped a photo on my phone and posted it to Facebook with the caption: "Dining by lantern light. #Sandy."

Day Five: I thought about packing a bag and going somewhere warm; several families had invited us to stay with them. Which would be worse: uprooting Mickey, or trying to explain his behaviors to people who hadn't met him? How could we leave our two cats? Fudge was elderly; she had a heart murmur. After I heard a policeman on the radio say, "Empty houses are a burglar's dream," I decided to stay put.

Our synagogue invited people without power for a Shabbat community dinner. "Can Wario come?" Mickey asked. Wario was the four-inch beanie baby Nintendo character he used to carry with him for comfort years earlier. He jammed Wario in his pocket. We entered the sanctuary, feeling shell-shocked in the dazzling light. Clutching Wario, Mickey bopped beside us in time to the music. Afterward, he worked the crowd. Attention must be paid. Mickey walked up to the new rabbi and introduced himself. "He's glad-handing like a politician!" Marc said, marveling.

"He feels safe here," I said.

Day Six: The cold was relentless. Our beds were piled high with quilts and comforters. Marc and I heard reports of gasoline shortages. Someone had pulled a gun on the gas line. Or maybe it was an axe.

On the way to the diner Mickey announced, "I'm going to order a burger and fries to cheer me up." He asked if he could get a new game for his Game Boy, and told me, "I'm going to stay in Best Buy till the cows come home."

Day Seven: Daylight Saving Time ended. Reluctantly we turned back our clocks. The house was dank, and we were dispirited. My muscles ached from shivering. A week in, our cat Fudge still waited patiently for warmth in her customary spot atop the kitchen heating vent. "Is Fudge dying?" Mickey asked fearfully.

"Of course not, honey," I told him. "She's just cold."

The temperature plummeted into the thirties. What if the pipes froze? The wind picked up; a radio announcer said a nor'easter was heading our way. How much longer would this last? Would we?

My friend Ellen had power, and we were grateful when she cooked and brought us a deliciously hot dinner. Mickey bolted his food, then climbed back into bed to cuddle under four quilts with Fudge. Marc opened a bottle of Chardonnay we'd been saving; it had chilled to perfection in our unheated house. We ate in front of the fireplace. It felt basic. Primitive. I thought of a refrain from the HBO show *Game of Thrones*: "The night is dark and full of terrors." I wondered what terror the dark held for Mickey. Our bit of heat didn't even reach the rest of the room; it was black beyond the fire's protective glow. We huddled close to the hearth in our circle of safety.

Marc attempted to read a book, finally putting it aside. "Maybe Abe Lincoln could read by firelight, but I can't."

"I'll never take our creature comforts for granted again," I said, even though I suspected I would be doing precisely that a month later.

Day Eight: Millwood reopened.

"I'm not going," Mickey said flatly. "First lights. Then school." He struggled to explain, and finally said, "I want to have an adventure with *you*."

Did he think "adventure" meant excitement, or deprivation? He had endured darkness and freezing temperatures, shortage of favorite foods, the disruption of comforting routines. He had seemed so resilient. It was the thought of leaving us that unhinged him.

"How do people die?" he asked.

"They get very old or sick," Marc said. "Or sometimes they have an accident."

"Did Aunt Tessie love me before she died? Did Uncle Stanley?" he asked.

"Of course," I said. "Very much."

"Because I'm a favorite kid?"

"Yes," I told him.

"I'm a cute little guy?" Sometimes his sweetness slayed me.

"I miss my friend Caitlin so much," he confided. His high school friend Caitlin was away at school. He was grappling with more loss than I'd realized.

We were recharging our devices in the synagogue library when our neighbor Nancy called to tell us our street had power.

"The adventure is over?" Mickey asked.

"It is," we reassured him. "Everyone is warm and safe."

But of course that wasn't true.

We take it as given that electricity will always flow. That fuel will be readily available. That the food supply is limitless. Superstorm Sandy had reminded us how vulnerable we were, and that safety was a fragile construct.

We'd no sooner gotten back on the power grid when Thanksgiving was upon us. As always, I reveled in it. But no matter how much fun we were having, no matter how full my heart was with goodwill and satisfaction and joy, each year I reached a moment when I needed to escape after cooking dinner for 24 people. A point when everything became too much. An aural assault. I felt an overwhelming need to step outside into the November night air. Each year I made the same excuse—"I just need to shake out the crumbs from the table cloth"—and stepped onto the front porch. The blast of cold air on my face was bracing. Reviving. Sound fell away and the world went silent.

That year, as I took in great gulps of wintry cold air, it struck me: this is how Mickey must feel when he reached the tipping point of sensory overload and said, "I've had enough."

When Mickey was eight and Jonathan 13, we'd flown to Arizona for our niece's bat mitzvah. Mickey fidgeted but managed to sit through the religious service, even singing along to familiar songs. At the end of the ceremony, we moved across the hall into the banquet room. We slammed up against a wall of thrumming music and flashing lights. Mickey flung himself to the floor and clutched his hands over his ears. People stared. Then they stepped over him.

Embarrassed, I'd tried to coax him up. He wouldn't budge. "This isn't going to work," Marc said. "I'll go back to the hotel with him."

"But your entire family is here, I don't want you to miss out," I said. "You and Jonathan should stay. I'll take Mickey back."

We'd returned to our spacious, serene suite. I called room service and ordered Mickey's comfort food: a burger and fries. After dinner he played with his Game Boy. I read a novel. We were both perfectly happy. The truth? I didn't like loud parties either.

 Having a child with these sensitivities opened a window into myself. I'd always hated crowded rooms. Strobe lights. Roller coasters. I'd thought it was a character flaw. I didn't realize it was just the way I was wired.

Just the way *he* was wired.

"I've had enough." He said it adamantly, often while the rest of us were still having fun. For years I cajoled. Reasoned. Even bribed him. I wanted him to sit longer at religious services. Stay later at the party. Last through the movie.

Did I have my own agenda? Was it more about my desires than his? Or had I been beating myself up too much? Mickey had always resisted anything unfamiliar, whether tasting a new food or trying a music program. I believed it was my job as his parent to expose him to as many new experiences as I could. I wanted to open the richness of the world to him. When was it okay to push? How hard? When to pull back? It was an intricate dance, and I was still learning the steps.

It took me a long time to understand that he didn't mean to be difficult or self-absorbed. He was simply advocating for what he needed. Just as I needed my moments of respite and retreat, Mickey did too.

Which was a good thing. A marvelous thing, in fact.

Standing there that Thanksgiving night, inhaling the cold, restorative air, I finally shook out more than table cloth crumbs.

∽୬

Chanukah followed right on the heels of Thanksgiving.

"Can I get Annie for Chanukah?" Mickey asked.

"You mean the musical?"

From his lack of reaction I could see he didn't know that word. "You mean Annie who sings?"

"Yes."

"What does she sing?" I asked him, just to be sure I understood what he wanted.

"'It's a Hard Knock Life.'"

"That's *Annie*, all right," I agreed. "Add it to your Chanukah list."

He liked making lists. That year's consisted of "dark green shirt, maroon shorts, Sonic the Hedgehog movie."

"Is there something you'd like for Chanukah?" I asked Jonathan.

"You can check my wish list on Amazon," he said. I did. As usual it was modest: books and a seltzer maker. Neither of the boys ever asked for much.

I wondered if they thought of Chanukah as the Jewish Christmas. I know I did at their age. We Jews frequently talked about the December Dilemma: how could we create a meaningful holiday for our kids without going completely overboard and trying to compete with Christmas? Chanukah was only a minor holiday in the Jewish calendar. A little history here: Chanukah celebrates the Jewish Maccabees' victory in 167 BCE over the Syrian-Greeks who had seized their temple and dedicated it to the worship of Zeus. When the Maccabees took back the Temple, they discovered they had only enough lamp oil to last a day; miraculously, it burned for eight. That's why we celebrated for eight days, and why we ate all that food fried in oil.

"Are my cats Jewish?" Mickey asked.

"Cats don't have a religion."

"They're Christian?"

"No, cats don't have a religion."

"My cats are Jewish," he insisted.

I didn't really know what being Jewish meant to Mickey, let alone Chanukah. I grew up in the parish of St. Andrew Avellino in Queens, where Catholic kids left school early Wednesday afternoons to attend catechism class. Every December I felt like an outsider when our family drove around the neighborhood at night to admire the lights. Year after year, we would marvel at a tinsel-draped tree in the large picture window of the white brick ranch house on the corner. It was glorious and greeting card perfect. It made me wistful, the same way Judy Garland's voice did when she sang "Have Yourself a Merry Little Christmas." I'd longed to live inside a cozy holiday movie like *Meet Me in St. Louis* or *White Christmas*. My friends' houses were filled with fragrant fir trees; I envied them all the sugar plums and Santa lore. I was mad for marzipan and meringue, peppermint canes and candied fruitcake. (Okay, the fruitcake not so much.) While they feasted on eggnog, sugar cookies and plum tarts, my family got to eat…fried potatoes latkes. Sure they were good, in their oily, artery-clogging way. But the chocolate gelt in gold mesh pouches my parents handed out couldn't compete with gingerbread houses. Norman Rockwell had a lot to answer for.

I wondered if Mickey or Jonathan felt any Christmas envy. Or was I projecting my own ambivalence? Did Mickey think of Chanukah with its eight days of presents as some kind of souped-up birthday?

This year, "eight days" had such personal resonance. During the ordeal of hurricane Sandy six weeks earlier, we'd lost power for… eight days. During those dank, dark nights, we'd huddled close to the hearth. It had been inky black beyond the fire's protective glow, and I'd found myself understanding on a visceral level why for millennia, people stared down darkness with celebrations of light. Every culture had its version: Chanukah. Christmas. Kwanzaa. St. Lucia's Day. Diwali. Yule.

Mickey added one more thing to his list. He asked to order a rare Jim Henson Sweetums Deluxe Action Figure. He found it on eBay. Together we placed the order. It arrived mid-week during Chanukah; I wrapped it and put it by the menorah, next to a sack of milk chocolate gelt. Mickey vibrated with excitement that evening, barely able to contain himself through the lighting of the candles, the chanting of the blessing. "Oh boy!" he chortled, tearing into the wrapping paper. "He's here! He's here!"

I watched his elated face in the flickering candlelight. Did it really matter what Chanukah "meant" to him? Couldn't it be enough for me, to see how happy something so simple made him?

Because oh, it did.

And what joy, to see such joy.

"I miss my friend Caitlin so much," Mickey told me again in January. He'd seen her briefly over the Christmas holiday.

"Would you like to write to Caitlin on Facebook?" I asked.

"Sure!" he said, excited.

Except that he wasn't on Facebook. When Alan had suggested setting up an account for him a year earlier, I'd resisted. It had stirred up my ever present fear of people taking advantage of Mickey's naïveté.

But now it seemed like a good opportunity. Mickey didn't love phone calls; maybe he would find it easier to communicate in writing, even though he still didn't particularly enjoy email. Lately he seemed to see it as a chore his teachers or we made him do.

I looked up articles on keeping kids safe online, eager for advice. All I found were safety measures I'd thought of already— telling him not to post his address, phone number or any other personal information. A year earlier there had been some talk that Facebook might introduce an "under 13" service, but that hadn't happened yet. Even if it did, it wouldn't replace parental supervision. It was still up to us.

One morning while Mickey was at Millwood, I set up a Facebook account for him. I applied the most stringent privacy settings possible. Then I hesitated. Besides Caitlin and other classmates, who would he friend? Family? Many of his cousins were typical teenagers, and I'd seen some of the wildly inappropriate stuff teens tend to post. Could I depend on them to exercise good judgment in what they shared with Mickey? Unlikely.

Then I thought about some of the things I'd posted myself, articles I wouldn't want him reading. But if I was even worrying about the stuff *I* posted, was anyone—except Grandma Bev, or my sister-in-law's dog Buddy (yes, even Buddy had his own Facebook page)—entirely safe for him to friend?

When I first suggested Facebook he seemed enthusiastic. But when I told him I had actually set up his page and wanted to show it to him, he looked nervous.

"Maybe later."

Was that his usual resistance to anything new? Or something else?

"You can look at all your friends' pictures," I coaxed. He loved poring over our cartons of family photos. He particularly enjoyed what he called "the married pictures"—my wedding album. I got it: pictures were safe. Predictable. The images never changed.

He shrugged me off. "Not now. I'm a little busy."

Briefly I considered sending out a few friend requests on his behalf, thinking to lure him in that way. But what would be the point? Then it would just become one more thing I did for him. It had to come from him because *he* wanted it. Otherwise it had no meaning.

I knew how much he wanted to be social. Mickey was never shy about approaching people; it was that once he got there, he didn't know what to say. He'd been verbal for so many years now, but I still often needed to stand alongside like an interpreter, explaining or prompting him. He still struggled to understand social nuances. Would it be easier for him to interact online, where he wouldn't have to worry if he was standing too close, or speaking too loudly? The down side, of course, was that if you stripped away all the visual cues imbedded in body language, it would be even easier to misinterpret what people were saying.

Facebook could be a minefield even for typical teens. Mickey was so literal; would he understand that sometimes a "friend" on Facebook wasn't really a friend? If he saw photos of his friends having fun without him, would he feel left out? He'd been through that in twelfth grade. I never wanted him to feel such misery again. What if he got de-friended on Facebook? I knew how hurtful it felt when it happened to me—and I was a grownup with emotional filters firmly in place.

As a journalist, I appreciated being able to crowd-source questions on Facebook, and to read and share articles. (And okay, yes, I enjoyed all those cat videos too.) That was *my* Facebook. But I envisioned Mickey's Facebook as something entirely different: a cyber mall, a place to hang out with some buddies.

Since the past spring when many of his classmates had graduated and gone on to post-secondary school programs, Mickey seemed very alone to me. He was watching far too many videos on YouTube. He'd taken to referring to movie characters as his "friends."

Which killed me.

Was he as lonely as I feared?

I desperately wanted him to have real friends. But was I projecting my own worry about his loneliness?

And if so, was setting up a Facebook account in his name really for him?

Or for me?

I let it go.

Later that month, after a long stretch of Mickey being seizure-free, the neurologist suggested we try to taper the Topamax. Mickey still took a hefty dose, but Marc and I began to notice subtle changes. Was Mickey scripting less? Speaking more spontaneously? Several people remarked that he seemed "more conversational."

"We're clearing the static," Marc said.

We were in the car with Mickey one afternoon when I mentioned to Marc that a friend had just dyed her hair.

"WHO DIED?"

I was startled. Mickey was wearing headphones and listening to music. How had he even heard me?

"No one died," I reassured him. "I was talking about hair dye."

"Die?" Mickey said. "Like passed away? Old or sick?"

"No, like dyeing your hair a different color. It's spelled differently. D-Y-E. Remember how you painted your hair blue for April Fool's Day last year?"

"Not D-I-E?"

"No. D-Y-E."

"Oh!" Mickey said. "They're homonyms."

Homonyms?

"Did you hear that?" I asked. Marc was grinning.

"I sure did."

Where had he dredged up that word? Okay, technically it wasn't a homonym, it was a homophone. *But still.* I dimly remembered an elementary school teacher sending home a work sheet on synonyms and antonyms. That was ten years ago. Had almost halving the dose on just one anti-epileptic drug made this huge a change?

Homonyms. I was stunned. Thrilled.

But once more, the what-ifs and the if-onlys pinched my heart. Who might he have been without those drugs?

"I have sad news," Mickey said, coming off the school bus in February. "Molly died."

Molly was a beloved administrative assistant at Millwood. I knew she'd been battling lung cancer for two years.

"I feel so sad," Mickey told me. "Even my Muppets are sad." His way of underscoring the intensity of his feelings.

All through dinner and into the evening, he continued to ask about Molly. "Why did she die?" "Was she old or sick?" "Does she have children?" "When will she be buried?"

Early the next morning I emailed his teacher Jackie a heads up that Mickey was upset. She wrote back:

Mickey was talking about Molly's death here, too. Another student made a big announcement in the classroom; we as teachers, felt it was up to parents to decide if and how they wanted to let their children know—it was unfortunate that [the other student] announced it that way, but that's the way it goes sometimes. We did acknowledge Molly's death to Mickey and helped him through it here. We will continue to do so should he continue to want to express himself.

We'd struggled down this road with him many times in the past ten years. I came from a large family, and most of my elderly aunts and uncles had died. Two of our four cats—Dizzy and Moxie — had died. Aunt Jill's dog Peetie had died; so had a neighbor's dog. Each time Mickey had asked the same *old or sick* question, followed by, "When are my other cats going to die?"

It's always hard to talk about death, but even harder to explain it to Mickey. We continued to emphasize that even after someone died, the love we felt for that person lived on forever in our hearts. But at 20, he continued to be literal and concrete in his thinking, so we weren't sure how he processed our explanation.

What we did know was that he was grappling with a lot of loss and change that year. All his friends from high school were gone. His best friend Jake, a few years younger than Mickey, was at a residential program for the next two years. Lauren had learned that New York wasn't building any new group homes for kids who would be aging out of the system in the near future; Jake's best shot at getting a good placement in a group home was by going the residential route now, before he turned 21. It was a painful choice. "We love him so much," she told me, "but on the other hand we know we have to think for his future for when we are not going to be here." Their friend James had gotten his driver's license and graduated. "He did everything the high school could offer and whatever they allowed him to participate in—sports, chorus, internships—but school had nothing left to offer him,"

Miriam said. James was headed to "Think College," a nationally affiliated, supportive program dedicated to developing, expanding and improving inclusive higher education options for people with disabilities. "He wants to feel like a college student," she said. "He's earned the right to have that experience."

Which meant that Mickey was spending his last year alone. He knew that Marc and I would soon be visiting day habilitation programs, trying to find one that would meet Mickey's needs. We didn't call it that, of course. We were still calling whatever came next "college."

"Do I have to take a plane to college?" he'd asked several times. We offered comfort and reassurance. "You'll still live here at home with us and the cats," we told him. Twice now in the last six months he'd wound up in the emergency room, first with the kidney stone, then with a flare-up of the pilonidal cyst. I knew he was feeling vulnerable. Again and again he said, "Come in my room and sit with me." Hoping to help him find words to express what he was feeling, I asked him, "Why do you want me to sit in here?"

He said simply, "Because I love you."

Getting on the school bus two days after he learnt of Molly's death, he noticed one child was missing. "Where is she?" I heard him ask the driver. "Did she die?"

[handwritten margin note: really cares about people]

He was brooding; his anxiety was palpable. All day I worried, knowing that when he felt that way, he sometimes got belligerent. Whenever the phone rang, I expected it to be Jackie, reporting a meltdown.

But the call didn't come. At the end of the day Jackie sent an email:

> Mickey and I talked about Molly this morning. I suggested he make a card for her family and he liked this idea and made three. He also wanted to buy flowers for the family from the A & P. A staff member who is going to the wake tonight will

take his cards and flowers to the funeral home; it was very thoughtful of Mickey to want to do these things. We know he has a good heart :0)

Indeed he did. And the heart, as they say, is a very resilient little muscle.

~ᴏ)

"Remember, no plane to college," Mickey said in March.

"No plane," Marc said. "You can go to college and still live here at home."

While many of our friends and their children were visiting campuses that spring, Marc and I were doing our own version of the college tour. We were finally visiting day habilitation programs.

Some context: in the later part of the nineteenth and earlier part of the twentieth century, people with disabilities were perceived as unproductive and in need of care, which led to the growth of institutions as the primary service system for persons with developmental disabilities. By 1965, Willowbrook State School on Staten Island in New York City, with a population of 6000, was the biggest state-run institution for people with mental disabilities in the United States. Senator Robert Kennedy toured the institution that year and said that people were "living in filth and dirt, their clothing in rags, in rooms less comfortable and cheerful than the cages in which we put animals in a zoo." In early 1972, Geraldo Rivera, then an investigative reporter for WABC-TV in New York, conducted a series of investigations at Willowbrook, documenting the deplorable conditions, as well as physical and sexual abuse of residents by members of the school's staff. The exposé, entitled *Willowbrook: The Last Great Disgrace*, drew national attention. The deinstitutionalization movement gained traction. People with disabilities began to challenge societal barriers that excluded them from their communities. Parents of children with disabilities began to fight against the exclusion and segregation of their children. In 1990, Congress passed the Americans with Disabilities Act, acknowledging that people with intellectual and developmental disabilities have a legal right to live in the community and receive necessary services and supports. This law was reinforced in 1999, when the United States Supreme Court held in *Olmstead v. L.C.* that unjustified segregation of persons with disabilities constitutes discrimination in violation of title II of the Americans with Disabilities Act. The courts have consistently upheld a person's right to receive services in the least restrictive environment possible.

Day habilitation programs typically operate Monday through Friday, from 9am to 3pm. They are Medicaid-funded and are built on a therapeutic model (i.e. the goal is to rehabilitate a client to whatever degree possible). The programs focus on giving participants the personal, social and vocational supports needed to live in their community. Ideally, a day hab program will be person-centered and provide a safe, respectful and stimulating environment that gives participants choices over their daily activities. The program should emphasize independence and opportunities to grow. A good program encompasses daily living skills, health and fitness, recreation, and educational opportunities. It should also foster employability, through meaningful volunteer projects at local businesses and agencies.

But just as with anything else, there is no such thing as a one-size-fits-all solution, and unfortunately, as we were about to see, quality varies widely from one day hab setting to the next.

"There's a Harvard for Mickey," my neighbor Amy insisted. She'd been saying this to me for years. "There's a great program out there. You'll find it."

I wasn't so sure.

Mickey wasn't ready yet for the kind of permanent, residential program Amy meant. We'd seen a "Harvard"; another neighbor's daughter had been there the past ten years and we'd visited. It was a vibrant, integrated community for developmentally disabled adults two hours away that offered employment, recreation and supervised living—a full life. What made it a Cadillac to us?

Everything. We liked their central philosophy: that the spirit, talents and hopes of their students are the strengths upon which to build. The program is a private, non-profit educational model serving 165 adults with a full range of individualized services and programs that blend direct instruction, individual counseling and experiential learning. Many things made it appealing to us: the caring, experienced and skillful staff; a safe and convenient campus along the beautiful Connecticut shoreline; good access to public transportation; and especially their commitment to serving the long-term needs of their members.

The entrance program is a three-year, post-secondary program for individuals 18 or older. It provides a two-year residential phase in a dorm-like setting, followed by a one-year phase in local transition apartments. After completing the program, individuals enter an outreach program and live independently in the community, while receiving support services as needed. They are well integrated in the community. They use the bank. The drug store. The health club. We met young adults in the program who reminded us of Mickey; all of them seemed happy.

The program has more than 100 staff members; 56 percent have been employed there for more than five years, and 27 percent for more than ten years, which is a far cry from employment statistics at typical day hab facilities, where, according to a federal Department of Health and Human Services report in 2004, the combined, annual average staff turnover rate for programs serving adults with developmental disabilities is 50 percent, a figure the report notes would be considered debilitating in most other industries. Among the reasons most often cited for such high turnover/vacancy rates: low pay/inadequate benefits, excessive client to staff ratios, physical or behavioral challenges presented by clients, inadequate training and limited professional status.

The key difference, of course, is that comparing the Connecticut program with a day hab made as much sense as comparing hair dryers to toasters. How could a government-funded program possibly measure up against a private, pay-for-it-yourself model? Nonetheless, that Connecticut program was our lodestar. Our hope.

But not yet. Mickey wasn't ready to leave home; he wasn't even ready for a day program "without walls." Programs without walls have no central location. They offer a daily and shifting roster of activities, all out in the community. Mickey still needed a home base. If he had a seizure he still needed to sleep it off. He couldn't do that if home base was hanging out in the local library or mall.

I obtained a directory of day hab programs from the County Department of Community Mental Health and started calling. I wanted to screen them before we brought Mickey. "What do you want for your son?" one social worker asked. I was taken aback; wasn't it apparent why I was calling? I told him about my son's medical needs; his anxiety; his quirky sense of humor. I rattled off the obvious: community integration, vocational skill building, volunteer work, social opportunities with his peers. Then unexpectedly my eyes welled up.

"I want him to be happy," I said.

What I didn't want for him was a sheltered workshop. Alan had often mentioned that as a possibility, based on his experience working in group homes years earlier. I had a horror of sheltered workshops. They may be appropriate for some people, but I don't think they should be the default mode. Typically they employ workers with disabilities at sub-minimum wages doing some kind of assembly work, such as collating products. I thought Mickey could do more.

Fortunately, this situation is changing for special education students. The US Senate recently voted to approve a sweeping jobs bill known as the Workforce Innovation and Opportunity Act, which would prohibit individuals with disabilities age 24 and younger from working in jobs paying less than the federal minimum unless they first try vocational rehabilitation services, among other requirements. The legislation also mandates that state vocational rehabilitation agencies work with schools to provide "pre-employment transition services" to all students with disabilities. In June 2014, the Department of Education announced a major, significant and long-overdue shift in the way it oversees the effectiveness of states' special education programs. Education Secretary Arne Duncan issued a new accountability framework that will raise the bar for special education and improve educational outcomes of America's 6.5 million children and youth with disabilities.

I made appointments to visit several day hab programs. Just as high school seniors know immediately—through some alchemy invisible to their parents—whether the school they're visiting is a good fit or not, Marc and I found we had immediate, visceral responses too. At the first day hab program we walked into, no one asked us anything about our son. We were assaulted by noise. Older adults in wheelchairs were crammed around tables; one woman read aloud from a newspaper though no one was listening. The administrator referred to the people in the room as "consumers." I didn't like that word. It was antiseptic. Dehumanizing. I didn't like that place. I hated the way the administrators spoke to the consumers with that false, hearty cheer and mock excitement people often use with children. Five minutes in, I was ready to bolt.

But Marc and I managed to walk politely through the facility and ask questions.

"What does a typical day look like here? What kind of training does your staff have?"

The response stopped me cold: "They all have high school diplomas, or high school equivalency."

Welcome to the world of adult services.

It felt like falling off a cliff.

In school, Mickey had been entitled to services. Now we had to seek help from social services, a fragmented system notoriously difficult to navigate. And adult services, I was realizing, were all about eligibility. We weren't guaranteed anything.

Peter Gerhardt, a nationally recognized expert on transition issues whom I've often heard speak at autism conferences, says:

> An entire generation of our nation's most vulnerable citizens is about to leave the entitlement-based world of special education and enter the already overwhelmed and under-funded world of non-entitlement adult services. And while exceptional adult programs and services exist in every state, they tend to be more the exception than the rule; leaving many individuals and their families to, in effect, fend for themselves. This should be considered completely unacceptable.

The second site we visited that afternoon was welcoming. Three administrators sat down with us in a conference room and invited us to tell them about our son. They took notes. They listened attentively, and asked good questions: what made Mickey happy? What were the signs he was about to have a meltdown? They described their program. We talked at least half an hour. We were impressed; I felt hopeful. Then they took us to tour the facility. We visited the "sensory enrichment room." Most of the people looked profoundly physically and developmentally disabled. We visited other rooms; again, I was struck by how much adaptive equipment I saw. I had a hard time picturing Mickey in that environment; I saw no one his age, so I asked.

"Our participants range from their thirties to sixties."

Mickey was used to being with students his own age. How could it be appropriate for our 20-year-old son to spend every day with people who were so much older?

That's when it sank in: school was truly over. "Adult services" weren't only for young adults like Mickey. "Adult" meant the entire lifespan.

We crossed that program off the list.

"But we're getting closer," Marc said reassuringly. "At least we liked the staff."

Two days later we visited another program. The director told us that they had four or five "consumers" who started their morning in the building, then went into the community. They spent afternoons hanging out at Dunkin' Donuts, or at the mall. I pictured Mickey wandering aimlessly through endless food courts. Overwhelmed. Purposeless.

"But what about the other ones who aren't out all day? Do they work on life skills?" Marc asked.

"We can't do that here," she told us. "Much of our population is medically fragile. We're just trying to keep them safe." It sounded like babysitting.

Still, we took the tour. The facility consisted of an open space as vast as a gymnasium. It contained bare tables, a couple of couches, and many idle "consumers." One woman stared at the ceiling, then stared down at her lap. Ceiling. Lap. Ceiling. Lap. Ceiling. Lap. The room had the hopeless feel of a nursing home. Averting my gaze, I asked the administrator about the age range of the people we were seeing.

"Twenties to fifties," she told us. But I saw a white-haired woman who looked well into her seventies, and a wizened old man who grinned at me. He had no teeth. I smiled and nodded back.

We peered into an alcove, and saw a sink and microwave. I thought about how much Mickey liked to bake. "Do you do any cooking with your 'consumers'?"

"We can't," she said. "Too many legal liabilities."

Marc and I couldn't find the exit fast enough.

"I'd sooner keep him home," I said fiercely.

"We will figure this out," Marc said. Trying to convince us both.

"It's grim out there," I told Amy. I knew there wasn't going to be a "perfect" program, just as there is no perfect college, no perfect job, no perfect anything. But what about *acceptable*?

I'd noticed that one of the first things some people at these programs asked about Mickey was "is he high functioning?"

I hated that question.

Were they asking his IQ score? If he spoke? Whether he'd ever live independently? I didn't know how to answer.

How well does anyone function all the time? Isn't it circumstantial? Mickey did well socially when he felt comfortable and safe with people he knew. He'd learned to ask socially appropriate questions such as "What did you do today?" or "How was your weekend?" He still struggled to sustain a complex conversation. If he didn't feel like interacting, he'd still say, "Leave me alone. I don't want to talk." Not exactly polite, but still functional. But put him in a room teeming with noisy, unfamiliar people or loud music? He'd be out the door so fast he'd leave skid marks.

I'd come to realize that all people are high functioning in some ways and less so in others. If you asked me to write an essay, I'd say—modestly—that I am fairly high functioning in that regard. But if you had to depend on me to rappel down the side of a cliff, or navigate a raft through white water, you'd be putting your money on the wrong gal. You'd never make it out alive.

As students, everyone is expected to do well in every subject. In reality, most of us are not good at everything. As we grow, we tend to narrow our focus. We specialize. We seek out work in areas where we can excel. Autistic or not, everyone has a mix of strengths and challenges.

If you could do calculus but couldn't tie your shoes, were you high or low functioning? Did high functioning mean you could live independently, but low meant you couldn't? Mickey couldn't turn on the stove to cook for himself yet. But he was adept at making his own sandwiches and reheating food in the microwave. He wouldn't starve. So where did he fall on the continuum? Just because an autistic person could speak, make great eye contact or perform academically didn't mean he didn't also have major social and behavioral challenges. Where was the arbitrary cut-off point between high and low? Who got to decide?

When Mickey had been 19 months old and saw his first speech therapist, she'd said he had a "mild" delay. Several months later, a different evaluator told us the delay was "severe." Mickey hadn't changed; he was still the same loving, lovable little boy. Nor had his challenges changed. What *had* changed? The evaluator.

It is human nature to want to categorize people and create hierarchies, but labels could be dangerous. They could so easily be used to dismiss people, to see them as "less than."

I wondered how I should respond the next time someone asked me where Mickey "fell" on the autism spectrum. His development was not linear. You couldn't measure it with a yardstick or clock. Maybe the only truthful answer to the question "Is your son high or low functioning?" was simply "Yes."

We continued to visit day habs. Finally, we walked into a program and saw several young men and women Mickey's age. They looked energetic. Engaged. The facility wasn't beautiful, but it was bright and cheerful.

"What's a typical day here?" Marc asked.

We heard the right words: functional academics. Community integration. Supported employment. They partnered with a program that offered life skill classes at local colleges for adults with developmental disabilities. Most of the people in the program were in their twenties. When we toured the building, we were pleased to see a computer lab, a fitness room and a fully equipped kitchen for program participants to practice cooking skills. "We'd be happy to have him come spend a day and try us out," the coordinator suggested.

"What do you think?" I asked Marc when we were back in the car. But I already knew.

"I can picture him here."

The following week we visited one more day hab. The young adults there looked comfortable too. Engaged with each other. The staff seemed warm and caring. We talked with them for more than an hour. "We'd love to meet Mickey," the coordinator offered.

"I can picture him here too," Marc said.

Such relief. We'd finally located two acceptable programs. If neither program lost its state funding, and if they had openings in the fall…we'd actually have a choice.

No. *Mickey* would have a choice. Because when all was said and done, this wasn't about us.

"Is it 'Harvard'?" Amy asked.

I thought wistfully of that residential program in Connecticut we liked so much.

"No," I said. "More like junior college."

But maybe—just maybe—it would be the best step toward developing the skills and social maturity Mickey would need to thrive someday at that "college" in Connecticut.

The following month we returned to see the neurologist. Mickey sat cross-legged on the bench in the neurologist's office to wait. A teenage girl and her mother were sitting catty-corner. I saw the girl's eyes widen. She smiled at my son. She was eyeing him as if she thought he was cute. Could she possibly be—flirting?

Mickey didn't look at her. Instead, he opened an oversized workbook called *Social Skills Activities for Special Children*. It was left over from Dori's sixth-grade class, but he still loved it. He read aloud, laughing a little too loudly. The girl glanced at her mother: the look they exchanged was unmistakable. I could practically see a cartoon thought bubble forming above her head:

What's wrong with him?

The girl's flirtatious smile faded to pity.

A nurse appeared. Mickey covered his ears. He crouched like a school kid in a duck-and-cover drill. "Don't say my name!" He was afraid the nurse was about to call him; he'd been fretting about this for weeks. Not happy about being there. He hated having to have yet another EEG. I'd promised over and over they wouldn't call his name. As soon as we checked in I'd made sure to tell the receptionist.

The girl whispered something to her mother. I wondered why she was there. This wasn't an ordinary waiting room. She wasn't there for a flu shot. This was the Epilepsy Center at NYU. There were children here wearing seizure helmets.

Mickey laughed to himself again. The girl darted sidewise glances. Then from across the room, I heard a man's irate and sibilant hiss. "Shush!"

Even here?

I bristled. Yes, Mickey was too loud. Sometimes he still had trouble modulating his volume.

"Mick?"

"Yeah, Mom?"

"Quieter voice, please." I patted the air in that downward motion that signaled him to speak more softly.

Welcome to Autism Awareness Month, I thought.

Yes, it was April, that cruelest month when everyone talked a good game about Autism Awareness.

But what I was acutely aware of at that moment was how people looked at him. Still. After all those blue light bulbs and puzzle piece car magnets and t-shirts and rubber bracelets.

The way they looked at my son.

Maybe they were just staring because people do that. Anything out of the ordinary catches the eye; it's a primitive itch. Twenty years ago, I might have looked too.

I didn't want to care so much that they stared.

But I still did.

Even though I was the one who always told other parents to ignore the stares. *Who cares what strangers think?* I'd say.

But I lied. It could still make me shrivel.

On a good day I'd tell myself that those stares were actually ones of understanding and support. Other days, the looks still felt accusatory: *Why can't you just control him?*

But what cut the most was the welling up with tears, there-but-for-the-grace-of-God-go-I Tragedy Look.

Because here's what those people weren't seeing. Mickey's sweetness. His sideways hugs. His silly sense of humor. The joyful way he confided, "I have delicious news." How fiercely I loved him.

So here we were again, back at April and Autism Awareness Month. In yet another doctor's waiting room. If I were a bigger person, I thought, I'd view this as a teachable moment. Start a conversation about autism. But sometimes, I just...couldn't.

Instead, I waited quietly for Mickey's name to be not-called. Silently, the nurse appeared and gestured; we stood. "Come, honey," I said. "It's your turn," and we traipsed past the staring girl, and her mother, and the man who hissed at my son.

I was tired of wearing ribbons. Awareness? We'd been working at that for years. What about acceptance?

Because I saw the way they still looked at him.

~♦~

"If you've met one person with autism, you've met one person with autism." To that I would add, and once you've met one family with autism, you've met one family.

Disability has a way of seeping into all the cracks, the corners, of a family's life. For years it was the emotional epicenter of our family, and the aftershocks lasted for years. Sometimes I'd felt as if other, typical families were feasting in a great restaurant, while the four of us were standing outside, noses pressed to the glass.

But as the years passed, I learned, at least most of the time, to wear emotional blinders. I'd stayed tightly focused on Mickey, celebrating every change we saw.

How do you do it? I was often asked. I gave the same answer each time. I wasn't given a choice. I just did it, one foot after the other. Marc and I had to be Mickey's advocates, because as wonderful as the therapists and teachers were, they went home every night. We were his ultimate teachers, the ones who were in it for the long haul. There was nothing particularly noble about it. We did it because it had to be done. We were his parents. No one could do it better.

Grief and anger could still rear up unexpectedly. They probably always would. Sometimes I still got tired of the relentless effort, the endless round of therapies and team meetings and fights with the insurance companies. The process of healing was a destination without an arrival. Joy and grief were joined in lock-step.

Ultimately, what buoyed our family was hope. Love is like this. When I looked at him, I did not see "autism." I now saw my nearly grown child: an animated, endearing, handsome young man with a mischievous sense of humor. Parenting this trusting, gentle boy had deepened me immeasurably. But would I trade in my hard-earned equanimity and expertise if someone could magically make his challenges go away tomorrow?

In a heartbeat.

Acceptance doesn't mean giving up.

Years earlier, I heard a story that changed the way I framed my feelings about having a child with a disability. Itzak Perlman was giving a concert. He made his way on crutches to the stage, seated himself and took up his violin. He began to play, when suddenly, a string snapped. Perlman looked around, seeming to measure the length of the stage, how far he would have to go on crutches to fetch a new string, and then seemed to decide that he would do without it. He lifted his violin and began to play, and even without that string, he not only played; he played beautifully.

That is what it felt like to have a disabled child. It felt as if we'd lost a crucial string. And then, painstakingly, we had learned to play the instrument we'd been given. Learned to listen to the voice of the instrument that was there all the time. Softly, differently, not playing the music we'd intended, but making music nonetheless.

The first we knew that Mickey's school was holding a student art auction later that April was from an email from Cindy, the school principal. When the state senator arrived, Cindy wrote, they called all the classrooms down to the lobby to cut the ceremonial ribbon. "I asked for volunteers to help and Mickey walked right up. He has a picture in our show too." She attached a photo of the painting, titled "My Favorite Meal," as well as an interview with the artist they'd posted beside the painting.

Q: *What is your inspiration?*

M: I want lunch.

Q: *What tools did you use? Why?*

M: Paint and paintbrush. So I can paint better.

Q: *What materials did you use?*

M: Color.

Q: *What do you like best about your piece?*

M: It's perfect. It's wonderful. I like the strawberry milkshake best.

Q: *What is it?*

M: McDonald's fast food.

Q: *What is your favorite part of the piece?*

M: All of it.

Q: *What were you trying to say in the work?*

M: I'd like to order these.

This was too delightful not to share. I sent out an email blast, and posted it to Facebook. The responses were immediate.

"Love you, love Mickey, love this," my friend Beth wrote.

"The interview is SO Mickey!" my college roommate Pat said.

"Okay, I liked the art, I even guessed what it was before reading the interview," my sister-in-law Susan said. "BUT it is the best interview ever! It reads like Woody Allen."

"Well I hope he got lunch," my brother Marty said. "Artists get very temperamental when they are hungry."

My friend Joelle, a writer and painter herself, had a different take. "I love Mickey's sensibility. I love his painting!... Mickey in his being literally tastes what he paints. An artist prays for this kind of immediacy. What we feel may be deadpan literal to him may well be sensual. 'What materials did you use'! And his answer is 'color.' I know exactly what he means. I called my last art show 'Color as Refuge.'"

Hmm. I hadn't even thought of it that way. I looked through a stack of Mickey's paintings over the years. Not masterful, but so self-assured. I stopped to study a sea of sapphire blue swirling beneath magenta mountains. Such bold brush strokes. Such saturated color. Joelle was right; I could feel Mickey's sheer exuberance.

I thought about all his fine motor challenges. His mixed reactivity to sensory input—how as a baby he couldn't tolerate the feel of sand at the beach, or grass beneath his bare feet. Couldn't bear to touch clay or glue. How he'd struggled to write, his pencil pressure so weak that for a long time we couldn't even make out the marks on the page. All those years of occupational therapy. How when he was in elementary school we'd covered the unfinished section of our basement in drop cloths, and filled the space with easels, tempura paint, brushes in different sizes and textures. Tubs of crayons and markers. Barrels of dried beans. Glitter glue and felt. Colored cotton pompoms and popsicle sticks. His creations adorned our walls. But after the nor'easter had flooded our basement with three feet of silty water, Mickey had shown no interest in setting up his "studio" again.

Color as refuge.

The dictionary defined refuge as: "a condition of being safe or sheltered from pursuit, danger, or trouble." Mickey would be exiting school soon. He was anxious about what was coming next. Perhaps color, as well as painting pictures of his favorite meal, provided a measure of comfort.

The current bid on the painting was $10. "We should bid," I told Marc. "It's a donation to the school."

"My Mick is worth $100," Marc said.

"No," I told him. "He's priceless."

One afternoon in May, Mickey came home from school and announced, "I have a girlfriend."

I was thunderstruck. "You do? Tell me about her. What's her name?"

"Caroline. She doesn't talk much," he said. "She's shy."

I'd heard about her a few weeks earlier, when Jackie had emailed me about the friendship that was blossoming between Mickey and the girl in the classroom next door.

> Caroline goes on a daily walk on the bike path and I have been letting Mickey go with her to offer encouragement—he quite enjoys this... I have to tell you that his mental demeanor is so improved when he gets that physical exercise—and it boosts his self-esteem, too because he thinks he is helping Caroline.

Soon after, Jackie emailed me this news:

> Just letting you know that Mickey asked his friend Caroline to the prom today... We will find out what color her dress is in case Mickey wants to get her a corsage.

Oh my.

"I think I need a tissue," I told my friend Beth.

"Are you kidding? I'd need a whole box," she said. "This is a monumental milestone moment."

I phoned the florist. The afternoon before the prom, I took Mickey to the shop. With a big smile, the florist produced a small white box and carefully peeled back layers of tissue paper to reveal a wrist corsage of rosebuds and ribbons nestled within. Mickey peered at it silently.

"She'll love it," the florist assured him.

Mickey nodded. All business, he pulled out his wallet. "How much does it cost?"

"$35."

Mickey placed two $20 bills on the counter, remembering
Cezanne's "dollar over" rule. He also remembered to wait for
his change. Then, as we walked back to the car, he confided, "I
hugged Caroline today."

"You did? What did she say?"

"She said, 'I love you.'"

"*Really*," I said, feigning nonchalance. "And what did you say?"

"I said, 'I love you too.'"

Oh my.

The prom took place in the school's gym. The theme was
"Candyland." There were rows of giant lollypops, and students
were decked out in colorful party best. Parents were invited too.
"But we shouldn't hover," I reminded Marc. (A reminder to me
as well.)

We watched from the sidelines as Mickey and Caroline
clasped hands. Together they jumped up and down, with looks
of sheer joy on both their faces. Each time he took her by one
hand and twirled her around, teachers and staff applauded. Marc
and I *kvelled*—a Yiddish word that means to burst with pride and
pleasure for one's child. It's related to the German word *quellen*:
"to well up."

Which I confess I was also doing. A lot.

Because here's the thing: I never expected him to go to a prom.
Prom was one of so many things in the litany of what we were told
he would never be able to do. He would never be social. Never do
pretend play. Never have empathy. Would always prefer solitude.

Why did professionals persist in telling these things to parents?
Especially when it was clear—even from the earliest days—that
our son liked—in fact, *craved*—connection?

Because here he was, at a prom. With a date. Maybe "prom"
didn't look the way I'd thought prom would look, but this wasn't
about me. It was time for me to let go of any lingering regret for

what wasn't—and to accept what was right in front of us. This was still a prom. *His* prom.

And Mickey was incandescent.

Mickey and Caroline jumped and twirled for 45 minutes before Mickey finally joined us to announce: "I've had enough."

"You need to tell Caroline," I told him. I watched him return to her side. He hugged her gently. Started back towards us. Stopped. Turned. Hugged her tenderly once more.

Then he asked Marc, "Was that appropriate?"

A lump in the throat moment. That he felt he had to ask… well, of course. Because for most of his life he's had teachers and therapists and parents guiding him on what is appropriate and inappropriate behavior.

Appropriate?

Was it ever.

~❧

June.

A few more weeks until Mickey's twenty-first birthday. He had been in Jackie's transition class for more than a year and was part of Millwood now. He continued to spend time with Caroline at school every day, as the weeks rolled on inexorably toward graduation.

In mid-June, we had our final Committee on Special Education meeting back at the high school. Karyn wasn't there; she had retired. Marc was out of town on business. I met in a small conference room with Alan, and Marie, who'd helped Karyn run the program and had been Mickey's social studies teacher in ninth grade. Millwood staff joined us by phone. The director of special education didn't bother to attend. I thought of saying something about it to Marie and Alan, then shrugged. It no longer mattered. This meeting was pro forma. Our district was finally closing the file on Michael Carter and his "difficult, demanding" family. We were *done*.

"It has been a privilege to work with your son," Marie said. "I know it was rocky at the start, but we've learned so much. I've loved working with Mickey, and I'm going to miss him. He is a delight."

Even during that terrible ninth-grade year, I thought, Marie had been in our corner.

"It's the end of an era," Alan said. "I have such a special spot in my heart for Mickey. My first pupil here. We have a special bond." We both welled up.

"Would it be possible to come to graduation at Millwood next week?" Alan asked. "Arthur would like to come too." Arthur, a retired grandfather, had worked as an aide in Alan's classroom for several years. A lovely man. Mickey was very fond of him.

"Mickey would be thrilled to see you both," I said.

That evening I told Marc about the meeting. "After all the years of drama, today was short and completely uneventful. You didn't need to be there, but I'm just sorry you weren't," I said. "They said such wonderful things about Mickey it made me weepy."

"Alan and Arthur are both coming? Wow, that's really nice," he said.

As soon as I heard the solemn strains of "Pomp and Circumstance," I was a puddle. (I'm like that. I cry at weddings too.)

Luckily, Cindy had already taken the precaution of passing out boxes of tissues just before the ceremony. I sat with Shana, Cezanne, Milagros, my sister-in-law Susan and my nephews Sam and Charles. Marc wielded the camera. Amidst applause and tears, we watched as the graduates in green caps and gowns marched into the gym.

Mickey's teacher Jackie had alerted us that he'd written a graduation speech. "There is no pressure for him to read it if he decides last minute that he does not want to," she'd emailed. "He's told me he wants to wear regular clothes under his cap and gown, so it's up to you if you want him to change. This is a stress-free event!"

Oh, but not for us.

This was the culmination of everything Marc and I had worked long and fought so hard for. Thousands of hours of therapy that began when Mickey was only 19 months old. Not knowing in those early years if he would ever learn to speak. Navigating medical crises. Fighting for services with the school district. Struggling for coverage with insurance companies. Years filled with fears and tears, but joy and pride too, for Mickey's many hard-won accomplishments.

Jackie had prepared personal remarks for each of her graduating students. "Mickey has been my biggest comedian in all my years of teaching," she told the audience. "Every day he arrives at school making jokes and pretending to be various characters—if we let him I bet he would spend the entire day acting silly and making silly remarks." She described skills mastered; friendships maintained. "I am going to miss Mickey," she said, "but I will be happy for him, too. I know he is going to be a success at whatever he chooses to do, because he already is."

Jackie motioned to Mickey. Beaming, he bounded up, speech in hand. He thanked everyone. "I learned much about working in the community and getting along with others," he said. "I had fun this year!"

I wondered: should we have also asked to let him walk in our high school's graduation ceremony? A small sliver of sadness. After all, he'd spent six years there. But Mickey was 21 now; his high school contemporaries were long gone. And Mickey didn't seem to think he was missing out on anything. Quite the contrary.

It was time to lose the hair shirt. I thought of Jonathan's wise advice the night before: "Focus on what you have; stop focusing on what you don't." Comparison is the thief of joy.

"I did it! Arthur? Mr. Cantor? Is that really you?" Mickey exclaimed.

"He looks great!" Arthur told me.

"So happy and fit," Alan added.

Hugs all around. We all adjourned to the conference room for lunch, and everyone posed for pictures with the graduates. I watched in awe as Mickey confidently worked the crowd, introducing family members, therapists and teachers to each other. So at ease. So appropriate.

"Look how exuberant he is," Marc marveled.

Carpe diem, I told myself. Seize this day and savor it. I hugged Mickey.

"So proud of you, hon," I said. "Love you."

"Love you too, Mom," he said.

When a baby is born, someone cuts the umbilical cord for you. How could we possibly loosen the thousands of threads that bind him to us? It's an endless unraveling, this process of letting go.

We call graduation "commencement." A beginning. But it is also an ending, the punctuation mark that seals off 16 years of formal education. The yellow school bus won't be stopping at our door anymore. Together we are crossing that bridge between childhood, and…whatever comes next. We will do this just as we have done everything else these past 20 years.

Pulling together as a family.

THE END

ACKNOWLEDGMENTS

I am grateful to my family for allowing me to tell our story.

The Art of the Memoir workshop at Sarah Lawrence College was the incubator for this book. Thank you to all my colleagues for their thoughtful critiques and unflagging optimism: Lisa Argrette Ahmad, Susan Amlung, Kathy Curto, Lucia Greenhouse, Inge Hershkowitz, Kuniko Katz, Samantha Knowlton, and Melanie Rock, and to Linda D'Arcy for reading successive versions of the manuscript. Thank you to our extraordinary teacher, Joelle Sander, for her penetrating insights and constant encouragement to dig deeper.

A huge thank you to Lisa Belkin, for publishing several of my essays at the *New York Times* Motherlode, many of which found their way into this book; my literary agent Allison Hunter, for her perseverance and belief in me; Alexis Hurley, who graciously provided input; Susan Senator, for her generosity and *menschlichkeit*; Claire LaZebnik, for her warmth, kindness, and early endorsement of this book; Susan Axelrod, Adam Feinstein, Arthur Fleischmann, Priscilla Gilman, Chantal Sicile-Kira, Steve Silberman, and Alison Singer, for their gracious support.

Thank you to Lisa Clark, Suzanne Connelly, Victoria Peters, Katelynn Bartleson, and the rest of the caring and collaborative staff at Jessica Kingsley for their skillful guidance, meticulous copy editing, and creative design.

I am thankful to friends and colleagues at Autism After 16, Autism Science Foundation, Center for Autism and the Developing Brain, CURE/Citizens United for Research in Epilepsy, Littman Krooks, Matan Kids, Ramapo for Children, and Westchester Reform Temple.

To the many self-advocates I've met on this journey, especially Scott Lentine, Paul Morris, and Chloe Rothschild, thank you for your friendship and invaluable insights.

I am indebted to the many doctors, teachers, and therapists who have shared their wisdom, insights, and perspectives: Todd Rosenthal, sports coach extraordinaire; Shana Gliksman-Ginipro, gifted therapist and kindred spirit; service coordinator Jeanne Feeney, who always looks out for Mickey; Eloisa Martinez, for trying to teach Mickey Spanish; Milagros Vargas, beloved babysitter, confidante, friend, and Mickey's biggest fan.

None of this would have been possible without my special needs parent posse: Beth Arky, Iris Bailey, Peter Bell, Miriam Beveridge, Ellen Cohen, Brenda Kosky Deskin, Cindy Dunne, Jody Isenberg, Marjorie Madfis, Robin Morris, Sandi Rosenbaum, Lisa Siegel, Lisa Tidball, Diane Towle, and Susan Wiener; Lauren Rimland, my trailblazer and touchstone; fellow special needs writers too numerous to name, especially Glen Finland, Leigh Merryday Porch, Laura Shumaker, Ellen Seidman, and Jess Wilson, for lighting the way.

Friends, family and neighbors are too numerous to name, but I would be remiss if I didn't give a special shout out to the Bauman and Clarvit families, for always having our backs; my extended family; my brother Marty Kupferberg, who always makes me laugh; Pat Zadok, for fortifying me with love, baked goods, and a restorative trip to Umbria.

To my parents, who didn't live long enough to read this book, but whose warmth and humor shaped every page, I love and miss you always. To my sons, Jonathan and Mickey, the beamish boys who gave me this story, love you both to infinity and beyond. To my husband Marc who has shared every step of this journey with me, thank you for your unwavering love, intelligence and wit, and for talking me off metaphoric ledges. "You are the butter to my bread, the breath to my life."